Stews, Bogs, and Burgoos

Stews, Bogs, and Burgoos

Recipes from

the Great American Stewpot

JAMES VILLAS

WILLIAM MORROW AND COMPANY, INC.

New York

It is the policy of William Morrow and Company, Inc., and its imprints
and affiliates, recognizing the importance of preserving what has been
written, to print the books we publish on acid-free paper,
and we exert our best efforts to that end.

Library of Congress Cataloging-in-Publication Data

Villas, James.
Stews, bogs, and burgoos / recipes from the great American
stewpot / James
Villas.—1st ed.
p. cm.
Includes index.
ISBN 0-688-15253-8
1. Stews. I. Title.

TX693.V55 1997
641.8' 23—dc21   96-50015
                                                                   CIP

Printed in the United States of America
First Edition

1 2 3 4 5 6 7 8 9 10

BOOK DESIGN BY DEBORAH KERNER
ILLUSTRATIONS BY RICHARD WAXBERG

FOR

Alice Marshall

An Acknowledgment

Today, more than ever before, a successful cookbook depends as much on the dedication, intelligent insights, and professional skills of its editor as well as its author's enthusiasm and ability; and in this capacity, Pam Hoenig at William Morrow is in a class by herself. Therefore, my most sincerest thanks to Pam for her keen involvement and suggestions, her uncanny dexterity editing recipes, her endless encouragement, and above all, her steadfast confidence and loyalty over the years. And now, I even forgive (and maybe thank) her for refusing resolutely to let me include "Ragouts" in the book's title for rhythmic effect. Even though the word is in every English dictionary, she insisted till the bitter end that "it still sounds too French to me."

Contents

Introduction

"In a large, heavy pot . . ." Just these five words, repeated over and over in recipes throughout this book, immediately evoke timeless memories of sitting around a big, wooden kitchen table with my family in North Carolina and watching my grandfather fill blue-and-white bowls with his steaming rabbit stew while Mother buttered a batch of fresh baking powder biscuits. The words also recall an inimitable cioppino that I first tasted as a teenager at a venerable, rather raucous seafood house in San Francisco called Bernstein's Fish Grotto, as well as the heroic burgoo made with squirrel served in the stately Louisville home of family friends when I attended my first Kentucky Derby. As a student one summer at Middlebury College in Vermont, I marveled at a kind old lady's earthy duck and rutabaga ragout in her downtown tavern, and later, when I lived in Missouri, there was catfish stew shared with colleagues at their rustic weekend retreat at Cape Girardeau, the aromatic flavor of which still lingers nostalgically. And how could I ever forget the luscious red snapper stew I was eventually introduced to at a restaurant in Tampa, or Paul Prudhomme's zesty chicken Gumbo Ya Ya when he was chef at Commander's Palace in New Orleans, or, indeed, the elegant beef stew with quinces at New York's famous Coach House restaurant.

American stews, ragouts, burgoos, mulls, braises, bogs, hotpots, kettles, gumbos, chilis, pilaus—the names go on and on, each suggesting certain culinary subtleties, some denoting highly regional distinctions, but all commingling to define one of the glories of world gastronomy: the great American stewpot. To be sure, there's not a country on the globe that can't boast of at least one type of stew or another, and no doubt the very practice of simmering solids in liquid till tender can be traced back to the beginnings of human history. America, on the other hand, seems to have been virtually founded on the stew tradition as the first settlers, faced with the same challenging hardships as the native Americans before them and the African slaves after, struggled to nourish themselves as easily, practically, and palatably as possible by cooking together in a single pot whatever ingredients might be available. Inherent in this immigrant tradition were stewing customs brought from the foreign lands, explanation of why, by the end of the nineteenth century, each territory in the United States had developed a variety of stews that reflected not only its multifaceted ethnic makeup but also the ingenuity with which its inhabitants adapted the rich regional bounty to an age-old cooking method. The Italian- and Portuguese-style fish stews of northern California and New England, respectively; the Russian soliankas, German goulashes, and Greek lamb stews of the Midwest; the Jewish cholents of New York and Dutch pepperpots of Philadelphia; the Mexican posoles, cocidos, and picadillos of the Southwest; the British mulls, African gumbos, and Middle Eastern pilaus of the South—these stews certainly had their foreign antecedents, but by the time they had been transformed in the all-American stewpot, there can be no doubt that they assumed an altogether new identity that will forever be part of our proud culinary heritage.

This cookbook, therefore, is devoted exclusively to American stews—their rich geographical history, their paramount role in the evolution of our cookery, their prodigious diversity, and, indeed, their unique succulence. Despite the curious, downright stupid neglect that stews have suffered in recent years thanks mainly to the frenzied ambitions of young superstar chefs oblivious to genuine regional cooking and determined to blindly modernize and fancify all American food, I must say that I've never met anyone anywhere who doesn't love a good stew. And why not? Nothing in this world is more comforting than the sight, tantalizing aroma, and intoxicating taste of a well-made stew capable of arousing our most primitive instincts, providing inimitable gustatory and spiritual satisfaction, and proving how so much homey pleasure can be derived from so little effort and expense. Whether it's a relatively plain, long-simmering meat, poultry, or bean concoction left to bubble on the stove till dinnertime for family or close friends, or a more sophisticated, last-minute seafood preparation redolent of wine, herbs, or exotic spices intended to impress guests, stew is one of the easiest and most practical dishes imaginable. Being generally a single-dish, one-pot affair, stew not only makes minimum demands on the cook, it usually requires little more accompaniment than maybe boiled rice or a nice green salad, plenty of good bread (preferably hot biscuits), a decent wine or other beverage, and possibly a simple dessert. Personally, I'd be happy eating or serving a hearty stew five nights out of the week—with hardly a second thought given to quick meat sautés, undergrilled poultry and vegetables, tasteless steamed fish, listless pastas, and all that other trendy stuff that makes a mockery of real American cookery.

While stew is (or should be) one of the most economical dishes you can serve, don't think for a second that all you have to do is clean out the refrigerator of leftovers or buy cheap, over-the-hill ingredients and dump everything in a pot. Yes, throughout the book I encourage the use of secondary but flavorful cuts of meat, unpopular but inexpensive types of fish, dried beans, and thrifty root vegetables, but I also insist that any stew is only as good as the quality of its ingredients. Never, for example, would I stew short ribs of beef or oxtails that are mostly bone and fat; never would I prepare a turkey mull or Brunswick stew with dry, darkly colored fowl or a shrimp bog with shrimp that have even a trace of strong odor; and just the thought of stewing overly large, tough okra, spotted yellow squash, or limp collard greens makes me cringe. I admit that I'm a sucker for any meat, poultry, fresh vegetable, or fruit that's on sale, and when it comes to stews, I'm particularly on the lookout for nice chicken giblets, lamb necks and shanks, pork shoulders, veal kidneys, catfish, and parsnips that might come at a bargain. To succumb to temptation, on the other hand, by buying sprouted onions, potatoes, or garlic at discount is not only false economy but also a patent invitation to disaster in the stewpot.

Throughout the book I also emphasize the cardinal role of quality stock in the execution of numerous recipes (especially those for seafood), and here I reiterate the view once more. Of course, not all stews involve a stock base, but for those that do, all I can say is that the difference between a full-flavored homemade beef, chicken, or fish stock and a commercial substitute can often distinguish a memorable from a mediocre stew. Making stock is, I realize, a bore, but once you've prepared a large quantity in your spare time and frozen it in individual containers, I can promise that you won't regret it when the time comes to put on the stewpot.

The recipes in this book have been developed or collected over many years, some going back as far as my childhood, others drawn from the various areas of the country where I've lived and traveled widely, and still others reflecting the hundreds of restaurants I've been led to cover as a professional stomach for hire and hungry nomad. No matter the occasion, I'm always on the lookout for great stew recipes, and while I'm forever changing or modifying many of my own stews, I do try to remain as faithful as possible to original recipes obtained from friends, colleagues, home cooks, professional chefs, restaurant personnel, and even family members. I'm certainly not about to reproduce a charming but untenable recipe for chicken stew that directs simply to "brown a good-size chicken, put it in a pot with lots of good vegetables, some nice seasonings, and a little liquid, and cook till done." Nevertheless, I do find that one of the real joys of stew making are the many different ways people go about it—ways that not only teach me new formulas and techniques but often challenge my preconceived notion of a given stew.

The stews included here, therefore, abound with inconsistencies, partly because I refuse to tamper inordinately (even while testing) with recipes received from or inspired by other stewheads I've respected over the years, and partly because I'm convinced that no two stews are ever exactly the same. Depending on the style of stew, there are differences in the quantity of base liquids (which determine a thick or soupy stew) and flour for dredging (if, indeed, flour is used at all); in the timing of vegetables that are browned; in the quantity and size of secondary ingredients; in cooking techniques; and in overall stewing times even within the same category of meats or poultry. I hope this is not perceived as indifference or sloppiness. There are literally dozens of stewing techniques intended to produce diverse flavors and textures, and if they were homogenized into a single method, all the wonderful flexibility and half the fun of stew making would be lost. Take Judy's Bonaker Beef Stew (page 8), for example. Never would I have cooked any beef stew this long or included so many onions until I made it exactly as Judy Mannes directed and I tasted the sapid results. And why so long and so many onions? "Because I love my meat falling apart, and I love lots of onions," she answered. That's the spirit, I say, and I hope you'll approach the recipes with the same sense of freedom to experiment and adapt things to your own taste—within reason, that is.

One of the greatest advantages of stews is that most made with any category of meat or poultry (and some of the vegetable ones, like succotash) are not only just as delicious when made in advance and reheated but they can also be very successfully frozen so long as they contain enough liquid. (Since the ingredients tend to break down, I never freeze seafood stews—not even gumbos.) For this reason, think seriously about doubling recipes, confident that your favorite pork, duck, or venison stew can be frozen in airtight plastic containers for up to three or four months and merely pulled out of the freezer, thawed, and heated whenever last-minute guests are expected or you simply don't feel like cooking. Rest assured that there's never a time when I haven't stored away at least two savory stews, each just waiting to make up to four people happy on a moment's notice.

Today, professional chefs (and some zealous home cooks) are trying to redefine American cookery, give it new character and dimension, and, under the rubric of "New American," generally elevate it to a level of sophistication equal to that of the world's finest and most respected cuisines. That's fine by me, since any style of cooking must be allowed to evolve if it's to survive the onslaught of progress and ever-changing tastes. To dismiss, on the other hand, such age-old dishes as stews in favor of facile novelty and wanton experimentation is not only to ignore the very foundation of our gastronomy but also to discredit the splendid regional culinary heritage of which we should be so proud. Stews make up a large and important segment of our cooking tradition. They are easy to prepare and utterly wonderful to eat, and those who have any doubts about their distinctive role in the American kitchen and on the table would do well to remember the wise words of that revered champion, James Beard: "Stewing is an essential part of our cooking, and a good stew, to my mind, is about as attractive a dish as you can offer."

Stews, Bogs, and Burgoos

Beef Stews

Beef Stock

Judy's Bonaker Beef Stew

Coach House Beef Stew with Quinces

Maytag Iowa Beef Stew in Ale

Liz Clark's Iowa Coffee Beef Stew

Julia Child's Favorite Beef Stew

Columbia County Applejack Beef Stew

Midwestern Beef Solianka

Jean Anderson's Jugged Beef with
Cranberries and Mushrooms

Michigan Barshch

Oklahoma Goulash

Twentieth Century Limited Hungarian Goulash

Braised Bourbon Rosemary Beef

Pearl's Bourbon Beef and Oyster Pot

Alabama Beef, Lima Beans, and Grits Scramble

Second Avenue Delicatessen Cholent

Arizona Cocido

Chicago Flank Steak and Green Pea Stew

New Orleans Daube Glacé

Sonoma Corned Beef Stewed in Beer

Prairie Oxtail Ragout

Oxtail and White Beans Braised in Stout

Paw Paw's Short Ribs of Beef

Sigrid's Meatball Stew

Tex-Mex Picadillo

Frank Tolbert's Original "Bowl of Red"

Tigua Green Indian Chili

Craig Claiborne's Beanless Chili

Chasen's Famous Chili

Cincinnati 4-Way Chili

Cuts of Beef
for Stewing

To most cooks studying the meat counters of American supermarkets, nothing can be more confusing than trying to determine the right cut of beef for stewing, the main problem being that both unregulated cuts and nomenclature tend to change radically, even from one local market to the next. "Flanken," "crossribs," "short plate," "shin," "hind shank," "top rib"—the variety of cuts and names is often enough to frustrate even the most seasoned shopper. Once was the time (and not that long ago) when you were safe just buying the cheapest (and most appropriate) cuts, but today I stand dumbfounded in some areas of the country to see short ribs of beef priced at $3.89 per pound, shin or shank in excess of $3 per pound, and brisket about $4—proof, no doubt, that stews must be making something of a comeback.

One solution, of course, is to depend on the advice of a good butcher and pay top dollar; another is to take a (pretty good) chance on what is widely packaged as "stew beef." But if you're really serious about producing great beef stews at minimum cost, you'll learn to recognize the various cuts generically without depending necessarily on unofficial labeling and to watch like a hawk for reduced prices.

Generally, cuts of beef for stewing come from the steer forequarter (neck, chuck, shoulder, shank or shin, short ribs, and brisket), underside (short plate and flank), and hindquarter (rump, round, shank or heel of round, and tail). The end pieces of various loin and sirloin steaks (often ground for hamburger) can also be used for making certain stews. Overall, chuck is the ideal and cheapest cut for stewing—so long, that is, as you use boneless steaks, roasts, and cutup "stew beef" and remember that there's little economy in such bone-in cuts as blade chuck, no matter how low the sale price. I also wait patiently for rump and bottom round roasts, "London broil" steaks cut from the shoulder or top round, oxtails, and thin-cut briskets to go on sale (sometimes as low as $1.59 per pound), but rarely do I find shin or shank, flank steaks, or my beloved short ribs at reduced prices. For specialized (but wonderful) cuts like flanken, my best advice is to deal directly with an expert kosher butcher.

Finally, don't forget that virtually all stew beef has a fair percentage of excess surface fat that should be at least partially trimmed off since the meat itself is usually flavorfully marbled with fat. The way this translates weight-wise (and money-wise) is that a three-pound brisket or chuck roast can easily be reduced by as much as a half-pound once it's been trimmed, affecting both the total amount of meat needed for a given recipe and the pocketbook. My strong suggestion is to inspect every side of the cut as shrewdly as possible, even to the point of demanding, if necessary, that a sealed package be opened.

BEEF STOCK

Bᴀꜱɪᴄᴀʟʟʏ, ʙᴇᴇꜰ ꜱᴛᴏᴄᴋ and beef broth are the same, the only difference being that stock might be more full-bodied and concentrated than broth. If a recipe calls for beef broth and the stock seems too concentrated, simply thin it with a little water.

4 pounds beef bones, hacked or sawed into 3-inch pieces
  if necessary
3 carrots, sliced
3 medium-size onions, sliced
¼ cup all-purpose flour
1 pig's foot or veal knuckle
2 medium-size, ripe tomatoes, chopped
2 medium-size leeks (white part and part of green leaves),
  thoroughly washed and chopped
2 celery ribs (leaves included), chopped
1 medium-size turnip, peeled and chopped
1 teaspoon dried thyme, crumbled
8 sprigs fresh parsley
1 bay leaf
4 cloves
8 black peppercorns
Salt to taste
4 quarts water

Preheat the oven to 450°F.

Place the beef bones and half the carrots and onions in a roasting pan, sprinkle with the flour, and brown in the oven for 30 minutes. Transfer the bones and vegetables to a large stockpot. Drain the fat from the roasting pan, deglaze the pan with a little water, scraping any browned bits off the bottom, and pour the juices into the stockpot. Add the pig's foot, the remaining carrots and onions, and all the other ingredients to the stockpot. If necessary, add more water to cover by 3 inches and bring the mixture to a boil, skimming the surface for scum. Reduce the heat to a low simmer, skim again for scum, cover partly, and simmer 3 to 4 hours, adding more water if necessary. Strain the stock through a double thickness of cheesecloth into a large bowl, let cool, chill thoroughly (preferably overnight), and remove the solidified fat from the top. Covered, the stock keeps 1 week in the refrigerator and, stored in freezer containers filled to within ½ inch of the top, up to 6 months in the freezer.

Makes about 2 quarts

STEW SAVVY When making chicken or beef stock that you don't plan to use immediately and intend to store in the refrigerator, don't skim off the fat, which helps seal out bacteria and keeps the stock fresh.

JUDY'S BONAKER
BEEF STEW

"BONAKER" IS THE NAME given to those who are native to the East End of Long Island, and none is more typical than my expert builder and handyman, Bob Mannes, and his wife, Judy. Not long ago, when Bob was constructing an addition to my house in East Hampton, I went outside when I saw his pickup pull into the drive at lunchtime, only to find him and a buddy wolfing down containers of this beef stew, which Judy had just prepared that morning. The aroma knocked me for a loop, so, to Bob's surprise, I asked for a taste. "It's just plain old beef stew," Judy apologized when I called her for the recipe and asked if she'd show me how she made it. Yes, it is just plain old classic American beef stew, and yes, Judy simmers it for a total of four hours. Do it just the way she does, however, and you'll understand why I got so excited.

*2½ pounds lean boneless beef chuck, trimmed of excess fat and
    cut into 1½-inch cubes*
3 tablespoons all-purpose flour
Salt and freshly ground black pepper to taste
3 tablespoons vegetable oil
3 cups beef broth (page 6)
1 cup water
1 large onion, chopped
6 medium-size carrots
6 medium-size potatoes
3 medium-size onions
*2 tablespoons all-purpose flour mixed with 2 tablespoons water
    (optional)*

On a large plate, dust the beef with the flour and salt and pepper, tapping off any excess. In a large, heavy pot, heat the oil over moderately high heat, add the beef, and brown on all sides. Add the broth, water, and chopped onion and bring to a simmer, scraping up any browned bits off the bottom. Cover the pot and simmer the beef about 3 hours.

Scrape the carrots, cut them into thirds, and add to the meat. Peel the potatoes, cut into halves or quarters, and add to the pot. Peel the onions, slice, and add to the pot. If necessary, add a little more broth or water just to cover the ingredients, return to a simmer, cover, and cook till the vegetables are very tender, about 1 hour.

The stew is pretty thick, but if you prefer even more body, transfer the meat and vegetables to a large platter, add the optional flour-and-water mixture to the liquid in the pot, and stir well till thickened. Return the meat and vegetables to the pot, stir, and simmer about 15 minutes longer.

Makes 4 to 6 servings

COACH HOUSE BEEF STEW WITH QUINCES

Before illness forced Leon Lianides to close his venerable landmark Coach House restaurant in New York a few years ago, I (and others, like James Beard and Craig Claiborne) would wait impatiently every October for Leon's call announcing the first beef stew with quinces and quince tart of the season. Succinctly, this is one of the greatest, noblest stews ever created, worthy of even the most elegant dinner party. Fresh quinces are still not that easy to find in many markets, though their popularity increases every day. No doubt the finest and largest quinces (especially the pineapple variety) are those grown in and shipped from California. When shopping for quinces, choose those that have ripened just to a golden yellow with a minimum of gray fuzz on the skins; never use one with small brown spots. Although Leon always marinated his beef for two days, I've learned that one day is usually quite sufficient for delicious results.

continued

2 cups dry red wine

½ cup red wine vinegar

1 medium-size onion, chopped

1 celery rib, chopped

2 garlic cloves, crushed

1 teaspoon dried thyme, crumbled

1 bay leaf

Salt and freshly ground black pepper to taste

*3 pounds lean boneless beef chuck, trimmed of excess fat and cut
    into 1½-inch cubes*

3 tablespoons vegetable oil

2 garlic cloves, sliced

1 large onion, chopped

2 tablespoons all-purpose flour

3 tablespoons canned tomato puree

½ cup dry red wine

1 celery rib, finely chopped

2 juniper berries, crushed

1 bay leaf

Salt and freshly ground black pepper to taste

2 large, ripe quinces, cored, peeled, and cut into 1-inch-thick slices

12 small white onions, peeled and scored on the root ends

1 tablespoon red currant jelly

Chopped fresh parsley leaves

Combine all the marinade ingredients in a large stainless steel or glass bowl and stir till well blended. Add the beef, stirring to coat it, and cover the bowl with plastic wrap. Place in the refrigerator and let marinate at least 1 day, turning once. Transfer the beef to paper towels, strain the marinade through a sieve set over a bowl, and discard the solids.

In a large, heavy casserole, heat the oil to moderately high. Add the garlic, stir for 1 minute, then discard it. In batches, brown the meat on all sides in the oil and transfer to a bowl. Add the onion to the pot and stir for 1 minute, then add the flour and stir for 2 minutes. Add the tomato puree, wine, celery, juniper berries, bay leaf, and salt and pepper and stir. Add the meat plus its juices, bring the liquid to the boil, then reduce the heat to a simmer, cover, and let cook about 1 hour. Add the quinces and white onions plus a little water if necessary to just cover the ingredients. Return to a simmer, cover, and cook till the beef and quinces are tender, about 1 hour longer.

Skim any fat from the stew and stir in the jelly till well incorporated. Transfer the stew to a heated platter and sprinkle with the parsley.

Makes 4 to 6 servings

MAYTAG IOWA BEEF STEW IN ALE

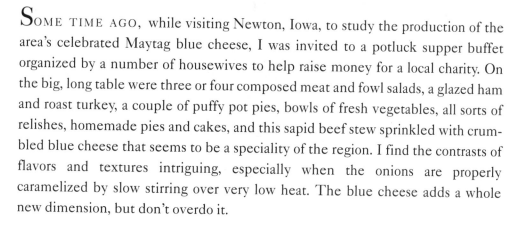

SOME TIME AGO, while visiting Newton, Iowa, to study the production of the area's celebrated Maytag blue cheese, I was invited to a potluck supper buffet organized by a number of housewives to help raise money for a local charity. On the big, long table were three or four composed meat and fowl salads, a glazed ham and roast turkey, a couple of puffy pot pies, bowls of fresh vegetables, all sorts of relishes, homemade pies and cakes, and this sapid beef stew sprinkled with crumbled blue cheese that seems to be a speciality of the region. I find the contrasts of flavors and textures intriguing, especially when the onions are properly caramelized by slow stirring over very low heat. The blue cheese adds a whole new dimension, but don't overdo it.

continued

5 strips bacon

3 large onions, coarsely chopped

2 tablespoons vegetable oil

2½ pounds beef shoulder, trimmed of excess fat and cut into 1½-inch cubes

3 tablespoons all-purpose flour

1 cup full-bodied ale

Pinch of dried thyme, crumbled

Pinch of dried rosemary, crumbled

2 bay leaves

Salt and freshly ground black pepper to taste

2 cups beef stock or broth (page 6)

1 tablespoon cider vinegar

1 cup crumbled Maytag blue cheese (available in finer markets)

In a large, heavy pot, cook the bacon over moderate heat till almost crisp and transfer to paper towels to drain. Add the onions to the bacon fat, reduce the heat to very low, and cook them slowly, stirring, till nicely caramelized, about 20 minutes. Transfer the onions to a plate, then crumble the bacon. Add the vegetable oil to the remaining fat in the pot and increase the heat to moderately high. On a large plate, dust the beef in the flour, tapping off any excess. Add to the pot and brown on all sides. Add the ale and stir, scraping any browned bits off the bottom. Return the crumbled bacon and onions to the pot and add the thyme, rosemary, bay leaves, salt and pepper, stock, and vinegar. Bring to a boil, reduce the heat to a simmer, cover, and cook till the beef is very tender, about 2 hours.

Serve the stew in bowls with a little blue cheese sprinkled on top.

Makes 4 servings

LIZ CLARK'S
IOWA COFFEE BEEF STEW

LIZ CLARK, WHO HAILS from Keokuk, Iowa, and conducts all sorts of cooking classes and food trips for her Midwestern public, learned from her mother this unusual technique of using strong coffee to make rich stew gravies.

Note that the gravy for this stew should be simmered till it's thick and glossy.

1 cup all-purpose flour

Salt and freshly ground black pepper to taste

3 pounds beef brisket (thin cut), trimmed of excess fat, sliced 1/4 inch thick across the grain, and cut into 2-inch pieces

6 tablespoons (3/4 stick) butter, or more as needed

3 large onions, diced

3 bay leaves

5 carrots, scraped and sliced into 1/2-inch-thick rounds

4 celery ribs, sliced 1/2 inch thick

1/4 pound mushrooms, sliced

2 teaspoons dried thyme, crumbled

1 cup strong black coffee

4 cups beef stock or broth (page 6)

Place the flour and salt and pepper in a brown paper bag, add the beef pieces, and shake to coat well. In a large, heavy enameled casserole, heat the butter over moderately high heat; meanwhile, shake the excess flour from the beef. Set the remainder of the flour aside. Brown the beef on both sides in the butter in batches and transfer to a platter. Add the onions and bay leaves to the pot and cook, stirring, for 1 minute. Add the carrots, celery, mushrooms, and thyme and continue to cook for 5 minutes, stirring. Push the vegetables to the side of the pot and, if no fat remains, add about 2 more tablespoons of butter. Add 2 tablespoons of the reserved flour and stir for 4 minutes. Add the coffee and stock and stir well. Add the beef pieces, bring to a simmer, cover, and cook till the beef is tender, 30 to 45 minutes. Taste for salt and pepper before serving.

Makes 4 to 6 servings

JULIA CHILD'S FAVORITE BEEF STEW

"BUT JULIA," I PROTESTED as the great lady explained in minute detail the beef stew at her home in Cambridge, Massachusetts, "is there no way to simplify the recipe?" "Not if you want it to be perfect," she admonished. Whether it's a question of a seafood terrine, or an elaborate sauce, or her beloved American beef stew, Julia Child simply never takes shortcuts or leaves anything to chance, which I suppose is the reason this is the most impeccable and elegant beef stew you'll ever prepare. Leftover stew freezes well.

One 5-ounce piece lean salt pork, rind discarded, cut into thin 1½-inch sticks (lardons)

1 tablespoon peanut oil, plus more as needed

3 pounds boneless beef chuck or shoulder, trimmed of excess fat, cut into 2-inch squares, and dried with paper towels

1 carrot, scraped and sliced

2 large onions, sliced

4 cups beef stock or broth (page 6)

1 large, ripe tomato, coarsely chopped

1 tablespoon tomato paste

2 garlic cloves, smashed

1 teaspoon dried thyme, crumbled

1 bay leaf
One 2-inch strip dried orange peel
Salt and freshly ground black pepper to taste
3 tablespoons all-purpose flour blended with 2½ tablespoons
*   soft butter*

Place the salt pork lardons in a large, heavy skillet, add 1 tablespoon of oil, and cook, stirring, over moderately high heat till lightly browned, about 5 minutes. Transfer the sticks to a plate. Add a little more oil to the fat in the skillet, heat to very hot, and, in batches, brown the beef on all sides, adding more oil as needed. Transfer the beef to a large, heavy casserole. Add the carrot and onion slices to the skillet, reduce the heat to moderate, brown lightly, and transfer to the casserole. Discard the fat from the skillet, add 1 cup of the stock, and scrape up the coagulated juices with a wooden spoon. Pour this over the beef and vegetables. Add the remaining 3 cups stock, the salt pork lardons, tomato, tomato paste, garlic, thyme, bay leaf, orange peel, and salt and pepper to the casserole. Bring to a simmer, cover, and cook till the beef is tender enough for a pleasant chew, about 2 hours.

Place a large colander over a saucepan and pour the contents of the casserole into the colander. Wash the casserole and return the meat to it. Press the juices out of the remains in the colander and discard the solids. Skim the fat from the liquid in the saucepan, taste for seasoning, and boil down till the stock is slightly concentrated. Remove the pan from the heat, whisk in the flour-butter blend, bring to a boil, and stir till it thickens into a light gravy. Pour the gravy over the meat and simmer for 2 to 3 minutes, basting the meat.

Serve the stew with boiled rice or noodles and a fresh green vegetable.

❧ *M a k e s   6   t o   8   s e r v i n g s* ❧

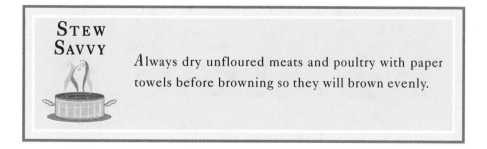

STEW SAVVY

*A*lways dry unfloured meats and poultry with paper towels before browning so they will brown evenly.

COLUMBIA COUNTY APPLEJACK BEEF STEW

So much did I rave about this boozy stew the first time my friend Don Erickson served it at his eighteenth-century farmhouse in Clinton Corner, New York, that I could depend on seeing the big pot on the stove every time I visited—especially during the snowy months. Applejack, which is brandy made from apple cider throughout much of New England and upstate New York, dates back in the United States to at least the early nineteenth century and can be traced even further to English "apple john," a variety of apple. Although we are still a major producer, you don't see or hear much about this potent, flavorful spirit outside the Northeast, which is a shame since applejack is not only a delectable restorative and important link with our culinary past but the ideal ingredient for adding new character to any number of meat stews. Don would often marinate his beef overnight, but I've found that a few hours is sufficient.

1 cup applejack (apple brandy)
¼ cup vegetable oil
4 shallots, chopped
2 garlic cloves, minced
Juice of 1 lemon
⅛ teaspoon dried thyme, crumbled
1 bay leaf
Salt and freshly ground black pepper to taste
Tabasco sauce to taste
3 pounds boneless beef chuck, trimmed of excess fat and cut into
* 1½-inch pieces*
2 cups beef stock or broth (page 6)
2 medium-size carrots, scraped and cut into 1-inch-thick rounds
2 small turnips, peeled and cubed
2 small parsnips, peeled and cubed

In a large bowl, combine the applejack, oil, shallots, garlic, lemon juice, thyme, bay leaf, salt and pepper, and Tabasco and stir well. Add the meat, cover with plastic wrap, and refrigerate 3 hours, turning the meat twice.

Transfer the meat and marinade to a large, heavy pot. Add the stock, bring to a simmer, cover, and cook for 2 hours. Add the carrots, turnips, and parsnips, return the stew to a simmer, and cook till the turnips and parsnips are tender, about 1 hour longer. Remove the top of the pot, increase the heat to moderately high, and cook the sauce down to a fairly thick gravy. Taste for seasoning.

Makes 6 servings

MIDWESTERN BEEF SOLIANKA

TRADITIONALLY IN RUSSIA, *solianka* is a distinctive, complex stew of mixed meats, salty pickles, olives, capers, and tomatoes—a one-pot meal consumed with sauerkraut and beets and served with lots of iced vodka. Although the stew was gradually modified by the Russian immigrants who settled in and around Chicago (and totally changed by those in the Pacific Northwest) at the turn of the century, to this day it's managed to retain most of its Old World integrity and can still be found in some of the Windy City's remaining authentic Russian restaurants. This recipe comes from my friend Anne Sonopol Anderson, who remembers her Russian mother, Proskovia, preparing the stew on cold winter days for a large family at their home in Argo, Illinois. "My father, who was also Russian, always had to have boiled potatoes with his solianka," says Anne, "but the rest of us preferred it with rice, beets, black bread, and, of course, good sturdy beer." Personally, I like to serve the stew with a big bowl of broad noodles—and extra dill pickles.

continued

2½ pounds boneless beef chuck, trimmed of excess fat and cut into
    1-inch pieces
2 tablespoons all-purpose flour
¼ cups (½ stick) butter
2 onions, chopped
1 garlic clove, minced
½ cup dry sherry
2 cups water
1 cup coarsely chopped dill pickles
½ pound mushrooms, quartered
⅓ cup tomato paste
1½ teaspoons imported sweet paprika
1 tablespoon snipped fresh dill
Salt and freshly ground black pepper to taste
½ cup sour cream

On a large plate, dust the beef with the flour, tapping off any excess. Heat 3 table-spoons of the butter in a large, heavy skillet over moderately high heat, add the beef, and brown on all sides. Transfer the beef to a large, heavy pot. Add the remaining 1 tablespoon of butter to the skillet, add the onions and garlic, cook, stirring, until softened, and add to the beef. Deglaze the skillet with the sherry, scraping up any browned bits, and pour over the beef and onions.

    Add the water to the pot, then stir in the pickles, mushrooms, tomato paste, paprika, dill, and salt and pepper and stir well. Bring to a simmer, cover, and cook till the meat is tender, about 1½ hours, adding a little more water if necessary to keep the stew very moist.

    Remove the pot from the heat and stir in the sour cream.

Makes 4 servings

JEAN ANDERSON'S JUGGED BEEF WITH CRANBERRIES AND MUSHROOMS

JEAN ANDERSON, ONE OF OUR FINEST cookbook authors and a fellow North Carolinean, lives in New York City as I do and can whip up quite a feast at her gracious old apartment on Gramercy Park. This, in my opinion, is one of Jean's greatest dishes, especially when she serves it with her broad buttered noodles and a loaf of homemade country bread. She simmers her stew in the oven, but it's just as good cooked on top of the stove—over very low heat. I'm sure that the origins of the stew are English, but the second cranberries are added, it instantly becomes American. Jean says this recipe works equally well for lamb, venison, even buffalo.

2½ pounds lean boneless beef chuck, trimmed of excess fat and
    cut into 1½-inch cubes

1 teaspoon salt

¼ teaspoon freshly ground black pepper

4 to 5 tablespoons all-purpose flour, as needed

½ pound slab bacon, cut into small dice

3 large onions, chopped

1 pound mushrooms, thinly sliced

8 large carrots, scraped and cut into 2-inch chunks

½ teaspoon dried rosemary, crumbled

½ teaspoon dried marjoram, crumbled

¼ teaspoon dried thyme, crumbled

⅛ teaspoon ground nutmeg

One 2-inch stick cinnamon

1 cup dry red wine

¼ cup dry port, Madeira, or sherry

½ cup whole-cranberry sauce

2 tablespoons minced fresh parsley leaves

continued

 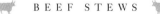

Season the beef with the salt and pepper, dredge in the flour, shaking off all excess, and set aside.

Preheat the oven to 300°F.

In a large, heavy casserole, fry the bacon over moderately high heat till crisp and drain on paper towels. Pour off all but about 3 tablespoons of the drippings, then brown the meat on all sides and transfer to a bowl. Add a little more bacon fat to the casserole, reduce the heat to moderate, add the onions and mushrooms, and stir till lightly browned, about 10 minutes. Add the carrots, rosemary, marjoram, thyme, nutmeg, and cinnamon; stir and cook about 1 minute more. Return the beef to the pot and add the red wine, port, and cranberry sauce. Bring to a boil, cover, and cook in the oven till the meat is very tender, 2 to 2½ hours. Crumble the bacon, add it to the pot along with the parsley, and stir well.

Makes 6 servings

MICHIGAN BARSHCH

I MUST SAY that I've never encountered much memorable food in Detroit (the old and wonderful London Chop House excepted), but when one local lady of Polish extraction prepared this hearty regional stew for me and other colleagues to judge at a March of Dimes Gourmet Gala, I proclaimed it to be exceptional—the deep flavors, texture, and stunning color. Note that this is an example of a beef stew where the meat is not browned before simmering, which necessitates considerable skimming. Also, the vegetables are quite overcooked. No matter. It all tastes wonderful if care is taken in the cooking. Do feel free (as I do) to add an extra beet if so desired.

2 pounds boneless beef chuck, trimmed of excess fat and cut into
1-inch cubes
1 beef soup bone
1 medium-size onion, chopped

3 celery ribs, cut into 2-inch pieces

3 carrots, scraped and cut into 2-inch chunks

Salt and freshly ground black pepper to taste

One 28-ounce can whole tomatoes with their juices, cut up

¼ head green cabbage, thinly sliced

3 fresh beets, peeled and grated

12 small red potatoes, peeled

1 tablespoon fresh lemon juice

1 teaspoon sugar

Sour cream

In a large, heavy stockpot, combine the beef, soup bone, onion, celery, carrots, and salt and pepper and add enough water to cover the ingredients. Bring the liquid to a boil and skim for fat, then reduce the heat to a simmer, cover, and cook for 2 hours, skimming from time to time.

With a slotted spoon, transfer the beef to another large, heavy pot, strain the stock over the beef, and discard the soup bone and vegetables. Add all the remaining ingredients except the sour cream and stir. Bring to a simmer, cover, and cook till the meat and vegetables are very tender, about 1 hour. Taste for salt and pepper.

Serve the stew in deep soup bowls and top each portion with a generous dollop of sour cream.

Makes 6 servings

STEW SAVVY

*R*emember that potatoes, rice, and okra serve as automatic thickeners in stews.

OKLAHOMA GOULASH

WHEN I WAS LIVING in Missouri, two friends and I crossed the Oklahoma border one weekend to visit the large Indian reservation just north of Tulsa, mainly out of curiosity but also to sample some genuine Indian cooking. Except for a very good red chili with bits of pork, the pickings were pretty slim, so the second night we headed for a small restaurant in Tulsa, run, we later learned, by a couple of German descent who prided themselves on a goulash that had been in the family since their ancestors immigrated to Texas and the Oklahoma Territory in the last century. Although the goulash was a far cry from the classic found throughout Germany, Austria, and Hungary, it was nonetheless one of the most remarkable stews I've ever eaten. Chatting with the lady of the house (and a couple of cowboys seated close by), I jotted down notes on a paper napkin and came up with what I think is a very credible version. They served their goulash with rice; I prefer buttered noodles—and fresh applesauce.

3 tablespoons all-purpose flour

1 teaspoon chili powder

*2½ pounds boneless beef chuck or shoulder, trimmed of excess fat
  and cut into 1½-inch cubes*

3 slices bacon

1 large onion, chopped

2 garlic cloves, minced

½ medium-size green bell pepper, seeded and chopped

2 cups water

Salt and freshly ground black pepper to taste

1 celery rib, coarsely chopped

1 carrot, scraped and cut into thin rounds

1 large potato, peeled and cubed

½ cup fresh or frozen lima beans

½ cup sour cream

Combine the flour and chili powder and dust the beef cubes on all sides, tapping off any excess. In a large, heavy skillet, fry the bacon till almost crisp over moderate heat, transfer to a paper towel to drain, and when cool enough to handle, crumble. Increase heat under the skillet to moderately high, add the beef, and brown it on all sides; transfer to a large, heavy pot. Add the onion, garlic, and bell pepper to the skillet, stir for about 2 minutes, and add to the beef. Add the water and salt and pepper to the pot, bring to a simmer, cover, and cook 1½ hours. Add the crumbled bacon, celery, carrot, potato, lima beans, plus a little more water if necessary, and simmer till the beef and vegetables are tender and the gravy fairly thick about 30 minutes longer. Remove the pot from the heat and stir in the sour cream.

Makes 6 servings

TWENTIETH CENTURY LIMITED HUNGARIAN GOULASH

THE GREAT NORTHERN, THE UNION PACIFIC, THE ILLINOIS CENTRAL, the Crescent Limited—the names of the great American railroads of our genteel past evoke childhood memories of my sitting down with my parents in a regal dining car and ordering crab gumbo, potted beef flank, pork pie, lamb fricassee with dumplings, and, best of all, every type of succulent stew imaginable. Until just a few years ago, when she made her final run, the Twentieth Century Limited was still my favorite means of transport between New York and Chicago; and while the food was generally pathetic compared to what was served back in the fifties and sixties, the tender, rich Hungarian goulash (with, alas, no potato dumplings) might well have been the sublime *gulzas* I remember my father ordering on the same train some thirty-five years before. I wish now that I or my mother had made the effort to somehow obtain the actual recipe (for this dish and what was called a baked pear crunch), but I must say I find this interpretation to be plausible. Note: the stew I remember had very large chunks of fork-tender meat (maybe 2½ inches thick), which you might try so long as you remember to simmer the goulash about twenty minutes longer.

¼ cup (½ stick) butter

2½ pounds boneless beef shin or shoulder, trimmed of excess fat
    and cut into 1½-inch pieces

2 large onions, chopped

2 garlic cloves, minced

2 ripe tomatoes, chopped

2 tablespoons imported sweet paprika

1 teaspoon crushed caraway seeds

Salt and freshly ground black pepper to taste

2 cups beef stock or broth (page 6)

1 bay leaf

2 medium-size potatoes, peeled and cut into small cubes

½ cup sour cream

In a large, heavy pot over moderately high heat, heat the butter, then add the beef and brown on all sides. Add the onions, garlic, and tomatoes and stir for about 2 minutes. Add the paprika, caraway seeds, and salt and pepper and stir well. Add the stock and bay leaf, stir, bring to a simmer, cover, and cook for 1½ hours.

Add the potatoes and stir, then return the goulash to a simmer, and cook till the meat and potatoes are tender, about 30 minutes longer. Discard the bay leaf and skim the surface for any fat. Whisk ½ cup of the cooking liquid into the sour cream, then return the mixture to the pot and stir till well blended.

Makes 4 to 6 servings

BRAISED BOURBON
ROSEMARY BEEF

I LOVE BEEF FLAVORED (lightly) with rosemary and came up with this stew one day when I had excess meat from a five-pound rump roast I'd bought on sale. Initially, I deglazed the pot with lots of red wine, but since that made the stew taste almost like *boeuf bourguignon*, the next time I used bourbon with delightfully different results. You might also think about adding a cup of corn kernels to this stew if you need to stretch it.

¼ cup (½ stick) butter

2 pounds boneless beef rump or bottom round, trimmed of excess fat, cut into bite-size strips, and patted dry with paper towels

½ cup bourbon

12 to 14 small white onions, peeled and scored on the root ends

6 carrots, scraped, halved, and cut into strips

½ pound mushrooms, sliced

3 cups beef stock or broth (page 6)

1 tablespoon chopped fresh rosemary, or 1 teaspoon dried, crumbled

Salt and freshly ground black pepper to taste

1 tablespoon cornstarch mixed with 1 tablespoon cold water

Heat half the butter over moderately high heat in a large, heavy pot, then add the beef strips and brown well on all sides. Transfer the strips to a plate. Add the bourbon to the pot, stir to scrape up the browned bits and pieces of meat, and pour over the strips.

In the same pot, heat the remaining 2 tablespoons butter over medium heat, then add the onions, carrots, and mushrooms, and stir gently till the mush room liquid has evaporated, about 8 minutes. Return the beef and juices to the pot and add the stock, rosemary, and salt and pepper. Bring to a simmer, cover, and cook till the beef is very tender, about 1 hour.

Stir in the cornstarch mixture over medium heat until the stew is thickened, about 5 minutes. Taste for salt and pepper before serving.

Makes 4 to 6 servings

PEARL'S BOURBON BEEF AND OYSTER POT

THE FORERUNNER OF WHAT today is called New American Cuisine was Pearl Byrd Foster, owner-chef of Mr. & Mrs. Foster's Place in New York City, a real Virginia lady and one of the great inspirations. When I once challenged her to create something similar to a delectable beef and oyster dish I'd just sampled at a country house hotel in England's West Country, this is the sensational stew that resulted and became a big hit at her tiny restaurant. "Honey," she said, "it proves just how sophisticated American stews can be."

¼ cup all-purpose flour
Salt and freshly ground black pepper to taste
*4 pounds beef top or bottom round, trimmed of excess fat and
    cut into 1½-inch pieces*
3 tablespoons vegetable oil
2 tablespoons butter
¾ cup bourbon
4 cups beef stock or broth (page 6)
4 cups water
1 large carrot, scraped and cut into 1-inch-thick rounds
2 celery ribs, cut into 1-inch-thick slices
1 large potato, peeled and cut into quarters
1 medium-size onion, peeled and studded with 2 cloves

2 tablespoons prepared tomato sauce
1 garlic clove, chopped
¼ teaspoon dried thyme, crumbled
1 bay leaf
Worcestershire and Tabasco sauces to taste
3 dozen shucked fresh oysters, plus their liquor
Toast points and watercress for garnish
Grated horseradish

In a bowl, combine the flour and salt and pepper and dust the beef with the mixture, tapping off any excess. In a large, heavy skillet, heat the oil and butter together over moderately high heat, then brown the meat on all sides. Pour ½ cup of the bourbon over the meat and, standing back at as safe a distance as possible, light the bourbon carefully with a long match. When the flames die out, transfer the meat to a large, heavy pot and pour the stock and water over it. Discard any fat in the skillet, add a little water to it, scrape up the browned bits, and add this to the meat. Add the carrot, celery, potato, onion, tomato sauce, garlic, thyme, and bay leaf to the meat and bring to a boil. Reduce the heat to a simmer, cover, and cook the stew until the meat is tender, about 3 hours.

Transfer the meat to a plate, pour the contents of the pot carefully into a blender or food processor (in batches if necessary), and reduce to a smooth puree. Return the sauce and meat to the pot, season with Worcestershire, Tabasco, and salt and pepper, and bring to a low boil. Add the oysters plus their liquor and heat just till the oysters curl. Heat the remaining bourbon in a small pan, pour over the beef and oysters, and flame as instructed above. When the flames die out, spoon the stew into heated serving bowls. Garnish each with toast points and watercress and pass the grated horseradish to be sprinkled on top.

Makes 8 servings

STEW SAVVY

When browning meats and poultry for stews, always use tongs or a spatula to turn the pieces, thus avoiding puncturing the seared crusts and releasing juices.

ALABAMA BEEF, LIMA BEANS, AND GRITS SCRAMBLE

THIS STICK-TO-THE-RIBS stew was made by the black cook of a friend's mother whom I visited at their gracious antebellum home in Huntsville, Alabama. Although I am Southern and was raised on every preparation of grits there is, this was the first and only time I ever saw them incorporated into a stew—or, as they call it, a "scramble." When I showed surprise at the dish, Mrs. Smith simply looked over at me and drawled playfully, "Well, son, y'all must not be very Southern over in North Carolina." Do not use quick grits for this recipe—for heaven's sake.

2 pounds boneless beef shank or shoulder, trimmed of excess fat
   and cut into 1½-inch pieces
½ cup all-purpose flour
¼ cup (½ stick) butter
2 onions, chopped
2 ripe tomatoes, chopped
3 carrots, scraped and cut into strips
Few dashes of Worcestershire sauce
Salt and freshly ground black pepper to taste
3 cups water
1½ cups fresh or frozen lima beans
1 cup regular grits

On a large plate, dust the beef with the flour well and shake off the excess. In a large, heavy pot, heat the butter over moderately high heat, then add the beef and brown on all sides. Add the onions and stir till softened. Add the tomatoes, carrots, Worcestershire sauce, and salt and pepper and stir. Add the water, bring to a simmer, cover, and cook 1½ hours. Add the limas and grits, stir well, and cook till the beef and limas are tender and the grits just soft, about 20 minutes longer.

Makes 4 to 6 servings

SECOND AVENUE
DELICATESSEN CHOLENT

CHOLENT IS ONE of the great hearty classics of Jewish delicatessen cookery, and none is more delicious than the late Abe Lebewohl's at the Second Avenue Deli in New York City. Since flanken (pronounced *flunken* by deli habitues) is a special cut of beef short ribs with its own distinctive flavor, you really should make the effort to find a good kosher butcher. Serve the stew steaming hot in bowls with good rye bread, perhaps a simple green salad, and a little coarse kosher salt to sprinkle on top; and remember that cholent only improves in flavor if prepared and kept chilled a day or so in advance. This is a soupy stew.

1½ pounds boneless beef flanken or chuck, trimmed of excess fat
and cut into 1½-inch pieces
1 onion, chopped
1 potato, peeled and diced
1 carrot, scraped and chopped
¾ cup dried white beans, rinsed and picked over
¼ cup pearl barley
4 cups chicken stock or broth (page 120)
4 cups beef stock or broth (page 6)
Salt and freshly ground black pepper to taste

In a large, heavy pot, combine all the ingredients, bring to a boil, and skim the froth from the surface. Reduce the heat to a simmer and cook till the meat falls apart to the touch and the beans are very tender, about 4 hours, stirring and skimming from time to time. Keep the ingredients well covered by adding more stock or water when necessary.

Makes 4 servings

ARIZONA COCIDO

FOR AGES IN SPAIN and Mexico, cocido has been a prized stew with endless variations of ingredients, a savory, soupy concoction that crossed the Mexican border with the development of our Southwestern states and quickly became part of Arizona and New Mexico's culinary traditions. I've sampled cocido made with every cut of meat and variety of bean, vegetable, and chili pepper imaginable, but this one with brisket, squash, and garbanzos, prepared at a March of Dimes Gourmet Gala I attended in Tucson, has to be one of the most memorable. Serve the stew with plenty of rice, tortillas, and ice cold beer, and remember that a real cocido should not be too thick.

2 pounds beef brisket (thin cut), trimmed of excess fat and cut into 1½-inch pieces

3 links chorizo sausages, cut into rounds

2 medium-size onions, chopped

2 garlic cloves, finely chopped

Salt and freshly ground black pepper to taste

3 cups beef stock or broth (page 6)

3 cups water

1 large potato, peeled and cut into medium-size cubes

2 carrots, scraped and cut into rounds

1 small acorn or butternut squash, peeled, seeded, and cut into cubes

One 15-ounce can garbanzo beans (chickpeas), drained and rinsed

2 small fresh ancho or jalapeño peppers, seeded and finely chopped

1 tablespoon chopped fresh oregano leaves, or 1 teaspoon dried, crumbled

1 tablespoon chopped fresh cilantro leaves

In a large, heavy pot, combine the brisket, sausages, onions, garlic, salt and pepper, stock, and water. Bring to a boil and let cook 5 minutes, skimming the scum as it rises to the surface. Reduce the heat to a simmer, cover, and cook 1½ hours, skimming from time to time if necessary. Add the remaining ingredients, return the stew to the simmer, cover, and cook till the beef and squash are tender, about 1 hour longer, adding more stock or water if the stew gets too thick. Taste for salt and pepper. Serve the stew in deep soup bowls.

Makes 6 servings

CHICAGO FLANK STEAK AND GREEN PEA STEW

MEMORY IS FAINT, but before the stockyards in Southside Chicago finally folded, nothing was more exciting than to venture out to one of the rough-and-ready restaurants, taverns, or roadhouses in the area that specialized in the succulent prime steaks that are now almost extinct, as well as savory stews like this one, made with every minor cut of meat imaginable. Ordinarily, flank or "London broil" (from the underside of the steer) must be marinated about six hours for perfect tenderness, but when simmered slowly a long time in liquid, no such prepping is necessary. Beef shank (with its rich marrow bone) works equally well in this simple stew.

continued

½ cup all-purpose flour

Salt and freshly ground black pepper to taste

2 to 2½ pounds flank steak cut about 1½ inches thick, trimmed
of excess fat and cut into 1-inch cubes

3 tablespoons vegetable oil

1 large onion, sliced

1 garlic clove, minced

3 cups beef stock or broth (page 6)

8 small red potatoes, peeled

2 cups fresh or frozen green peas

In a bowl, combine the flour and salt, and pepper until well blended. In batches, add the steak cubes and toss until well coated, tapping off any excess. In a large, heavy pot, heat the oil to moderately high, add the cubes, and brown evenly. Add the onion and garlic, and stir 1 minute. Add the stock, bring to a boil, reduce the heat to a simmer, cover, and cook 2 hours. Add the potatoes and simmer 20 minutes longer, adding a little more stock if necessary. Add the peas, stir, and cook till the potatoes and peas are tender, about 15 minutes longer.

Makes 4 to 6 servings

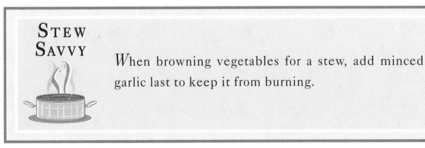

STEW SAVVY

When browning vegetables for a stew, add minced garlic last to keep it from burning.

NEW ORLEANS
DAUBE GLACÉ

T̲RADITIONALLY, C̲REOLE ̲DAUBE ̲GLACÉ, made from beef and veal shin bones stewed with pigs' feet, is one of the most elaborate, elegant, and time-consuming dishes on earth, intended for formal buffets like those set up for special occasions in the grand old mansions of New Orleans's Garden District. The chilled daube can either be in the form of a large, jelled loaf or served as individual molds. This much-simplified version (which originated when I once found an exquisite piece of brisket on sale and wanted to get rid of two pigs' feet taking up room in the freezer) takes considerably less time and effort and never fails to impress my luncheon guests. If you want to be fancy, you can make the daube in an attractive mold, but normally I just use a colorful big bowl and let my friends serve themselves. To start, I like to serve a simple gumbo or chowder, and nothing goes better with this type of food than plenty of hot buttered biscuits.

One 3-pound beef brisket (thin cut) or boneless rump roast,
 trimmed of excess fat and cut into 1½-inch cubes
2 pig's feet, scrubbed and rinsed
3 onions, coarsely chopped
2 celery ribs (leaves included), coarsely chopped
1 garlic clove, finely chopped
3 sprigs fresh parsley
2 cloves, pounded to powder
2 bay leaves
1 teaspoon dried thyme, crumbled
1 teaspoon cayenne pepper
Salt and freshly ground black pepper to taste
½ cup dry sherry

continued

Place the beef and pig's feet in a large, heavy pot, add enough cold water to cover, bring to a boil, and skim off the foam. Reduce the heat to a simmer, cover, and cook 1 hour. Skim carefully for foam and fat.

Add all the remaining ingredients except the sherry, return the stew to a simmer, cover, and cook till the meat is tender, about 2 hours longer, skimming from time to time and adding more water if necessary.

With a slotted spoon, transfer the beef to a large, deep bowl. Transfer the pig's feet to a chopping board; remove the meat from the bones, mince the meat, and discard the bones. Add the minced meat to the beef.

Strain the stock through a piece of cheesecloth into another bowl; discard the solids and stir the sherry into the stock. Pour the stock over the meats, stir, and let cool to room temperature. Cover the meats with plastic wrap and chill at least 6 hours, stirring from time to time to distribute meats evenly.

Makes 6 servings

SONOMA CORNED BEEF
STEWED IN BEER

WHEN VISITING THE FAMOUS food writer M.F.K. Fisher at her modest Glen Ellen ranch in California's Sonoma Valley, I never knew what Mary Frances might come up with for one of our long, chatty, wonderful lunches. On a rather chilly fall day redolent of eucalyptus, she had prepared this spicy beef stew made with half of a whole corned brisket she said she didn't "care to have sitting around." Served with fresh sourdough bread baked by a neighbor and glasses of pinot noir, followed by vanilla-flavored custard, it was one of my most memorable lunches.

½ cup Dijon mustard

½ cup firmly packed light brown sugar

*One 3-pound corned beef (thin cut), trimmed of excess fat and
    cut into 1½-inch cubes*

3 tablespoons vegetable oil

6 cloves

6 black peppercorns

Salt to taste

4 cups full-bodied beer

3 medium-size onions, quartered

2 carrots, scraped and cut into thirds

1 celery rib (leaves included), coarsely chopped

On a large plate, stir together the mustard and brown sugar till well blended and lightly coat the beef cubes in the mixture. In a large, heavy pot, heat the oil to moderately high, then add the cubes and brown evenly, turning carefully so as not to burn the sugar. Add the cloves, peppercorns, salt, and beer, bring to a simmer, scraping any browned bits off the bottom, cover, and cook 2½ hours. Add the onions, carrots, and celery, stir, and cook till the beef and vegetables are tender, about 40 minutes longer.

Makes 4 to 6 servings

PRAIRIE OXTAIL RAGOUT

"WHAT IS THAT?" I asked the butcher at Snow's meat market in Kansas City, Kansas, pointing to a long object in the case. It was a whole oxtail, of course, skinned and ready to be hacked into two-inch pieces, and my first exposure to one of the most neglected yet delicious cuts of beef there is. When the butcher told me how to prepare the joints, I ordered four or five pounds along with the prime K.C. strip steaks I'd come in for. I proceeded to drive to Lawrence where my friend's wife, accustomed to cooking oxtails since a young girl, only smiled as she plopped them in a big pot with lots of vegetables and placed the steaks in the refrigerator. Since then, I've learned that oxtails were not only a readily available and inexpensive staple during the days of pioneer expansion but that they are still highly prized throughout the Plains states and in Texas—stewed, braised, and even browned under the broiler. Today, you can find disjointed, fairly meaty oxtails (usually frozen and no longer that cheap) in most major supermarkets, and when slowly simmered in a ragout like this one, their rich, satiny, gelatinous flavor and texture are utterly sublime. This is another dish that improves when made a day or so in advance, chilled, defatted, and reheated after the flavors have had a chance to mellow.

4 pounds oxtail, disjointed

½ cup all-purpose flour

6 tablespoons vegetable oil

3 medium-size onions, sliced

2 garlic cloves, minced

1 small turnip, peeled and sliced

*1 medium-size leek (white part only), thoroughly washed and
    sliced into rounds*

2 ripe tomatoes, chopped

2 cups beef stock or broth (page 6)

2 cups dry red wine
½ teaspoon dried thyme, crumbled
½ teaspoon dried rosemary, crumbled
1 bay leaf
Salt and freshly ground black pepper to taste

Wash the oxtail, then flour the pieces well, tapping off any excess. In a large, heavy skillet, heat 5 tablespoons of the oil over moderately high heat, then add the oxtail in batches and brown on all sides. Transfer to a large, heavy pot. Add the remaining tablespoon oil to the skillet, reduce the heat to moderate, add the onions and garlic, and brown lightly, stirring; transfer to the pot. Add to the pot the remaining ingredients, bring to a boil, and let boil 5 minutes, skimming the scum as it rises to the surface. Reduce the heat to a simmer, cover, and cook the ragout till the oxtail pieces are very tender, about 3 hours, skimming from time to time.

Makes 6 servings

STEW SAVVY

*T*o get a rough idea of the various degrees of doneness when browning onions for any stew (depending on the volume), follow the timing for 1 medium-size onion cooked in vegetable oil over moderate heat: 2 minutes, soft; 4 minutes, golden; 7 minutes, lightly browned; 9 minutes, browned. Note also that oil browns faster than butter or margarine.

OXTAIL AND WHITE BEANS
BRAISED IN STOUT

Although relatively still unknown in the United States, Delia Smith is the Julia Child–Martha Stewart of Britain, an indefatigable cook and food personality who has authored numerous cookbooks and appears regularly on London TV. When, during a recent dinner, she mentioned this sumptuous oxtail stew braised in stout, I wasted no time jotting down the cooking directions so I could reproduce the dish at my home in East Hampton. As usual, I've tampered a bit with the recipe to give it more American character, but I doubt that Delia would disapprove. If you can find cannellini (white Italian kidney) beans, they're utterly delicious in this stew. (If you don't have time to soak the beans overnight, a quick method is to boil them 10 minutes, then soak them for six hours.) Likewise, any variety of wild mushroom (substituted for the button ones) adds even more depth.

8 ounces (1¼ cups) dried white peas or navy beans

8 cups cold water

¼ cup vegetable oil

3½ pounds oxtail, disjointed

2 to 3 tablespoons all-purpose flour

2 large onions, thickly sliced

4 garlic cloves, peeled

2 sprigs fresh thyme, or 1 teaspoon dried, crumbled

2 bay leaves

Salt and freshly ground black pepper to taste

1 pound mushrooms, quartered

2 cups beef stock or broth (page 6)

1½ cups stout or dark ale (like Guinness)

In a large bowl, combine the beans and water and soak overnight.

In a large, heavy skillet, heat 2 tablespoons of the oil over moderately high heat. On a large plate, dust the oxtail pieces with the flour, tapping off any excess, then brown them in the oil till nutty in color. Transfer to a large, heavy pot. Add the remaining 2 tablespoons of oil to the skillet, reduce the heat to moderate, add the onions, and brown them slightly. Add them to the oxtail. Remove the pan from the heat.

Drain and pick over the beans, then add them to the oxtail and onions along with the garlic, thyme, bay leaves, and salt and pepper and stir. Return the skillet to moderate heat, add any remaining flour, and stir well to soak up the juices. Gradually add the stock and stout, increasing the heat and whisking well till the liquid reaches a simmer. Pour over the oxtail, cover the pot, bring the stew to a simmer, and cook for 3 hours; the meat will be extremely tender. Skim any fat from the surface, then taste for seasoning.

Makes 6 servings

PAW PAW'S
SHORT RIBS OF BEEF

THIS WHOLESOME, INCREDIBLY FLAVORFUL STEW has been in my Southern family at least four generations, and I can still see my grandfather Paw Paw arguing with the butcher over whether the ribs being proffered were large and meaty enough. My mother still won't touch ribs that aren't at least four inches wide and three inches thick, while what I rage about mostly these days is the high cost of this minor cut of beef that used to be cheap as dirt ($3.89 per pound, indeed!). Just lately, beef short ribs have become rather popular in even the most fashionable American restaurants, but I've yet to sample a preparation that comes close to this sumptuous stew I serve at least once a month—religiously with hot buttermilk biscuits.

continued

6 meaty short ribs of beef, trimmed of excess fat
Salt and freshly ground black pepper to taste
12 small onions, peeled and scored on the root ends
10 small red potatoes, peeled
One 16-ounce can whole tomatoes with their juices
Beef stock (page 6; optional)

Place the short ribs in a large saucepan or pot with enough water to cover and season with salt and pepper. Bring to a boil, then reduce the heat to low, cover, and simmer at least 3 hours, adding more water if necessary to cover. During the last hour of simmering, add the onions. During the last 30 minutes, add the potatoes.

Preheat the oven to 375°F.

Transfer the meat to a shallow baking dish with a slotted spoon, place the onions and potatoes around the meat, and add the tomatoes with their juices. If the juices do not fill the baking dish by three-quarters, add a little of the cooking liquid or stock. Season with salt and pepper, place in the oven, and cook till the top is slightly crusted, about 45 minutes. Serve directly from the dish.

Makes 4 to 6 servings

SIGRID'S MEATBALL STEW

WHEN I WAS A CHILD in North Carolina, nothing was more special than the Sunday nights when my Swedish grandmother would serve her spicy meatball stew accompanied by tiny parsleyed boiled potatoes and homemade applesauce. Later, I knew Swedes in Minnesota who also prepared a *frikadeller* stew (always served with a big bowl of beets and plenty of limpa bread to sop up the gravy), but to my mind, Mama's remains the quintessential version, a dish that fills the house with the most intoxicating aroma.

1 tablespoon butter

1 medium-size onion, minced

2 pounds ground beef round or boneless shank

½ teaspoon ground cinnamon

Pinch of ground nutmeg

Salt and freshly ground black pepper to taste

1½ cups beef broth (page 6)

Juice of 1 lemon

2 tablespoons lingonberry jam

2 teaspoons snipped fresh dill

1 bay leaf

In a small skillet, heat the butter over moderate heat, then add the onion, cook, stirring, till softened, and transfer to a large bowl. Add the beef, cinnamon, nutmeg, and salt and pepper to the bowl and with your hands mix all the ingredients until well blended. Roll the mixture into 1-inch balls.

In a large, heavy pot, brown the meatballs over moderately high heat on all sides, transfer to paper towels, and discard any fat from the pot. Return the meatballs to the pot and add the remaining ingredients. Bring to a simmer, cover, and cook 45 minutes, adding a little more stock or water if necessary. Discard bay leaf before serving.

Makes 4 to 6 servings

TEX-MEX PICADILLO

IN MEXICO, WHERE THE PIG is king, picadillo is always made with cubed or shredded pork and used primarily to stuff chilies and tortillas. However, as it has been transformed in Texas and other border states, the spicy dish is usually prepared with chopped beef or a combination of chopped beef and pork and served over rice. One lady I know in Brownsville, Texas, simply serves her sensational picadillo by itself in big colorful bowls (like chili) with lots of fresh wheat tortillas on the side. Personally, I love to use the thick stew to stuff baked green bell peppers, a dish that's always a big hit at a casual luncheon or summertime dinner buffet—served with slaw and either biscuits or corn sticks. I must say also that when I barbecue a whole huge pork shoulder in the Southern manner, I often use some of the shredded meat in this same recipe in place of the beef. And one of my next projects is to do the same with a large barbecued brisket of beef. Why not?

3 tablespoons corn oil

2 pounds boneless beef chuck or shoulder, trimmed of excess fat and coarsely chopped

1 pound boneless pork shoulder, trimmed of excess fat and coarsely chopped

2 medium-size onions, finely chopped

2 garlic cloves, minced

1 fresh green Anaheim or jalapeño pepper, seeded and finely chopped

2$^{1}/_{3}$ cups dark raisins

4 ripe tomatoes, coarsely chopped and juices retained

2 teaspoons chili powder

$^{1}/_{2}$ teaspoon ground cinnamon

$^{1}/_{2}$ teaspoon ground cloves

$^{1}/_{2}$ teaspoon ground cumin

Salt and freshly ground black pepper to taste
½ cup water
¼ cup cider vinegar

In a large, heavy pot, heat the oil over moderate heat, then add the beef and pork and stir till lightly browned, about 10 minutes. Add the onions, garlic, and jalapeño, stir, and cook till softened, about 5 minutes. Add all the remaining ingredients, bring to a simmer, cover, and cook till the stew has thickened nicely, about 1 hour.

Makes 6 servings

STEW SAVVY *T*o make your own chili powder for Southwestern stews, place dried hot peppers on a baking sheet, toast 10 to 15 minutes in a 250°F. oven, remove the stems and seeds, grind to a powder in an blender or spice mill, and store in plastic bags.

FRANK TOLBERT'S ORIGINAL "BOWL OF RED"

Mastermind behind the world Championship Chili Cookoff at Terlingua, Texas, author of the definitive *A Bowl of Red*, and owner of two famous chili parlors in Dallas, Frank Xavier Tolbert is still recognized as the world's greatest expert on chili con carne. Although the much-sought-after recipe he gave me might sound a bit complex and involved, I reproduce it here in his own words with minimum editing and tampering. Read the recipe carefully at least three times to absorb the facts and get in the chili-making mood, then get to work and learn what truly great Texas chili is all about.

continued

The main vehicle in the formula is three pounds of mature beef or venison, and we usually call for lean beef when we can get it. I successfully made the chili on the North Cape in Norwegian Lapland, hundreds of miles above the Arctic Circle, with reindeer meat, and my brother in Alaska uses caribou (same as reindeer) and moose.

At the start, we marinate the beef in beer and keep this liquid in the cooking process. Cut the meat into thumb-sized pieces or put it through a grinder at the coarsest setting. We sear the beef until it is gray in rendered beef kidney suet, which adds a sweet flavor, but you will probably do the searing in vegetable oil. Vegetable oil is okay, I guess. The searing will seal in meat flavors and solidify the beef for the cooking process, same as you would sear a steak. I use about an eighth of a pound of rendered kidney suet, and a like amount of vegetable oil should do. Many old-time chili cooks sprinkle some chopped-up onions on the meat while it is being seared. Go ahead if you think it'll suit your taste.

Chili peppers, such as sun-dried anchos or jalapeños, can be obtained in most Mexican food stores. For mild chili use two average-sized chili pepper pods for each pound of beef. For "elevated" chili use four pods. Put chili peppers in a blender along with enough water to make a puree, transfer to a large pot along with the beer marinade and meat, and cook the seared meat, first bringing it to a boil and then simmering for about 30 minutes. Take the pot off the stove for a while.

Add fresh garlic to taste, two level tablespoons of crushed cumin seed or powdered *comino*, one level tablespoon of salt, one level tablespoon of cayenne pepper, and a few pinches of oregano. We go very slow with the oregano. Too much oregano can give a spaghetti sauce flavor. If you use yellowish, greenish, or purplish chili peppers, you can sprinkle in some paprika to add a reddish hue to the chili. It won't affect the taste. Wick Fowler, one of the greatest of chili cooks, put 15 ounces of tomato sauce in a recipe calling for three pounds of meat. He said it adds color and thickening and most of the tomato flavor surrenders to the more powerful spices. Wick also "tightened" the chili with *masa harina* [corn flour], but I think it gives too much of a tamale taste.

With the spices in there, put the pot back on the stove, bring to a boil, and then simmer about 45 minutes, stirring some but keeping the lid on as much as possible. This last time for simmering isn't arbitrary. Cook the meat till it's tender and has the taste you're looking for. Keep the chili in the refrigerator overnight to seal in the spices. This also makes it easy to spoon off any grease at the top, which you don't want in your chili. Actually, though, a little grease helps the flavor.

If you want pinto or red beans with your chili, for God's sake cook the beans separately, and there's no need to make the beans highly flavored. I'm constantly running into people who cook beans in with the meat in making chili con carne. These people flunked chemistry.

Yield: "Can't say. Depends on appetites. But there ought to be enough chili here for at least 4 or 5 hungry people."

TIGUA GREEN INDIAN CHILI

WHILE IN TUCSON to eat barbecue, I was encouraged by my colleagues Jane and Michael Stern to make the detour down to El Paso just to sample this distinctive and rare chili served at the colorful Tigua Indian Restaurant. They also serve a mean red chili, but it was the fiery green one speckled with pepper seeds (and sometimes made with mutton instead of beef) that taught me what the flavor of Southwestern chili is really all about. Needless to say, nobody at the restaurant was about to part with the exact recipe, but after a lengthy conversation with a group of Indians at the next table, I came up with this version that comes pretty close to the slightly soupy, intensely flavored chili that forced me to gasp (delightfully) for breath after every spoonful. Rice and hearty Indian bread were served with it, but I find that cornbread makes a very acceptable substitute—and helps to placate the heat.

continued

2 tablespoons lard

2 pounds boneless beef shank or chuck, trimmed of excess fat and
　　cut into 1-inch cubes

1 medium-size onion, finely chopped

1 garlic clove, minced

1 ripe tomato, diced

¼ cup ground dried hot peppers (like Anaheims, anchos,
　　or serranos)

2 fresh jalapeño peppers, finely chopped

1 teaspoon ground cumin

½ teaspoon dried oregano, crumbled

1 tablespoon chili powder

1 tablespoon finely ground cornmeal

Salt to taste

2 cups beef stock or broth (page 6)

1 cup water

1 tablespoon cider vinegar

2 medium-size potatoes, peeled and cut into tiny chunks

In a large, heavy pot, melt the lard over moderately high heat, then add the beef, and brown on all sides. Reduce the heat to moderate, add the onion and garlic, and stir 2 minutes. Add all the remaining ingredients except the potatoes, stir well, and bring to a simmer. Cover and let cook for 2 hours, adding a little more water if necessary. Add the potatoes, stir, and cook till the meat and potatoes are tender, about 30 minutes longer. Serve the chili in deep bowls.

❧　*M a k e s　4　t o　6　s e r v i n g s*　❧

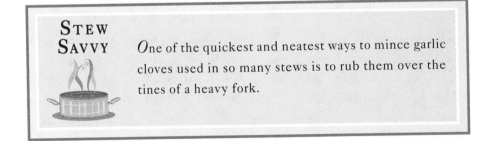

STEW SAVVY

*O*ne of the quickest and neatest ways to mince garlic cloves used in so many stews is to rub them over the tines of a heavy fork.

CRAIG CLAIBORNE'S
BEANLESS CHILI

OF ALL THE CHILIHEADS I've known and shared "bowls of red" with, none is
more passionate about the dish than my neighbor Craig Claiborne. And nobody is
more adamant about beans being wrong in chili than Craig. Served on the side,
yes, but not *in* the chili. It doesn't matter to him that I disagree, nor does he care
that I disapprove of browning the meat for chili in olive oil (too pungent, I say). On
the other hand, I have to admit that Craig's finished product is intriguing, partly
because of the technique of rubbing the spices between the palms to release the
flavors—a trick he learned from a lady down in San Antonio, Texas. With this chili,
Craig likes to serve an array of garnishes: chopped lettuce, sour cream, grated
Cheddar cheese, chopped fresh cilantro leaves, and hot pepper flakes.

½ cup olive oil

5 pounds lean chuck roast, trimmed of excess fat and cut into
1-inch cubes

½ cup all-purpose flour

½ cup chili powder

2 teaspoons cumin seeds

2 teaspoons dried oregano

8 garlic cloves, minced

4 cups beef broth (page 6)

Salt and freshly ground black pepper to taste

In a large, heavy pot, heat the oil over moderate heat, then add the beef and stir
until the meat loses its red color. Sift together the flour and chili powder, sprinkle
the mixture over the meat, and stir well. Rub the cumin seeds and oregano
between the palms of your hands and sprinkle over the meat. Add the garlic and
stir. Add the broth, stirring constantly. Add the salt and pepper and bring to a boil,
then reduce the heat to a simmer, cover, and cook till the meat almost falls apart,
3 to 4 hours, adding more broth if necessary.

Makes at least 8 servings

CHASEN'S FAMOUS CHILI

UNTIL JUST A COUPLE of years ago when it finally closed, Chasen's was one of the most fashionable and legendary restaurants in Los Angeles, partly because of this chili (along with what was called a "Hobo Steak"). In the early sixties, while they were filming *Cleopatra*, Elizabeth Taylor and Richard Burton would cable Dave Chasen to fly ten frozen quarts of the chili to Rome; whenever my neighbor and colleague Craig Claiborne happened to be in town over the past decades, a stop at Chasen's for a bowl of chili was always at the top of his agenda. Ditto yours truly, who, like Craig, spent years begging Maude Chasen for the exact recipe, each time being given just a slightly different formula. Here, therefore, is my last version of a chili that's really not that unusual—just damn good. I do think that one secret to Chasen's chili is that it never had too many beans.

¼ cup corn oil

3 medium-size onions, chopped

1 large green bell pepper, seeded and chopped

2 garlic cloves, minced

¼ cup (½ stick) butter

2½ pounds ground beef chuck

1 pound ground pork

6 tablespoons chili powder, or to taste

1 teaspoon dried oregano, crumbled

1 teaspoon crushed cumin seeds

Salt and freshly ground black pepper to taste

One 28-ounce can crushed tomatoes

One 16-ounce can pinto or kidney beans

In a medium-size skillet, heat 2 tablespoons of the oil over moderate heat, then add the onions, bell pepper, and garlic, and cook till softened, about 5 minutes, stirring. Set aside.

In a large, heavy pot, heat the remaining 2 tablespoons oil plus the butter over moderate heat, then add the beef and pork, and cook, stirring and breaking up the meats till lightly browned, about 10 minutes. Sprinkle with the chili powder, stir well, and cook, stirring occasionally, 10 minutes longer. Add the contents of the skillet to the meat, along with the oregano, cumin, and salt and pepper, and stir. Add the tomatoes and their juices plus the juice from the beans and stir. Bring to a simmer, cover, and cook till slightly thickened, about 1 hour.

Tilt the pot and skim off and discard as much fat as possible. Add the beans, return to a simmer, cover, and cook the chili about 1 hour longer.

Makes 8 to 10 servings

CINCINNATI 4-WAY CHILI

People either love or hate Cincinnati chili. No doubt it is an acquired taste for those chiliheads accustomed to the Southwestern "bowl of red" or classic chili con carne. I can only say that the second I arrive in Cincinnati, the first parlor I hit is either Camp Washington Chili or one of the many branches of Empress Chili located around town that specialize in 2-way chili (over spaghetti), 3-way (with grated cheese), 4-way (chopped onions added), or 5-way (with kidney beans). They say that Cincinnati chili was invented by Greek immigrants, which makes sense since the dish is so spicy and since so many of the chili parlors have been (and still are) run by Greeks. How the addition of chocolate came about still baffles me, but believe me, it's one of the ingredients that makes this chili distinctive and unique.

2 pounds ground lean beef chuck
2 medium-size onions, finely chopped
2 cups canned crushed tomatoes
2 garlic cloves, minced
2 cups strong black coffee
2 cups water
2 tablespoons chili powder
1 teaspoon ground cumin
1 teaspoon ground cinnamon
½ teaspoon ground ginger
½ teaspoon ground cloves
Salt and freshly ground black pepper to taste
Big dash of cayenne pepper
½ ounce (½ square) unsweetened chocolate
1 pound spaghetti
2 cups grated Cheddar cheese
2 medium-size onions, chopped

In a large, heavy skillet, cook the beef over moderate heat till all the pink is gone, about 5 minutes, stirring and breaking up the meat. Transfer to a large pot, discarding any fat in the skillet. Add the onions, tomatoes, garlic, coffee, and water to the beef, stir well, and bring to a low boil. Add all the seasonings and chocolate, and stir well. Reduce the heat to a simmer and cook, uncovered, till desired consistency is reached, about 2½ hours.

Cook the spaghetti according to the package directions, drain in a colander, then divide among 6 soup bowls. Ladle equal amounts of chili over the spaghetti and garnish the tops with the cheese and chopped onions.

Makes 6 servings

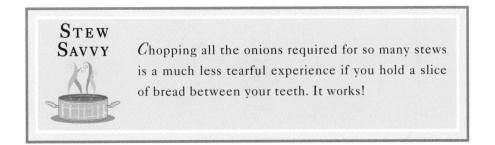

STEW SAVVY *C*hopping all the onions required for so many stews is a much less tearful experience if you hold a slice of bread between your teeth. It works!

Pork Stews

Pork Stew with Prunes and Apples

New England Pork and Clam Stew

Santa Fe Posole

*The Curmudgeon's
Pork and Onion Stew in a Pumpkin*

Sheboygan Cider Pork and Apple Stew

Spicy Pork and Red Plum Stew

Curried Pork and Yellow Squash Ragout

Napolean Pork, Vegetable, and Olive Ragout

Pork Goulash Ritz-Carlton

Charlevoix Pork and Sauerkraut Goulash

Gray Kunz's Braised Pork Butt with Maple Syrup

Colorado Chile Verde

Hoosier Pork Spareribs and Sweet Potato Stew

Pork Chili with Corn

Mrs. Zodas's Glazed Sausage and Chickpea Stew

Uncle Tom's Sausage Pilau

Cajun Ham, Sausage, and Shrimp Jambalaya

Georgia Ham and Black-Eyed Pea Stew

Garden State Sausage and White Bean Pot

Ranch Ham Hocks with Sauerkraut

Kentucky Stewed Ham Hocks and Lima Beans

Cuts of Pork
for Stewing

No meat makes more succulent stews than pork, and except for the back (fat back), head, tail, and belly, there's virtually no part of the hog that can't be used successfully. Pork flesh is generally firm and short-fibered, meaning that, unlike most other meats and poultry, it maintains its integrity even when subjected to unusually long simmering. Owing to modern breeding and feeding methods, of course, hogs today contain about 30 percent less fat than just ten years ago, an innovation that might please those obsessed with cholesterol but one that deprives the meat of much flavor and moisture—except, that is, when it's properly stewed.

I use ribs, meaty necks, feet and hocks, fresh and smoked hams, sausage meat, and, on occasion, even expensive loins to make stew, but my favorite cut by far is the shoulder (often marketed as Boston butt, picnic, jowl butt, or blade roast). Not only is shoulder more readily available and modestly priced but it also contains just the right amount of fat and sinew for delicious eating. A pork shoulder is a big hunk of meat, but what I don't use for stewing I either freeze for future dishes or cook slowly over hickory coals for delectable chopped pork barbecue.

When shopping for any pork, remember that the meat should have a fresh, fairly sweet aroma and the fat should be firm and pure white. Because of potential bacteria and bone dust left on the meat from butchering with power saws, I also wash pork carefully before cooking.

A savory pork stew simmered with vegetables needs little more accompaniment than a basket of hot biscuits, but when side vegetables are in order, think of such sturdy, full-flavored ones as parsnips, Brussels sprouts, turnips, cabbage, and rutabagas.

PORK STEW WITH PRUNES AND APPLES

THIS IS MY TRIED-and-true, old-fashioned pork stew with prunes and apples—simple and utterly delicious. For years, I served it with boiled parsleyed potatoes and a green salad, but I've begun spooning the stew over split buttermilk biscuits.

2½ pounds boneless pork shoulder, trimmed of excess fat and cut into 1-inch cubes

¼ cup all-purpose flour

3 tablespoons butter

1 large onion, chopped

1 celery rib, chopped

1 large cooking apple (like Granny Smith), cored and fairly thinly sliced

12 pitted prunes

⅛ teaspoon dried sage, crumbled

2 cups dry red wine

Salt and freshly ground black pepper to taste

Beef stock or broth (page 6) as needed

Dredge the pork cubes in the flour, tapping off any excess. In a large, heavy pot, heat 2 tablespoons of the butter over moderately high heat, then add the pork, brown on all sides, and transfer to a bowl. Heat the remaining 1 tablespoon of butter in the pot, then add the onion and celery, and cook, stirring, till softened, about 2 minutes. Return the pork to the pot and add the apple, prunes, sage, wine, salt and pepper, and enough stock to just cover the ingredients. Bring the liquid to a gentle simmer, cover, and cook till the pork is tender, about 1½ hours.

Makes 4 to 6 servings

NEW ENGLAND
PORK AND CLAM STEW

THE PORTUGUESE HAVE ALWAYS been an important ethnic influence in New England, not only because they are responsible for much of the commercial fishing but also because their unusual style of cooking has contributed lots to the region's cuisine. Pork with clams might sound like an odd pairing, but I've loved the exotic combination ever since tasting the great Boston chef Jasper White's pork ribs chops with clams and garlic sauce—the inspiration behind this savory stew. This is one of the rare occasions when I use a relatively expensive boneless pork loin, the rationale being that the clams should not be overpowered by the more aggressive flavor of shoulder or other lesser cuts. Notice that the loin requires a shorter cooking time, and remember when seasoning that the clams provide a good deal of salt. This stew is also delicious when small linguiça sausages (so beloved by the Portuguese) are substituted for the pork.

2½ pounds boneless pork loin, trimmed of excess fat and silverskin and cut into 1½-inch cubes

3 tablespoons all-purpose flour

3 tablespoons olive oil

1 large onion, chopped

1 celery rib, chopped

1 garlic clove, minced

½ cup dry white wine

2 large, ripe tomatoes, chopped

5 cloves

1 bay leaf

Salt and freshly ground black pepper to taste

2 cups beef stock or broth (page 6)

12 to 18 littleneck clams, well scrubbed and rinsed

Dust the pork cubes with the flour, tapping off any excess. In a large, heavy pot, heat the oil over moderately high heat, then brown the pork on all sides and transfer to a plate. Add the onion, celery, and garlic, cook, stirring, till softened, about 2 minutes, and transfer to the plate. Add the wine to the pot and stir. Return the pork and vegetables to the pot, add the tomatoes, cloves, bay leaf, salt and pepper, and stock, and stir. Bring to a boil, then reduce the heat to a gentle simmer, cover, and cook until the pork is tender, about 45 minutes. Add the clams, increase the heat to moderately high, cover, and cook just till the clams open, about 7 minutes (discard any that do not open).

Serve equal amounts of pork and clams on each plate.

Makes 4 to 6 servings

SANTE FE
POSOLE

In Mexico, cooks still add a pig's foot and tripe to their posole, but since I've never once seen these savory but rather greasy ingredients in the many posoles I've been served in New Mexico and Arizona, they must have been discarded at some point after the soupy stew crossed the border. "It might be good, but it's not genuine posole," my friend Diana Kennedy once huffed. Whatever, I find this Sante Fe version utterly delectable—especially when such garnishes as chopped red onion or radishes and grated Monterey Jack cheese are sprinkled over the top. Also, corn sticks are perfect with this stew. Make sure to wear rubber gloves when working with the hot peppers, and remember the next time you're in Sante Fe to try the exceptional posole at a popular restaurant called La Tertulia.

2 medium-size dried jalapeño or ancho peppers

1 cup warm water

¼ cup corn oil

*2 pounds boneless pork shoulder, trimmed of excess fat, cut into
    1-inch cubes, and patted dry with paper towels.*

1 pound chicken wings, tips removed

1 large onion, chopped

2 garlic cloves, finely chopped

4 cups chicken stock (page 120)

1 teaspoon dried oregano, crumbled

Salt to taste

1 cup canned hominy, drained

Remove the stems and seeds from the peppers, then tear them into strips and soak for 1 hour in the water.

In a large, heavy skillet, heat half the oil over moderately high heat, then add the pork, brown on all sides and transfer to a large, heavy pot. Heat the remaining 2 tablespoons of oil in the skillet, then add the chicken wings, cook until golden on all sides, and transfer to the pot. Pour off all but about 1 tablespoon of fat from the skillet, then add the onion and garlic, cook, stirring, till softened, about 2 minutes, and transfer to the pot. Add the stock and stir well.

Drain the peppers, place in a blender or food processor, and reduce to a puree. Add the puree, oregano, and salt to the pork and chicken. Bring the liquid in the pot to a boil, reduce the heat to a gentle simmer, cover, and cook till the pork is tender, about 2 hours. Stir in the hominy, return the stew to a simmer, and cook 15 minutes longer.

Serve the stew in deep soup bowls.

Makes 4 to 6 servings

THE CURMUDGEON'S PORK AND ONION STEW IN A PUMPKIN

DAN GOLDBERG, WHO PUBLISHES a delightful offbeat food newsletter in Yountville, California, called "The Curmudgeon's Home Companion," came up with this novel way to serve his pork stew. At first, I sort of smirked at the overly dramatic idea, but after I prepared and tasted the stew and heard guests rave over the presentation, I immediately became more respectful. Since the width of flesh can differ radically in pumpkins, Dan wisely advises to make the stew well in advance in order not to risk undercooking.

continued

¼ cup (½ stick) butter

1 pound small white onions, peeled and scored on
the root ends

4 garlic cloves, finely chopped

1 medium-size onion, finely chopped

4 pounds boneless pork shoulder, trimmed of excess fat, cut into
1-inch cubes, and patted dry with paper towels

1 teaspoon curry powder

3 cups chicken stock or broth (page 120)

1 teaspoon salt

1 teaspoon freshly ground black pepper

1 herb bouquet (1 bay leaf, 1 sprig fresh parsley, and 8 crushed
juniper berries wrapped in cheesecloth)

One 12-pound pumpkin

2 cups half-and-half or heavy cream

2 tablespoons chopped fresh parsley leaves

In a large, heavy skillet, heat half the butter over moderate heat, then add the onions and garlic, and stir gently till softened, about 5 minutes; transfer to a large, heavy pot. Add the chopped onion to the skillet, stir till softened, about 2 minutes, and transfer to the pot. Heat the remaining 2 tablespoons of butter in the skillet, then add the pork in batches, transfering it to the pot when browned on all sides. Sprinkle the curry powder into the skillet and stir a few seconds, then add the stock, stirring to scrape up any browned bits off the bottom of the skillet. Pour the curried stock over the pork and onion and add the salt, pepper, and herb bouquet. Bring the liquid to a gentle simmer, cover, and cook till the liquid has thickened slightly, about 2 hours.

Meanwhile, preheat the oven to 375°F. Wash the pumpkin well, then cut out a lid about 6 inches across and remove and discard the seeds and fibers. Cut away and discard about a pound of flesh to form a hollow, being careful not to cut too deeply. Replace the lid, place the whole pumpkin in a large baking dish, and bake till the flesh is tender, about 1½ hours. Remove from the oven.

To serve, remove and discard the herb bouquet from the hot stew and stir in the half-and-half. Remove the pumpkin lid and gently ladle the stew into the hollow. Sprinkle the parsley on top, replace the lid, and carry the pumpkin (on a platter) to the table. Ladle the stew into heated bowls, scooping out bits of pumpkin flesh for each portion.

Makes 8 servings

STEW SAVVY *T*o prevent small whole onions from coming apart during the cooking of stews, take a knife and score the root ends with an X.

SHEBOYGAN CIDER PORK AND APPLE STEW

I DON'T KNOW WHAT'S STRONGER in Sheboygan, Wisconsin: the nasal local accent or the German influence on cooking. Delectable sausages, of course, abound throughout the upper Midwest, but none is more distinctive than the garlicky "Sheboygan brat" served with sautéed onions on a hard roll. Nor will you find better German-style pork stews like this spicy one, prepared by a friend who moved some years ago from New Jersey to Sheboygan and quickly began collecting earthy recipes from neighbors. Although this stew contains no wine, Bill feels (and I agree) that its immigrant roots must be the classic German beef sauerbraten.

continued

*3 pounds boneless pork shoulder, trimmed of excess fat and
  cut into 1½-inch pieces*

3 tablespoons all-purpose flour

¼ cup (½ stick) butter

1 large onion, chopped

1 celery rib, chopped

2 garlic cloves, minced

2 cups beef broth (page 6)

2 cups apple cider

*1 tablespoon chopped fresh sage leaves, or ½ teaspoon dried,
  crumbled*

1 teaspoon peeled and grated fresh ginger

6 cloves

One 2-inch stick cinnamon

Grated rind of ½ lemon

Salt and freshly ground black pepper to taste

*2 large cooking apples (like Granny Smith), cored, peeled,
  and sliced*

Dredge the pork pieces in the flour, tapping off any excess. In a large, heavy pot, heat the butter over moderately high heat, then add the pork, brown it on all sides, and transfer to a platter. Add the onion, celery, and garlic to the pot and stir till softened, about 2 minutes. Return the pork to the pot, add everything but the apples, and stir. Bring the liquid to a boil, reduce the heat to a gentle simmer, cover, and simmer till the pork is tender, about 1½ hours. Add the apples and simmer about 10 minutes longer, adding a little more cider or water if necessary. Pick out the cinnamon stick, and, with a slotted spoon, transfer the pork and apples to a large heated platter.

Makes 4 to 6 servings

SPICY PORK
AND RED PLUM STEW

Here is a spicy pork stew that lends itself to the addition of any number of fresh fruits, depending on what's in season. Originally, I made the stew with firm apricots, then apples, and even grapes and oranges. Slightly tart red plums, however, are ideal, so long as you don't overcook them. Check after about ten minutes to make sure they aren't falling apart.

3 tablespoons Dijon mustard
¼ teaspoon ground cloves
⅛ teaspoon ground allspice
Dash of cayenne pepper
3 tablespoons all-purpose flour
3 tablespoons firmly packed light brown sugar
2½ pounds boneless pork shoulder, trimmed of excess fat and cut
    into 1½-inch pieces
2 tablespoons vegetable oil
1 tablespoon butter
1 large onion, chopped
Salt and freshly ground black pepper to taste
3 cups chicken stock (page 120)
6 firm red plums, halved and pitted

In a small bowl, combine the mustard, cloves, allspice, and cayenne and stir till well blended. On a small plate, combine the flour and brown sugar and stir till well blended. Brush the pork pieces with the spice mixture, then roll them in the flour-sugar mixture, tapping off any excess.

In a large, heavy pot, heat the oil and butter together over moderately high heat, then add the pork and brown on all sides. Add the onion and salt and pepper, and stir till softened about 2 minutes. Add the stock and bring to a boil. Reduce the heat to a gentle simmer, cover, and cook till the pork is tender, about 1½ hours. Add the plums, stir, and cook till they are tender, about 20 minutes longer.

Makes 4 servings

CURRIED PORK AND YELLOW SQUASH RAGOUT

"THIS STEW IS GOOD but bland," an outspoken colleague once commented, criticizing a sacred recipe that has been in my Southern family for generations and one that my Georgia grandfather prided himself on making. We discussed adding a few splashes of cider vinegar, more herbs, even chiles, but when I tried the stew with a tablespoon of curry powder, the results were sensational. This stew should not be at all soupy, so if there appears to be too much liquid after the squash is added, pour off a little of the stock.

2½ pounds boneless pork shoulder, trimmed of excess fat and
cut into 1½-inch pieces
3 tablespoons all-purpose flour
3 tablespoons peanut or vegetable oil
2 medium-size onions, chopped
2 garlic cloves, minced
1 tablespoon curry powder
1 teaspoon dried summer savory, crumbled
Salt and freshly ground black pepper to taste
3 cups chicken stock (page 120)
3 tablespoons tomato paste
1 pound (about 3 medium-size) yellow crookneck squash,
scrubbed, ends trimmed, and cut into
½-inch-thick rounds

Dredge the pork pieces in the flour, tapping off any excess. In a large, heavy pot, heat the oil over moderately high heat, then add the pork, brown it on all sides, and transfer to a platter. Reduce the heat to moderate, then add the onions, garlic, curry powder, summer savory, and salt and pepper, and stir till well blended, about 2 minutes. Add the stock and tomato paste, and stir till well blended, then return the pork to the pot. Bring the liquid to a boil, then reduce the heat to a gentle simmer, cover, and cook about 1 hour. Add the squash, return the stew to a simmer, cover, and cook till the pork is very tender, about 45 minutes.

Makes 4 servings

NAPOLEON PORK, VEGETABLE, AND OLIVE RAGOUT

My NAME FOR THIS unusual dish refers not to an emperor or French pastry but to a small town in Missouri between Columbia and Kansas City, where an old friend's family produces a limited number of Boone County country-cured hams and where his mother once treated us to her "olive ragout." When I asked Mrs. Singleton why she happened to put black olives in a pork and vegetable stew, she looked at me as if puzzled and responded simply, "Because we love black olives." Fair enough, I commented meekly while jotting down the family recipe. Mrs. Singleton probably would never approve of my adding a cup of wine to her prized ragout, but I do think it gives it a bit more character.

continued

2 tablespoons vegetable oil

2 pounds boneless pork shoulder, trimmed of excess fat, cut into
    1-inch cubes, and patted dry with paper towels

1 large onion, chopped

1 garlic clove, minced

1/4 teaspoon dried thyme, crumbled

1/4 teaspoon dried sage, crumbled

1 bay leaf, finely crumbled

1 tablespoon all-purpose flour

1 cup dry white wine

1 cup water

1 large carrot, scraped and cut into 1-inch-thick rounds

3 medium-size potatoes, peeled and quartered

1/2 cup pitted black olives

Salt and freshly ground black pepper to taste

1 cup fresh or frozen green peas

In a large, heavy pot, heat the oil over moderately high heat, then add the pork and brown on all sides. Add the onion, garlic, thyme, sage, and bay leaf and stir till the onion is softened, about 2 minutes. Sprinkle the flour over the top and stir 2 minutes longer. Add the wine and water, and stir well. Add the carrot, potatoes, olives, and salt and pepper and stir. Bring the liquid to a boil, reduce the heat to a gentle simmer, cover, and cook till the pork is tender, about 1 hour. Add the peas, return the stew to a simmer, cover, and cook 10 minutes longer, adding a little more water if necessary.

Makes 4 to 6 servings

STEW SAVVY

Since mealy, starchy potatoes like Idahos tend to disintegrate when simmered a long time in stews, try to use red, waxy boiling potatoes.

PORK GOULASH
RITZ-CARLTON

When a very suave gentleman named James Bennett ran the Ritz-Carlton in Boston some years ago, there were three signature dishes that helped to keep the elegant dining room packed: stuffed lobster with whiskey sauce, roast truffled pheasant, and this humble pork goulash served with buttered noodles. Since my publisher at that time was just across The Commons, lunch at the Ritz was almost a ritual after hours of tense business; and eventually, when I'd call Jim to make me a reservation in the restaurant, he'd end the short conversation by stating, "And no doubt you'll be having the goulash again." Yes, of course, I'd confirm, the result being that, shamefully, I never got around to even tasting the other two famous specialties. I don't know if the hotel still serves this wonderful goulash, but thanks to Jim's sending me the recipe, I certainly do.

3 tablespoons vegetable oil

2½ pounds boneless pork shoulder, trimmed of excess fat, cut into 1-inch cubes, and patted dry with paper towels

2 medium-size onions, thinly sliced

1 medium-size red bell pepper, seeded and cut into thin strips

3 garlic cloves, minced

1 teaspoon dried marjoram, crumbled

½ teaspoon dried thyme, crumbled

1 bay leaf

1 tablespoon caraway seeds

2 tablespoons imported medium-hot paprika

Salt and freshly ground black pepper to taste

2 cups beef stock or broth (page 6)

1 bottle full-bodied beer

3 tablespoons tomato paste

continued

In a large, heavy pot, heat the oil over moderately high heat, then add the pork and brown on all sides. Reduce the heat to moderate, add the onions, bell pepper, and garlic and stir till the onions are browned, about 3 minutes. Add the marjoram, thyme, bay leaf, caraway seeds, paprika, and salt and pepper and stir well. Add the stock, beer, and tomato paste and stir till well blended. Bring the liquid to a boil, reduce the heat to a gentle simmer, cover, and cook till the pork is very tender, about 1½ hours.

Makes 4 servings

CHARLEVOIX PORK AND SAUERKRAUT GOULASH

THIS RECIPE COMES FROM Sue Bolt who, along with her husband, Russell, is not only a highly respected ceramic artist and painter in Charlevoix, Michigan, but also an enthusiastic cook. Here is an example of a pork stew where the meat is not initially browned—which doesn't affect the overall sumptuous flavor. Sue recommends serving the goulash with buttered noodles, a fresh green salad, a nice dry white wine, and—I love this—"candles and Vivaldi's music."

3 tablespoons vegetable oil

4 onions, sliced

1 garlic clove, minced

1 tablespoon snipped fresh dill, or ½ teaspoon dried, crumbled

1 teaspoon caraway seeds

Salt and freshly ground black pepper to taste

*2½ pounds boneless pork shoulder, trimmed of excess fat
        and cut into 1½-inch cubes*

2 cups water

1 pound sauerkraut, rinsed and drained

1 tablespoon imported paprika

½ cup sour cream

In a large, heavy pot, heat the oil over moderate heat, then add the onions, garlic, dill, caraway seeds, and salt and pepper, and stir till the onions are golden brown, about 8 minutes. Arrange the pork on top, add the water, bring to a gentle sim mer, cover, and cook 30 minutes. Add the sauerkraut and paprika and stir well. Return to a simmer, cover, and cook till the pork is tender, about another hour, adding a little water if the stew looks too dry. Stir in the sour cream and serve.

Makes 6 servings

GRAY KUNZ'S
BRAISED PORK BUTT
WITH MAPLE SYRUP

Although four-star chef Gray Kunz is acclaimed nationwide for the fancy, highly complex dishes he serves at Lespinasse in the St. Regis hotel in New York City, he also loves to prepare a large, earthy whole pork butt braised slowly for three hours in a 300-degree oven. Adapting the recipe for my own homestyle purposes, I found no problem cutting up the meat and turning the dish into a relatively simple stew. Gray's addition of maple syrup, vinegar, and beer is nothing less than a touch of genius, and this is one time when the use of fresh herbs is absolutely obligatory.

4 pounds boneless pork shoulder, trimmed of excess fat, cut into 2-inch pieces, and patted dry with paper towels

Salt and freshly ground black pepper to taste

¼ cup corn oil

½ pound celery root, peeled and cut into 2-inch pieces

3 carrots, scraped and cut into 1-inch-thick rounds

3 medium-size onions, coarsely chopped

2 garlic cloves, finely chopped

½ cup pure maple syrup

¼ cup white wine vinegar

2 cups full-bodied beer or ale

2 cups water

1 spice sachet (2 cloves, ½ teaspoon allspice berries, 10 black peppercorns, and 5 juniper berries wrapped in cheesecloth)

1 herb bouquet (1 sprig fresh rosemary, 2 sprigs fresh thyme, and 1 sprig fresh parsley wrapped in cheesecloth)

1 tablespoon mixed chopped fresh tarragon, parsley, and chives

2 tablespoons butter

Season the pork pieces with salt and pepper. In a large, heavy skillet, heat the oil over moderately high heat, then add the pork, brown on all sides, and transfer to a large, heavy pot. Add the celery root, carrots, onions, and garlic to the skillet and stir till they just begin to brown, then transfer to the pot with the pork. Deglaze the skillet with the maple syrup and vinegar, scraping any browned bits off the bottom, and reduce by half. Add the beer and water, bring to a boil, and pour over the pork and vegetables. Add the spice sachet and herb bouquet and bring the liquid to a boil. Reduce the heat to a gentle simmer, cover, and cook over very low heat till the pork is tender, about 2 hours.

Strain the liquid into a saucepan, bring to a boil, and reduce by half. Remove the pan from the heat, stir in the chopped herbs and butter, and taste for salt and pepper. Arrange the pork and vegetables on a large heated platter and pour the gravy over the top.

❧ Makes 6 to 8 servings ❧

COLORADO
CHILE VERDE

GREEN CHILI STEWS ARE indigenous to and ubiquitous throughout Arizona and New Mexico, but few know that one of the greatest and most authentic is served at a kitschy but very popular restaurant in Denver called La Casa de Manuel. "All I know is you gotta use lard, lots of meat, and good green chiles," the cagey waitress informed me when I asked about the recipe, forcing me to follow my palatal instincts when trying to reproduce the spicy dish. My version is pretty hot (like most of the chile verdes found in New Mexico), so if you prefer a tamer stew, cut down on the hot peppers. To prepare the peppers, blister them under the broiler till crinkly, remove the skins (wearing rubber gloves), and, if you prefer a milder stew, scrape out part or all of the membranes and seeds. Rice and corn tortillas are ideal with this dish.

3 tablespoons all-purpose flour

Salt and freshly ground black pepper to taste

2½ pounds boneless pork shoulder, trimmed of excess fat and cut into 1½-inch cubes

3 tablespoons lard

2 medium-size onions, finely chopped

2 garlic cloves, minced

4 medium-size, ripe tomatoes, peeled, chopped, and juices retained (about 3 cups)

10 fresh green hot peppers, blistered (see Note), peeled, and finely chopped

1 teaspoon dried oregano, crumbled

½ teaspoon ground cumin

1 tablespoon finely chopped fresh coriander (cilantro) leaves

1½ cups chicken stock (page 120)

On a plate, combine the flour and salt and pepper and dredge the pork cubes in the mixture, tapping off any excess.

In a large, heavy pot or saucepan, heat the lard over moderately high heat, then add the pork and brown on all sides. Add the onions and garlic and stir till softened, about 2 minutes. Add the tomatoes, hot peppers, oregano, cumin, and coriander and stir well. Add the stock, bring to a boil, reduce the heat to a gentle simmer, cover, and cook until the pork is very tender, about 1½ hours.

N O T E : *To blister the peppers, either hold them with tongs directly over a gas burner and turn until evenly charred, or lightly grease them and blister under a hot oven broiler until charred, turning from time to time.*

Makes 4 to 6 servings

STEW SAVVY

When cooking tomatoes in a stew, avoid ever bringing them to a rolling boil, which causes them to burst and turn acidic.

HOOSIER PORK SPARERIBS AND SWEET POTATO STEW

"HONEY, WE DON'T MAKE SPARERIBS here, only the pork tenderloin with cinnamon apples," the old waitress at Groves' Restaurant in Bloomington, Indiana, informed me. "Oh, you love the ribs? Well, so do I, specially those fat country-style ones, and if you'd like me to tell you how I fix mine at home with sweet potatoes and mustard and orange juice. . . . Simple as pie, and the best you ever put in your mouth."

> 8 meaty country-style pork spareribs (about 3 pounds)
> 1 cup red wine vinegar
> 1½ cups orange juice, preferably freshly squeezed
> 1 medium-size onion, minced
> 1 tablespoon Dijon mustard
> 2 garlic cloves, minced
> 1 teaspoon Worcestershire sauce
> 1 teaspoon dried sage, crumbled
> 3 tablespoons vegetable oil
> 1 cup water
> 3 large sweet potatoes, peeled and quartered

Trim and discard any excess fat from the ribs and, using a meat cleaver, heavy knife, or hatchet, whack the ribs in half.

In a baking dish or large bowl, combine the vinegar, ½ cup of the orange juice, the onion, mustard, garlic, Worcestershire, and sage and stir till well blended. Arrange the ribs in the marinade, baste well, cover with plastic wrap, and let marinate at least 6 hours in the refrigerator, basting from time to time.

Remove the ribs from the marinade and pat dry, reserving the marinade.

In a large, heavy pot, heat the oil over moderately high heat, add the ribs, and brown on all sides. Add the reserved marinade plus the water and scrape the bottom of the pot to get up any browned bits. Bring to a boil, reduce the heat to a gentle simmer, cover, and cook for 1 hour. Add the sweet potatoes and the remaining 1 cup of orange juice, return the stew to a simmer, and cook till the pork and sweet potatoes are very tender, about another hour.

Makes 4 to 6 servings

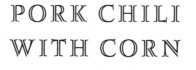

PORK CHILI
WITH CORN

WHILE MOST SOUTHWESTERN PORK CHILIS include either pinto or black beans, I find the authentic Indian examples with corn to be one of the greatest contributions to American cookery. Today, a lot of to-do is made about cooking with Southwestern blue corn, and I have indeed had chili in New Mexico with this exotic substitute. The truth is that the taste and texture of blue corn are exactly the same as those of regular Indian corn, so unless you want to appear trendy, there's no reason to go to all the trouble of acquiring blue corn just to impress a few people. Fresh ham is also a wonderful cut of pork to use in this recipe, so the next time you're faced with a huge ham found on sale and don't care to bake it all, think chili.

continued

¼ cup corn oil

*8 meaty country-style pork spareribs (about 3 pounds), meat
removed from bones, cut into ½-inch cubes, and patted dry
with paper towels*

2 medium-size onions, finely chopped

1 small green bell pepper, seeded and finely chopped

3 garlic cloves, minced

2 tablespoons chili powder

1 teaspoon ground cumin

1 teaspoon dried oregano, crumbled

Salt and freshly ground black pepper to taste

Tabasco sauce to taste

3 large, ripe tomatoes, peeled and chopped

2 cups water

1 cup beef broth (page 6)

Two 12-ounce cans corn kernels, drained

In a large, heavy pot, heat the oil over moderately high heat, then add the pork and brown on all sides. Add the onions, bell pepper, and garlic and stir till lightly browned, about 5 minutes. Sprinkle the chili powder, cumin, and oregano over the pork and vegetables and stir well. Add the salt, pepper, and Tabasco, stir, and continue cooking for 2 minutes. Add the tomatoes, water, and broth and stir well. Bring the liquid to a boil, reduce the heat to a gentle simmer, cover, and cook for 1 hour. Add the corn, stir well, return the chili to a simmer, and cook till the chili has the desired consistency, about 30 minutes.

Makes 6 servings

MRS. ZODAS'S GLAZED SAUSAGE AND CHICKPEA STEW

THE ANNUAL BAZAAR held at the Greek Orthodox Church in Charlotte, North Carolina, is a gastronomic event that has to be seen to be believed, a feast where Greek ladies in the community seem to go all out to surpass one another in culinary prowess. Over the years, I must have sampled hundreds of dishes proudly displayed on the long tables, but never was I so impressed as by this sumptuous glazed stew of sausage, chickpeas, and tangy feta cheese prepared by a Greek-American friend of my family's. Since domestic feta is insipidly mild, do make the effort to find the imported (Greek or Armenian), always sold fresh in barrels in Greek delis and usually available in jars in supermarkets.

½ pound dried chickpeas (garbanzo beans), rinsed and picked over

2 tablespoons olive oil (preferably Greek)

1½ pounds fresh pork sausage links, cut into ½-inch-thick rounds

2 medium-size onions, thinly sliced

2 garlic cloves, minced

1 teaspoon dried oregano, crumbled

One 14½-ounce can whole tomatoes with their juices, chopped

Salt and freshly ground black pepper to taste

¼ pound feta cheese, crumbled

½ cup dry bread crumbs

Place the chickpeas in a medium-size saucepan with enough water to cover, bring to a boil, and cook for 2 minutes. Remove from the heat, cover, and let stand for 2 hours. Return to the heat, bring to a boil again, reduce the heat to a gentle simmer, cover, and let cook for 1 hour.

continued

Meanwhile, heat the oil in a large, heavy pot over moderately high heat, add the sausages, and brown on all sides. Drain the sausages on paper towels, then pour off all but 2 tablespoons of the fat. Add the onions, garlic, and oregano to the pot and stir until softened, about 2 minutes. Return the sausages to the pot. With a slotted spoon, transfer the chickpeas to the pot, stir in the tomatoes plus their juices, then add the salt and pepper and just enough of the bean water to barely cover the ingredients. Bring the liquid to a boil, reduce the heat to a gentle simmer, cover, and cook 1 hour.

Preheat the broiler.

Pour off most of the liquid from the pot, transfer the contents to a large, ovenproof baking dish, and sprinkle the cheese on top. Sprinkle on the bread crumbs and brown the top of the stew about 4 inches from the heat for about 3 minutes.

Makes 4 to 6 servings

STEW SAVVY

If a stew calls for canned chopped tomatoes and you have only the whole ones, slash at them right in the can with a knife or kitchen shears to avoid mess on the counter. Otherwise, if the stew is long-simmering, simply dump the tomatoes in whole and crush them with the back of a wooden spoon.

UNCLE TOM'S
SAUSAGE PILAU

IN THE CAROLINA and Georgia Low Country, pilau (or purloo or perlo) is usu-ally made with chicken, shrimp, ham, or a combination of seafood. Why my Geor-gia grandfather used sausage in the pilau remains a mystery. Maybe it was because originally it was the most economical pilau he could imagine; perhaps it was because Paw Paw (known to adults in the family as Uncle Tom) loved fresh sausage more than I do. Whatever, it's still one of the best (and easiest to prepare) pilaus I know. I remember that Paw Paw would serve his pilau with a big spinach salad redolent of bacon; today, I tend to settle for a mixed green salad with a mus-tardy vinaigrette.

1 pound country-style link pork sausage, cut into 1-inch-thick rounds
¼ cup (½ stick) butter
1 medium-size onion, chopped
1 celery rib, chopped
½ medium-size green bell pepper, seeded and chopped
1 medium-size, ripe tomato, chopped
1 teaspoon dried sage, crumbled
¼ teaspoon red pepper flakes
Salt and freshly ground pepper to taste
1 cup uncooked rice
2 cups chicken stock (page 120)

In a large heavy skillet, fry the sausage over moderate heat till cooked through, then drain on paper towels. In a large, heavy pot, heat the butter over moderate heat, then add the onion, celery, and bell pepper and stir till golden brown, about 10 minutes. Add the tomato, sage, red pepper flakes, and salt and pepper and stir. Add the sausage, rice, and stock and stir. Bring to a simmer, cover, and cook 30 minutes without lifting the lid. Fluff the pilau before serving.

Makes 4 servings

CAJUN HAM, SAUSAGE, AND SHRIMP JAMBALAYA

ALTHOUGH AUTHENTIC CAJUN JAMBALAYA seems more and more difficult to find in the increasingly trendy restaurants of New Orleans, drive west to Roussel's in La Place, Louisiana, or even farther west to The Cabin at Burnside (near Monroe Plantation), and you'll hunker down with local Cajuns to eat stew that is prepared as it was a century ago. Of course, the ingredients can change from day to day, but this jambalaya with Cajun tasso (smoked ham), spicy sausage, and Gulf shrimp is the one I always hope has been prepared every time I venture out to The Cabin. Tasso can now sometimes be found in specialty food shops. Do remember that any great jambalaya must remain slightly moist (but not gloppy) and be served as quickly as possible after cooking.

6 tablespoons (¾ stick) butter

1 pound tasso (or other smoked ham), cut into
½-inch cubes

½ pound spicy garlic sausage (such as Spanish chorizo),
thinly sliced

2 medium-size onions, chopped

1 celery rib (leaves included), chopped

½ green bell pepper, seeded and chopped

3 garlic cloves, minced

3 medium-size, ripe tomatoes, chopped

½ teaspoon dried thyme, crumbled

¼ teaspoon ground cloves

Pinch of ground nutmeg

1 bay leaf

Cayenne pepper to taste

1½ cups uncooked rice

3 cups beef broth (page 6)

1 pound small shrimp, shelled and deveined

Salt and freshly ground black pepper to taste

¼ cup finely chopped fresh parsley

In a large, heavy pot, heat half the butter, then add the ham and sausage, cook over moderate heat till lightly browned, and transfer to a bowl. Heat the remaining 3 tablespoons of butter in the pot, then add the onions, celery, bell pepper, and garlic and stir till softened, about in 2 minutes. Increase the heat to moderately high, add the tomatoes, thyme, cloves, nutmeg, bay leaf, and cayenne, stir well, and cook about 2 minutes. Add the rice and stir the mixture about 2 minutes. Add the broth, shrimp, and salt and pepper, stir, and bring the liquid to a boil. Reduce the heat to a gentle simmer, cover, and cook till the rice is tender, about 45 minutes, adding a little more broth if necessary to keep the jambalaya moist. Add the parsley and stir till well blended

Makes 6 servings

STEW SAVVY *T*omatoes for most stews should never be peeled since the skins not only add texture but contain good fiber and nutrients.

GEORGIA HAM AND BLACK-EYED PEA STEW

THIS HAS TO BE the most unsophisticated stew recipe I know, but it's a delicious dish that both my mother and I have been preparing ever since one of my great aunts outside Macon, Georgia, served it to the family after a day of peach picking. (No doubt it was one of her many ways to use up a large smoked ham.) If you can't find fresh black-eyed peas, boil the same quantity of dried ones for two minutes, let soak about one hour off the heat, and substitute the soaking liquid for the fresh water. The stew is best when left overnight in the refrigerator and reheated, and we can't imagine serving it any other way than over rice—with hot biscuits on the side, of course.

3/4 pound shelled fresh black-eyed peas (1 1/2 pounds unshelled peas), rinsed and picked over

1 pound cooked smoked ham, cut into small cubes

1 large onion, chopped

1 celery rib, chopped

1/2 green bell pepper, seeded and chopped

1 bay leaf

1/4 teaspoon dried sage, crumbled

Salt and freshly ground black pepper to taste

3 cups water

2 tablespoons tomato catsup

Worcestershire and Tabasco sauces to taste

1 tablespoon all-purpose flour mixed with 1 tablespoon water

In a large, heavy pot, combine the peas, ham, onion, celery, bell pepper, bay leaf, sage, and salt and pepper. Add the water and stir. Bring to a boil, reduce the heat to a gentle simmer, cover, and cook for 1 hour. Add the catsup, Worcestershire, and Tabasco and cook till the peas are tender, about another 30 minutes. Add the flour-and-water mixture and stir till the stew is thickened. Serve immediately.

Makes 6 servings

GARDEN STATE
SAUSAGE AND
WHITE BEAN POT

NEW JERSEY PROBABLY HAS the largest Italian-American population in the United States, and over the years when I lived in East Brunswick, I never had better Italian food than that prepared by the wife of a colleague who taught at Rutgers. When Alicia would make this sausage and white bean pot, she thought nothing of keeping the stew at a very low simmer for as long as four hours while we drove around "antiquing," and somehow the beans never seemed to be overcooked. When I tried the same procedure on more than one occasion, however, they never failed to end up mushy. The age of dried beans, of course, can produce radically different cooking results, so begin checking the texture after about 1½ hours of simmering.

*1 pound (2½ cups) dried Great Northern beans, rinsed and
    picked over*

1 tablespoon olive oil

*2 pounds thick Italian sausage links, cut into 2-inch-thick
    rounds*

2 medium-size onions, chopped

2 garlic cloves, minced

3 cups beef stock or broth (page 6)

1½ tablespoons tomato paste

*1 herb bouquet (¼ teaspoon each dried thyme and rosemary,
    1 bay leaf, and 2 sprigs fresh parsley wrapped in
    cheesecloth)*

Salt and freshly ground black pepper to taste

Place the beans in a bowl with enough cold water to cover and let soak overnight. Drain the beans and pick them over again for any loose hulls.

continued

In a heavy pot, heat the oil over moderately high heat, then add the sausages and brown on all sides. Pour off all but about 2 tablespoons of the fat, add the onions and garlic, and stir till softened, about 2 minutes. Add the beans to the pot, then the stock and tomato paste and stir well. Add the herb bouquet and salt and pepper and bring the liquid to a boil. Reduce the heat to a gentle simmer, cover, and cook till the beans are tender but not mushy, about 2 hours. Remove and discard the herb bouquet before serving.

Makes 4 to 6 servings

RANCH HAM HOCKS WITH SAUERKRAUT

WHEN TEXAS WAS STILL a republic in the last century, the largest number of European immigrants to settle in the southeastern Hill Country were Germans, most of whom quickly adapted their style of cooking to what was available in the region—explanation enough for the ethnic blend of hearty smoked sausages, dumplings, barbecue, bean stews, and biscuits still found from New Braunfels up to Taylor. It is in this same area that two of my stylish Houston friends have a ranch retreat near Lockhart, and while I doubt that their cook, Edna, has a trace of Germanic blood, these ham hocks slowly cooked with sauerkraut, which she often prepares when Rebecca and Sam invite lots of hungry friends for the weekend, are not unlike those I've eaten in the *stuben* of Munich and Wiesbaden. (P.S. If you're ever in Lockhart, don't miss some of the greatest Texas pit-cooked barbecued brisket at the venerable Kreuz market, which has been around since 1900.)

> *6 meaty smoked ham hocks, trimmed of tough skin and scrubbed well*
> *under running water*
> *1 quart water*
> *1 large onion, coarsely chopped*
> *1 herb bouquet (celery leaves, 5 fresh sage leaves, 2 bay leaves,*
> *8 black peppercorns, and 5 cloves wrapped in cheesecloth)*
> *2 pounds cooked sauerkraut, drained and rinsed*

In a large pot, combine the hocks, water, and onion and add the herb bouquet. Bring the liquid to a boil and skim off the scum. Reduce the heat to a gentle simmer, cover, and cook till the meat is very tender, about 2½ hours. Remove and discard the herb bouquet and let the pot cool. Chill for about 2 hours, covered, then remove the fat from the top.

To serve, reheat the hocks, add the sauerkraut, and simmer for 10 minutes. Arrange the hocks on a large platter and spoon the sauerkraut around the sides.

Makes 6 servings

KENTUCKY STEWED HAM HOCKS AND LIMA BEANS

KENTUCKY PRODUCES COUNTRY HAMS that almost equal those cured in the mountains of North Carolina, and I never visit friends in Lexington without visiting Stanley Demos's legendary Coach House just to order that great Southern specialty—fried with red-eye gravy. These same friends, however, pride themselves on this sumptuous stew made with regular ham hocks, often substituting black-eyed peas or field peas for the lima beans, depending on what looks best in the market. You almost have to have a deep freezer to store the number of hocks I regularly saw off all the shanks I bake, but whether you save hocks or buy them in the market, this simple way of preparing them is hard to beat.

4 slices bacon
1 large onion, chopped
1 celery rib, chopped
½ green bell pepper, seeded and chopped
2 garlic cloves, minced
2 large, ripe tomatoes, chopped and juices retained
1 tablespoon chopped fresh thyme leaves
1 tablespoon chopped fresh sage leaves
1 tablespoon Dijon mustard
Salt and freshly ground black pepper to taste
6 meaty smoked ham hocks, trimmed of skin
5 cups water
1 pound fresh or frozen lima beans

In a large, heavy pot, fry the bacon over moderately high heat till crisp, then drain on paper towels, and when cool enough to handle, crumble. Add the onion, celery, bell pepper, and garlic to the pot and stir over moderately high heat till softened, about 2 minutes. Add the tomatoes and their juices, the thyme, sage, mustard, and salt and pepper and stir well. Add the ham hocks and water, bring to a boil, and skim any froth from the top. Reduce the heat to a gentle simmer, cover, and simmer about 2 hours. Add the reserved bacon and the beans, return to the simmer, and cook about 30 minutes longer.

With a slotted spoon, transfer the hocks to a large platter and arrange the beans around them.

Makes 6 servings

Lamb and Veal Stews

Leon's Dilled Lamb and Leek Stew

Irish Lamb Stew with Root Vegetables

Lamb and Apricot Stew

Paula's Autumn Lamb, Squash, and Chickpea Stew

New England Hot Pot

An American Lamb Curry

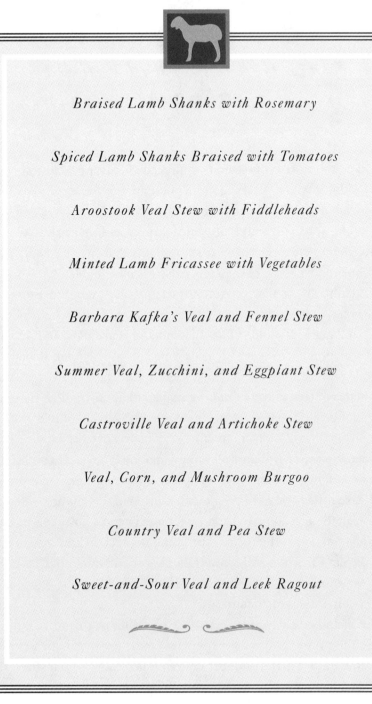

Braised Lamb Shanks with Rosemary

Spiced Lamb Shanks Braised with Tomatoes

Aroostook Veal Stew with Fiddleheads

Minted Lamb Fricassee with Vegetables

Barbara Kafka's Veal and Fennel Stew

Summer Veal, Zucchini, and Eggplant Stew

Castroville Veal and Artichoke Stew

Veal, Corn, and Mushroom Burgoo

Country Veal and Pea Stew

Sweet-and-Sour Veal and Leek Ragout

Cuts of Lamb and Veal
for Stewing

A lthough Americans now seem to appreciate lamb and veal stews more than they did just twenty years ago, the popularity of these meats is still hardly comparable to that of beef or pork. Blame it on the notions that all lamb is offensively strong and gamy and that veal is stringy and tough, but whatever the (usually erroneous) perceptions, the truth remains that, when handled properly, both meats can produce some of the greatest stews imaginable.

No doubt the quality of American lamb and grass-fed European-style veal today has never been finer, and unlike in the old days, when the most you might find in the market was leg of lamb, lamb and veal chops, and perhaps a few reddish veal scaloppine, now such ideal stewing cuts as shoulder, shank, and neck are available almost everywhere. My real regret, though, is the virtual absence in the United States of fine mutton (and the explanation of why I've not included a few recipes for mutton stew). Mutton, which is lamb aged about two years or more, has an undeniably pungent flavor, but anyone who has ever savored a rich mutton stew in France, Spain, or Britain knows how glorious the meat can be. Unfortunately, our sheep farmers cater only to popular tastes and thus the most lucrative market, so I have little hope of finding much mutton in this country any time soon. If you should come upon some mutton by remote chance, however, do try substituting it for lamb in one of the recipes using shoulder. (I do know that two restaurants, Jack's in San Francisco and Keens Chophouse in New York City, serve what are pegged as "mutton chops"—rather tame for my taste—so aged lamb does apparently exist in minuscule quantities.)

The main point to remember when choosing lamb and veal for stews is never to buy the prime (and most expensive) cuts, none of which contains the appropriate amount of fat and connective tissue necessary to transform the meat by way of long, moist simmering into gelatinous succulence. The more tender cuts (chops, leg of lamb, steaks, veal scaloppine) tend to become dry and stringy when stewed since heat shrinks the muscle tissue, whereas the tougher cuts (even lamb neck and veal breast), filled with cartilage and sinew, just get juicier and more tender. Since most of the meat labeled "lamb stew," "veal cubes," and the like in supermarkets is cut from the shoulder, it is generally perfectly acceptable for making stews.

When shopping for lamb, do try to make sure that the meat is firm, rosy colored, ungreasy to the touch, and with only a slightly pungent aroma. A certain amount of fat is necessary to ensure succulence, but since lamb fat tends to be indigestible, excessive surface amounts should always be trimmed off before stewing.

Whereas most veal dishes call for the palest, fine-grained, milk-fed variety, this is just the opposite of what you want for stewing. Select, instead, veal that is rosy pink and speckled with fat—indications that the calf was grain-fed long enough (eight to twelve months) to develop sufficient fat and connective tissue.

LEON'S DILLED LAMB
AND LEEK STEW

CREATED BY LEON LIANIDES at his legendary Coach House in New York City, this lamb and leek stew frothy with egg and lemon is without doubt one of the most sophisticated dishes I know. As at the restaurant, you can opt to brown the meat in a shallow pan in a 500 degree oven, transfer it to a pot with the other ingredients, and simmer the stew slowly at about 300 degrees for about 1½ hours. Since I always prefer to do stews on top of the stove (where it's easy to peek into the pot from time to time), Leon instructed me how to modify the technique without compromising the dish's integrity. Whichever method you choose, the major secret is to not stir the leeks into the stew during the simmering, lest they cloud the broth.

2 tablespoons butter

1 tablespoon vegetable oil

*3 pounds boneless lamb shoulder, trimmed of excess fat, cut into
    2-inch cubes, and patted dry with paper towels*

2 medium-size onions, finely chopped

1 tablespoon finely chopped fresh parsley leaves

1 teaspoon finely snipped fresh dill

Salt and freshly ground black pepper to taste

1 cup dry white wine

1 cup water

½ cup chicken stock or broth (page 120)

*6 medium-size leeks, most of the green and any discolored leaves
    removed, the white parts thoroughly washed, and cut into
    2-inch pieces*

4 large eggs

2 tablespoons fresh lemon juice

1 teaspoon cornstarch

In a large, heavy pot, heat the butter and oil together over moderately high heat, then add the lamb and brown on all sides. Add the onions, stir, and cook till softened, about 2 minutes. Add the parsley, dill, salt and pepper, wine, water, and stock and bring to a boil. Reduce the heat to a gentle simmer, cover, and cook for 1 hour. Add the leeks but do not stir, spooning a little liquid from the pot over the leeks. Return the liquid to a simmer, cover, and cook till the lamb and leeks are tender, about 30 minutes. Remove the pot from the heat.

In a large bowl, whisk the eggs vigorously till frothy. In another bowl, combine the lemon juice and cornstarch, stir, and whisk into the eggs. Add about 1 cup of hot liquid from the pot to the eggs, whisking constantly till well blended. Pour the mixture over the stew and stir gently till well blended.

Makes 4 to 6 servings

IRISH LAMB STEW
WITH ROOT VEGETABLES

THERE MUST BE HUNDREDS of ways to make Irish stew, but according to my Irish-American friend Patrick (who happens to be a professional chef), for a stew to be authentic, neither the meat nor vegetables should be browned, and the ingredients must be layered. It is permissible to blanch the lamb initially for a few minutes in boiling water (to render the fat), and there are purists who wouldn't dream of making an Irish stew that didn't include cabbage. Nonetheless, if you don't agree this is one of the simplest and most delicious versions you've tasted, you must be English!

continued

3 medium-size potatoes, peeled and cut crosswise into ¹/₂-inch-thick slices

2 medium-size onions, cut into ¹/₂-inch-thick slices

2 medium-size carrots, scraped and cut into ¹/₂-inch-thick rounds

1 medium-size parsnip, peeled and cut into ¹/₂-inch-thick slices

*2¹/₂ pounds boneless lamb shoulder, trimmed of excess fat and
    cut into 1-inch pieces*

¹/₄ teaspoon dried thyme, crumbled

3 dashes of Worcestershire sauce

Salt and freshly ground black pepper to taste

2 cups beef broth (page 6)

In a large, heavy pot, layer half the potato slices over the bottom. Cover with half the onion slices, then top with the carrot rounds and parsnip slices. Layer the lamb pieces evenly over the top, sprinkle over the thyme, Worcestershire, and salt and pepper, and layer the remaining potatoes and onions. Pour the broth over the ingredients, bring to a simmer, cover, and cook slowly till the lamb is very tender, about 1½ hours.

Makes 4 to 6 servings

STEW SAVVY *If* you plan to freeze a stew containing potatoes, remove and discard the potatoes since they become mushy when frozen. When ready to thaw and reheat the stew, simply parboil a few new potatoes and let simmer in the stew until tender.

LAMB AND
APRICOT STEW

No matter what the international provenance, lamb stewed with apricots is one of those culinary marriages blessed from above, and this version, prepared by a former colleague at the University of Missouri in Columbia, is a prime example—especially when spooned over rice pilaf. The spicy Middle Eastern influence is obvious, but when I first tasted it at a weekend retreat in the Ozarks, it couldn't have seemed more down-home American. I've also made this stew with fresh kumquats, in which case it helps to add about a tablespoon of sugar along with the spices.

½ pound dried apricots
2½ pounds boneless lamb shoulder, trimmed of excess fat and
    cut into 1½-inch cubes
3 tablespoons all-purpose flour
¼ cup (½ stick) butter
1 tablespoon vegetable oil
2 medium-size onions, finely chopped
2 garlic cloves, minced
½ teaspoon ground cinnamon
¼ teaspoon ground ginger
¼ teaspoon ground allspice
Salt, freshly ground black pepper, and cayenne pepper to taste
2 cups beef stock or broth (page 6)

Cut the apricots into quarters, place in a bowl with enough warm water to cover, and let soak for 45 minutes. Meanwhile, dredge the lamb in the flour, tapping off any excess.

In a large, heavy pot, heat the butter and oil together over moderately high heat, then add the lamb and brown on all sides. Add the onions, garlic, and, if necessary, a little more oil, and cook till browned, about 5 minutes, stirring. Add the cinnamon, ginger, allspice, salt, pepper, and cayenne and stir 1 minute longer. Add the stock, bring to a boil, reduce the heat to a gentle simmer, cover, and cook for 45 minutes. Stir in the apricots, return to a simmer, cover, and cook till the lamb is very tender, about 30 minutes.

Makes 4 to 6 servings

PAULA'S AUTUMN LAMB, SQUASH, AND CHICKPEA STEW

ALTHOUGH MY OLD FRIEND Paula Wolfert is famous mainly for her exotic and sublime Mediterranean dishes, it is never beneath her to prepare a relatively simple stew such as this at home for family and friends. "I'm obsessed with layers of taste in whatever I cook," she says, "and nothing exemplifies the principle better than when I put together a hearty stew." Warning: Some of Paula's cooking techniques (her little tricks) might seem too time-consuming, but if you want the stew to taste right, follow the directions to the letter.

1¼ teaspoons freshly ground black pepper

1 pound boneless lamb shoulder, trimmed of excess fat, cut into 1-inch cubes, and patted dry with paper towels

3 tablespoons olive oil

1 medium-size onion, chopped

1 tablespoon tomato paste

1½ cups water

4 pounds hubbard or butternut squash, peeled, seeded, and cut into 1-inch cubes

1½ cups cooked chickpeas

1 large, ripe tomato, peeled, seeded, and chopped

1 garlic clove, minced

½ teaspoon salt

¼ cup fresh lemon juice

2 teaspoons imported hot paprika

1 teaspoon red pepper flakes

Sprinkle half the black pepper over the lamb. In a large pot, heat 2 tablespoons of the oil over moderate heat, then add the lamb and cook, stirring, till all the juices have evaporated, about 7 minutes. Add the onion and cook, stirring, till lightly browned, about 7 minutes. Add the tomato paste and cook, stirring, till the mixture begins to caramelize, about 10 minutes. Add the water and bring to a boil. Reduce the heat to a gentle simmer, cover, and cook till the meat is tender, about 45 minutes.

Add the squash, chickpeas, tomato, garlic, salt, and enough water to barely cover the ingredients. Return the stew to a simmer, cover, and cook till the squash is tender, about 30 minutes. Stir in the lemon juice and remove the pot from the heat. Season with salt to taste and transfer the stew to a shallow serving dish.

Rub the paprika, red pepper flakes, and the remaining black pepper through a fine sieve. In a small saucepan, heat the remaining 1 tablespoon of oil over high heat till sizzling. Add the sieved seasonings and stir for an instant. Swirl the seasoned oil into the stew and serve hot.

Makes 4 to 5 servings

NEW ENGLAND HOT POT

No DOUBT THE PROTOTYPES of this layered lamb stew, traditionally simmered in the oven throughout the countryside of New England, are Britain's Lancaster hot pot and Irish lamb stew. Overseas, of course, the slightly bland stew would be made with fresh lamb and only potatoes and onions, whereas in its Yankee transformation the custom often is to use leftover lamb and include all sorts of vegetables and seasonings. Unfortunately, most of our leftover lamb usually comes from the leg, which tends to be dry, so if you don't want to start from scratch, remember this stew the next time you're braising lamb shanks or baking shoulder chops. Served in a handsome earthenware casserole, this hot pot is perfect on a buffet.

Vegetable shortening

3 large potatoes, peeled and cut into medium-size dice

2 pounds boneless lamb shoulder, chops, or neck, trimmed of excess fat and cut into 1-inch cubes

2 large onions, diced

2 carrots, scraped and sliced

1 celery rib, sliced

2 large, ripe tomatoes, peeled, coarsely chopped, and juices retained

1 tablespoon chopped fresh rosemary leaves, or ½ teaspoon dried, crumbled

Salt and freshly ground black pepper to taste

1 cup beef stock or broth (page 6)

Preheat the oven to 325°F.

Grease a medium-size heavy casserole or large baking dish with shortening and layer the bottom with the potatoes. Layer the lamb over the potatoes, then add the onions, carrots, celery, tomatoes, rosemary, and salt and pepper. Add the stock, cover, and cook in the oven till the lamb is tender, about 1½ hours. Remove the lid and cook about 30 minutes longer to brown the top.

Makes 4 to 6 servings

AN AMERICAN
LAMB CURRY

I'M OBSESSED WITH LAMB CURRY, and while I seek out and relish those authentic Indian concoctions made with coconut, chutney, and numerous individual spices that are usually baked in the oven, I have equal admiration for this intriguing American version created by the private cook of a certain lady I knew for many years who also loved lamb curry but couldn't abide exotic seasonings. This is a delicious stew as is, but I must confess that sometimes I do add pinches of ground cloves and allspice, so feel free to play around.

1½ cups peanut oil

¼ cup red wine vinegar

2 tablespoons fresh lemon juice

3 garlic cloves, minced

3 pounds boneless lamb shoulder, trimmed of excess fat and cut
    into 1½-inch cubes

3 tablespoons all-purpose flour

1 large onion, finely chopped

1 large carrot, scraped and finely chopped

1 large celery rib, finely chopped

1 medium-size cooking apple (such as Granny Smith), cored,
    peeled, and cut into small cubes

3 tablespoons medium-hot curry powder, or to taste

½ teaspoon dried thyme, crumbled

3 cups chicken broth (page 120)

3 tablespoons tomato paste

Salt and freshly ground black pepper to taste

½ cup heavy cream

continued

In a large glass bowl, combine 1¼ cups of the oil, the vinegar, lemon juice, and 2 of the garlic cloves and whisk till well blended. Add the lamb, stir till well coated with the mixture, cover, and let marinate 1 hour.

Transfer the lamb cubes to a plate and discard the marinade. Dredge the cubes in the flour, tapping off any excess.

In a large, heavy pot, heat the remaining ¼ cup of oil over moderately high heat, then add the cubes and brown on all sides. Add the onion, carrot, celery, apple, and remaining garlic clove and stir till softened, about 2 minutes. Sprinkle the curry powder and thyme over the top and stir. Add the broth and stir in the tomato paste. Add the salt and pepper, bring the liquid to a boil, reduce the heat to a gentle simmer, cover, and cook till the lamb is very tender, about 1½ hours. Stir in the cream and heat a few more minutes.

Makes 6 servings

STEW SAVVY

*T*o ensure even browning, always brown large quantities of meat and poultry in batches, allowing sufficient space between each piece.

BRAISED LAMB SHANKS
WITH ROSEMARY

THERE'S NO MORE SAPID DISH in the world than aromatic, moist, fork-tender lamb shanks that have been braised slowly till the meat falls from the bone. Here I use the whole shanks, but if you'd like a nicer presentation and are handy with a hacksaw, try my technique of sawing the shanks into halves or thirds and producing a more legitimate stew. If the shanks are particularly fatty, I often preboil them as long as fifteen minutes before dredging in flour and browning. While this does render fat, it can also reduce flavor as well as simmering time. So long as you have a large enough pot, double this recipe since the shanks freeze beautifully.

4 meaty lamb shanks (about 1¼ pounds each), trimmed of
    excess fat
¼ cup all-purpose flour
3 tablespoons olive oil
1 medium-size onion, chopped
2 garlic cloves, minced
1 tablespoon chopped fresh rosemary leaves, or ½ teaspoon
    dried, crumbled
Salt and freshly ground black pepper to taste
1 cup water
½ cup dry red wine
1 tablespoon tomato paste
Tabasco sauce to taste

Dredge the shanks in the flour, tapping off any excess. In a large, heavy pot, heat the oil over moderately high heat, then add the shanks and brown evenly on all sides. Add the onion and garlic and, turning the shanks, cook 1 minute. Add the rosemary, salt and pepper, water, and wine and turn the shanks again. Stir in the tomato paste and Tabasco, bring the liquid to a gentle simmer, cover, and cook till the shanks are fork-tender, about 2 hours.

Makes 4 servings

SPICED LAMB SHANKS
BRAISED WITH
TOMATOES

"THESE TASTE ALMOST LIKE PAPA'S," exclaimed my dad at Santorini's restaurant in Chicago, referring to the spicy lamb shanks his Greek father used to braise when I was growing up and that Mother still cooks occasionally. As usual, nothing would do but to call over the manager and listen intently to the recipe. While I still love the way my Greek grandfather did shanks, I must say that these are better—maybe it's the added touch of brandy. And if you really want something good, serve orzo on the side with a little juice from the stew spooned over it.

4 meaty lamb shanks (about 1¼ pounds each), trimmed of excess fat
¼ cup all-purpose flour
¼ cup olive oil
1 large onion, chopped
3 garlic cloves, minced
¼ cup brandy
4 large, ripe tomatoes, chopped and juices retained
1 cup dry red wine
1 cup water
½ teaspoon ground allspice
2 bay leaves
One 2-inch stick cinnamon
Salt and freshly ground black pepper to taste

Place the shanks in a large pot and add enough water to cover. Bring to a boil, reduce the heat to moderate, and cook for 10 minutes. Drain the shanks, then wash out and dry the pot. Dredge the flanks in the flour, tapping off any excess.

Heat the oil in the pot over moderately high heat, then add the shanks and brown on all sides. Add the onion and garlic and stir about 1 minute. Add the brandy and stir about 1 minute, scraping up all the browned bits and pieces on the bottom of the pot. Add the tomatoes and their juices and the remaining ingredients and stir. Bring to a boil, reduce the heat to a gentle simmer, cover, and cook till the lamb is very tender, about 2 hours.

Makes 4 servings

AROOSTOOK
VEAL STEW
WITH FIDDLEHEADS

"COME ON UP TO MAINE this spring and we'll hunt fiddleheads," an old friend urged some years ago. Only once had I tasted fiddlehead ferns (at The Four Seasons restaurant in New York City), so, eager to see how these mysterious greens are harvested on home territory, I took him up on the invitation and came away with one of the most exciting stew recipes (his wife's) in my collection. By early spring, fiddleheads (the tender shoots of ferns just emerging from the soil, shaped like a violin neck) can be found along riverbanks and in other moist areas throughout northern New England, and their savor is somewhere between asparagus and broccoli (an acquired taste for some people). Fresh fiddleheads are seen in Northeastern U.S. markets from May into June; frozen ones are usually now carried in specialty shops and better supermarkets in many areas of the country. To prepare them for cooking, discard any brown husks, trim the stems, and wash carefully to remove all traces of sand and dirt. I like to serve this stew over rice, picking out a few of the elegant fiddleheads and positioning them on top of each serving.

continued

*3 pounds boneless veal stew meat, trimmed of excess fat and cut
    into 1½-inch pieces*

2 tablespoons all-purpose flour

3 tablespoons butter

1 large onion, chopped

1 medium-size carrot, scraped and cut into small cubes

½ teaspoon dried tarragon, crumbled

Salt and freshly ground black pepper to taste

1½ cups water

1 cup cider vinegar

1 cup or more fresh or frozen fiddleheads

Dredge the veal in the flour, tapping off any excess. In a large, heavy pot, heat the butter over moderate heat, then add the veal and brown on all sides. Add the onion and carrot and stir till softened, about 3 minutes. Sprinkle the tarragon over the top and add the salt and pepper, water, and vinegar. Bring the liquid to a boil, reduce the heat to a gentle simmer, cover, and cook 1½ hours. Add the fiddleheads, stir, return to a simmer, cover, and cook till the veal is tender, about 30 minutes longer.

Makes 4 to 6 servings

MINTED LAMB FRICASSEE WITH VEGETABLES

What better time to search for sweet, inexpensive lamb neck in the supermarket (or to ask a butcher to save you some) than early summer, when spring lamb is still readily available and the first fresh vegetables are starting to bear. Because of all the sinew, lamb neck is a tough cut of meat, but when it is stewed, it is this connective tissue that is almost magically transformed into gelatinous tenderness. Like short ribs of beef, lamb neck can be wonderfully meaty or disgustingly bony, so shop carefully and opt for shoulder if you're not satisfied with neck. Also, you may have to pay extra, but if you don't relish hacking the neck into pieces the way I do, most butchers will do the job for you.

3 pounds meaty lamb neck, trimmed of excess fat

3 tablespoons all-purpose flour

3 tablespoons peanut oil

1 large onion, chopped

2 garlic cloves, minced

2 large, ripe tomatoes, chopped and juices retained

2 tablespoons chopped fresh mint leaves

1 tablespoon chopped fresh rosemary leaves, or ½ teaspoon dried, crumbled

Salt and freshly ground black pepper to taste

1½ cups beef broth (page 6)

1 cup water

2 medium-size yellow squash, scrubbed, ends trimmed, and cut into 2-inch-long fingers

1 large carrot, scraped and cut into 2-inch-long fingers

1 cup fresh or frozen green peas

continued

Using a cleaver, hack the lamb necks into 1-inch pieces. Dredge the pieces in the flour, tapping off any excess. In a large, heavy pot, heat the oil over moderately high heat, then add the lamb and brown on all sides. Reduce the heat to moderate, add the onion and garlic, and stir till softened, about 2 minutes. Add the tomatoes and their juices, the mint, rosemary, salt and pepper, broth, and water. Bring the liquid to a boil, then reduce the heat to a gentle simmer, cover, and cook for 1 hour. Tilt the pot and skim off as much fat as possible. Add the squash and carrot, stir, return to a simmer, and cook for 1 hour. Add the peas, stir, and cook 10 minutes longer.

Makes 4 to 6 servings

STEW SAVVY

If a stew ends up too salty, either add a peeled, quartered potato, turnip, or carrot, simmer 10 minutes, and discard, or add a small can of pinto or white beans, simmer 10 minutes, and using a slotted spoon, remove and discard. In both cases, the vegetables and beans will absorb the offending salt.

BARBARA KAFKA'S
VEAL AND FENNEL STEW

My friend Barbara Kafka is one of the most respected food experts and cooks in this country, and perhaps no dish better illustrates her originality than this beguiling veal and fennel stew with scallions and lemon peel. Actually, Barbara browns her veal by roasting it for 18 minutes at 500 degrees, and she would probably kill me for using butter instead of canola oil and for simmering my stew a full two hours. No matter. We argue all the time.

> 2 tablespoons butter
> 2 pounds veal stew meat, trimmed of excess fat, cut into
>   1½-inch cubes, and patted dry with paper towels
> 2 cups beef broth (page 6)
> 1 medium-size fennel bulb, fronds removed, fibrous outer layers
>   of bulb removed with a vegetable peeler, quartered length-
>   wise, and sliced into long, thin strips
> 2 bunches scallions, white parts cut into 2-inch lengths and
>   green parts thinly sliced crosswise (keep them separate)
> Three 1-inch strips lemon peel
> 2 tablespoons cornstarch
> ¼ cup water
> Salt and freshly ground black pepper to taste
> 2 tablespoons fresh lemon juice

In a large, heavy pot, heat the butter over moderately high heat, then add the veal and brown on all sides. Add ½ cup of the broth, scraping any browned bits off the bottom, and bring to a boil. Reduce the heat to a gentle simmer and cook about 15 minutes, stirring occasionally. And the remaining 1½ cups broth, the fennel, scal lion whites, and lemon peel and return the stew to a boil. Reduce the heat to a gentle simmer, cover, and cook till the veal is tender, about 2 hours.

continued

In a bowl, whisk together the cornstarch and water, add about ½ cup of liquid from the pot, stir well, and return the mixture to the pot, stirring. Bring to a boil, reduce the heat to moderate, add the scallion greens, and simmer for about 3 minutes, stirring. Add the salt and pepper and lemon juice, stir well, remove the pot from the heat, and let rest for 5 minutes.

Makes 4 to 6 servings

SUMMER VEAL, ZUCCHINI, AND EGGPLANT STEW

LET'S FACE IT: Veal is a pretty bland meat that almost demands additional flavors to give it character. Veal partnered with such wonderful summer vegetables as zucchini, yellow crookneck squash, eggplant, or sugar snap peas no doubt makes a subtle combination, but to add spark you almost have to include a little wine and other seasonings. Here's your chance to really experiment with fresh herbs. I've used only thyme, but you might also think about fresh summer savory, oregano, tarragon, even dill. Just don't overdo it.

3 tablespoons vegetable oil

1½ pounds boneless veal shoulder, trimmed of excess fat, cut into 1½-inch cubes, and patted dry with paper towels

2 medium-size onions, chopped

1 garlic clove, minced

2 tablespoons all-purpose flour

1 small zucchini, scrubbed, ends trimmed, and cut into 1-inch-thick rounds

1 small eggplant, peeled and cut into 1-inch cubes

2 medium-size, ripe tomatoes, coarsely chopped and juices
   retained
1½ cups chicken broth (page 120)
½ cup dry white wine
1 tablespoon tomato paste
1 tablespoon chopped fresh thyme leaves, or ½ teaspoon dried,
   crumbled
Salt and freshly ground black pepper to taste

In a large, heavy pot, heat the oil over moderately high heat, then add the veal and
brown on all sides. Add the onions and garlic and stir about 1 minute. Sprinkle on
the flour and stir so that the meat is evenly coated. Add the zucchini and eggplant
and stir. Add the tomatoes and their juices, the broth, and wine and stir well. Stir in
the tomato paste and add the thyme and salt and pepper. Bring the liquid to a boil,
reduce the heat to a gentle simmer, cover, and cook till the veal is tender, about 2¼
hours.

Makes 4 to 5 servings

CASTROVILLE VEAL AND ARTICHOKE STEW

"THIS IS THE REGIONAL WINNER, no doubt about it," Craig Claiborne
whispered to me as we tasted the veal and artichoke stew being judged at a March
of Dimes Gourmet Gala in Monterey, California. I agreed wholeheartedly, first
because the dish was indeed sumptuous and second because the artichoke capital
of America was just north in Castroville, and the lady who'd prepared the stew was
a grower. Served over rice, this is truly a lovely combination that almost demands
the use of fresh tarragon.

continued

*2 pounds boneless veal shoulder, trimmed of excess fat and cut
    into 1½-inch pieces*

3 tablespoons all-purpose flour

2 tablespoons butter

1 tablespoon vegetable oil

2 medium-size onions, chopped

1½ cups chicken stock (page 120)

2 tablespoons fresh lemon juice

*1 tablespoon chopped fresh tarragon leaves, or ½ teaspoon
    dried, crumbled*

Salt and freshly ground black pepper to taste

*One 10-ounce package frozen artichoke hearts, thawed
    and cut in half*

2 tablespoons chopped fresh parsley leaves

Lightly dredge the veal pieces in the flour, tapping off any excess. In a large, heavy pot, heat the butter and oil together over moderately high heat, then add the veal and brown on all sides. Add the onions, stir, and cook till softened, about 2 minutes. Add the stock, lemon juice, tarragon, and salt and pepper, bring the liquid to a gentle simmer, cover, and cook till the veal is tender, about 2¼ hours. Add the artichoke hearts and parsley, stir, return the stew to a simmer, and cook till the hearts are tender, about 15 minutes longer.

Makes 4 to 6 servings

VEAL, CORN,
AND MUSHROOM BURGOO

WHILE ATTENDING KENTUCKY DERBYS in Louisville, I must have sampled dozens of classic beef and chicken burgoos, but none sticks in my memory like this one with veal breast, fresh corn, and mushrooms served at a special dinner sponsored by the good people who produce my beloved Jack Daniel's whiskey. Since veal breast is so flavorful (and cheap), it's a shame it's not used more in stews. Yes, there can be a lot of fat and cartilage; yes, you often have to plan on one pound of breast per person; and yes, if the butcher won't cooperate, you have to cut up the breast yourself with a cleaver or hacksaw. But when you do find a meaty breast and stew it long and slowly, there's really nothing like it. Since veal breast can render considerable fat, be sure to pour some off after browning the meat if it seems necessary.

One 5-pound breast of veal, trimmed of excess fat and cut into
    2-inch pieces
2 tablespoons all-purpose flour
¼ cup (½ stick) butter
1 tablespoon vegetable oil
2 large onions, chopped
1 garlic clove, minced
1 cup chicken stock or broth (page 120)
1 cup water
2 tablespoons tomato paste
2 large, ripe tomatoes, chopped and juices retained
½ teaspoon dried thyme, crumbled
Salt and freshly ground black pepper to taste
12 medium-size mushrooms, quartered
2 cups fresh or frozen corn kernels

continued

Dredge the veal pieces in the flour, tapping off any excess. In a large, heavy pot, heat 2 tablespoons of the butter plus the oil over moderately high heat, then add the veal and brown on all sides. Tipping the pot, pour off all but about 1 tablespoon of the fat, then add the onions and garlic, and stir for 1 minute. Add the stock, water, and tomato paste and stir till well blended. Add the tomatoes and their juices, the thyme, and salt and pepper. Bring the liquid to a boil, reduce the heat to a gentle simmer, cover, and cook till the veal is tender, about 2¼ hours.

In a medium-size skillet, heat the remaining 2 tablespoons of butter over moderate heat, then add the mushrooms and stir till slightly browned, about 5 minutes. Add the mushrooms to the veal along with the corn, increase the heat to moderately high, and stir for 2 to 3 minutes before serving.

Makes 4 to 6 servings

COUNTRY VEAL AND PEA STEW

THIS SIMPLE DISH came about when my mother and I wanted to include a fairly elegant stew to be served over rice on a buffet and we saw veal shanks on sale for something like $1.99 per pound. Cubed carrots, zucchini, or mushrooms can be substituted for the peas, but remember that they should be added about 30 minutes before the simmering is over. Don't forget that if you use boneless shank meat, you'll have to buy about four shanks (preferably cut from the hind leg).

1 tablespoon butter
1 small onion, chopped
2 tablespoons vegetable oil
2 pounds boneless veal shank or shoulder, trimmed of excess fat,
*   cut into 1-inch pieces, and patted dry with paper towels*
Salt and freshly ground black pepper to taste

¹⁄₂ teaspoon dried sage, crumbled

1 sprig fresh parsley, finely chopped

2 medium-size, ripe tomatoes, coarsely chopped and juices
    retained

1 cup dry white wine

One 10-ounce package frozen green peas, thawed

In a large, heavy pot, heat the butter over moderately high heat, then add the onion and stir for 1 minute. Add the oil, then the veal, and stir till browned, about 5 minutes. Add the salt and pepper, sage, parsley, tomatoes and their juices, and the wine, bring the liquid to a gentle simmer, cover, and cook till the veal is tender, about 2¼ hours. Add the peas, stir, increase the heat slightly, and cook till the peas are tender, about 10 minutes.

Makes 4 servings

STEW SAVVY *T*o speed the important conversion of sinew into gelatin when stewing tough secondary cuts of veal (like shank), add acid ingredients such as tomatoes.

SWEET-AND-SOUR VEAL AND LEEK RAGOUT

"WOULDN'T THIS MEAT by itself be great in a simple stew?" my friend Pat asked Tony Vallone as she wrestled with the huge (but delicious) veal shank (*osso buco*) at Tony's restaurant in Houston. Such a suggestion, of course, would be sacrilege to a traditionalist like Tony, and no doubt he would disapprove of my transforming the Italian classic into this boneless variation with oriental overtones. Tough veal shanks, on the other hand, lend themselves to endless experimentation, and while the meat itself is pretty bland, stewing it with any number of flavorful vegetables, herbs, or spices can make for memorable eating. To get three pounds of stew meat you'll probably have to buy five or six meaty shanks (preferably cut from the hind leg), and if you want a really luscious stew (and the pot is big enough), toss in a couple of the bones so they will yield their sweet marrow during the simmering—discarding them, of course, before serving.

3 pounds boneless veal shank, trimmed of excess fat and cut into 1½-inch pieces

3 tablespoons all-purpose flour

2 tablespoons butter

2 tablespoons vegetable oil

1 medium-size leek (white part only), thoroughly washed and cut into ½-inch-thick rounds

1 large, ripe tomato, chopped and juices retained

1½ cups chicken stock or broth (page 120)

½ cup fresh lemon juice

½ cup seedless golden raisins

3 tablespoons sugar

1 teaspoon ground ginger
¼ teaspoon ground nutmeg
Salt and freshly ground black pepper to taste

Dredge the veal pieces in the flour, tapping off any excess. In a large, heavy pot, heat the butter and oil together over moderately high heat, then add the veal and brown on all sides. Add the leek, stir, and cook till the leek has softened, about 7 minutes. Add the remaining ingredients and stir well. Bring the liquid to a gentle simmer, cover, and cook till the veal is tender, about 2½ hours.

❧ *Makes 4 to 6 servings* ❧

Poultry Stews

Chicken Gumbo Ya Ya

Plantation Chicken, Sausage, and Hominy Gumbo

Georgia Brunswick Stew

Traditional Kentucky Burgoo

Craig's Ragout of Chicken Giblets and Root Vegetables

Adobe Chicken and Black Bean Chili

Squab and Mushroom Stew

Turkey, Corn, and Lima Bean Mull

Turkey Wing, Ham, and Pea Bog

Turkey Gumbo

Key West Turkey, Sweet Potato, and Mango Pot

Tex-Mex Turkey Chili

Minnesota Duck and Onion Stew

James Beard's Duck and Pinto Bean Stew

Duck Braised with Fresh Figs

Middlebury Duck and Rutabaga Ragout

East Hampton Goose, Sausage, and Chestnut Stew

Poultry for Stewing

I f I could have my way, I'd use nothing but tough, old, mature hens in virtually every chicken stew I simmer for the simple reason that they have so much more flavor than tender young fryers, broilers, roasters, and even capons. I'm not naive, however, and I'm as aware as any other stew fanatic that meaty six-pound hens are now as rare in supermarkets as the proverbial hen's teeth. As a result, I'm usually forced to settle for commercial battery chickens whose feet never touch the ground—much less scratch around for months in barnyard dirt full of the nutriments and savors that once made broody Leghorns and Rhode Island Reds taste so good. Stewing hens (often free-range) do exist at fine butcher shops for a hefty price, and from time to time I do find a few (curiously on sale!) at my local A & P—at which moment I snap up as many as my freezer will hold. Otherwise, the chickens I prefer mostly for stews are large, four- to five-pound roasters (usually about sixteen weeks of age) or fat five- to seven-pound capons. Of course, young fryers and broilers (no more than six to seven weeks old) are the most readily available chickens and can make delicious stews so long as they're not overcooked. Older birds, on the other hand, stand up well to relatively long, slow simmering, and as far as that ornery, flavor-packed old stewing hen is concerned, it's almost impossible to cook it too long.

For turkey stews, I prefer wings, drumsticks, and thighs; I rarely use breast meat since it tends to be dry and stringy. Individually packaged fresh turkey parts in the supermarket are usually cheap, but since they're not always available, I take no chances and either buy them in quantity for freezing or collect (and freeze) wings from the turkey breasts I love to roast.

Although virtually all ducks (ten to twelve weeks old) and ducklings (seven to eight weeks) are marketed frozen today (I'm lucky to get fresh birds from a duck and goose farm not far from my home on Long Island), they both make sumptuous stews—especially when simmered with robust vegetables and fruits.

Descended from White Pekins introduced to Long Island a century ago, our ducks have wonderful flavor but also lots of indigestible fat and bone. This means not only that measures should be taken to minimize the fat in stews as much as possible (by cutting away excess fat from the birds, pricking the skins before preroasting or browning and pouring off fat, and careful skimming) but also that you usually can't count on more than about 1¼ pounds of uncooked duck per person. Of course, some ducks are meatier than others, but generally when I buy a five-pound duck for a stew, I know I'm taking a chance inviting more than two—at the very most, three—guests. A much safer bet is to purchase two four-pound ducks, adjust the recipe accordingly, and perhaps have some duck stew left over for another meal.

Geese, always marketed frozen, are certainly larger (eight to fourteen pounds) and might be a little meatier than ducks, but rarely have I produced a stew from a nine-pound goose that would feed more than five or six souls. Like ducks, geese have an inordinate amount of fat (which is why they're so flavorful and make such savory stews), so the same defatting techniques applied to ducks should be used for cooking the heftier birds.

While squabs (invariably frozen) are little more than young domesticated pigeons, the meat is milder and sweeter than that of their wild cousins. Like Cornish hens, these tasty lightweights (about one pound apiece) can make fascinating stews—so long, that is, as they're not overcooked, which toughens the meat. When buying squabs or Cornish hens, plan on one bird per person.

Finally, although I'm certainly no health fanatic, I take few risks in the handling and storage of any poultry—despite recent progress made in our inspection programs that promise to minimize exposure to salmonella and other harmful bacteria. Frozen birds cause me no initial concern whatsoever (and I actually prefer frozen turkeys to fresh ones), but I still wash with soap and water my hands and any utensils and surfaces that come in contact with uncooked fowl. When buying fresh chickens, refuse any that have a break in the plastic packaging, as well as those which appear dry or darkly colored around the wing tips and drumsticks. If there is a slightly strong aroma when the plastic is removed at home, don't panic: most likely this is simply a bit of oxidation that will quickly disappear. If it does not, return the chicken to the market. A sound chicken will remain fresh (and safe) for two days in the refrigerator; frozen ones maintain their integrity for up to six months.

CHICKEN STOCK

L IKE BEEF BROTH, chicken broth is little more than a concentrated chicken stock that has been thinned slightly with water. In most recipes, chicken stock and broth can be used interchangeably.

One 5-pound stewing hen, neck, giblets, and liver included, cut up
4 quarts water
2 medium-size onions, peeled and cut in half
2 carrots, cut in half
2 celery ribs (leaves included), broken in half
2 medium-size leeks (white part and part of green leaves
*   included), thoroughly washed and chopped*
Salt to taste
1 herb bouquet (1 teaspoon dried thyme, 1 peeled garlic clove,
*   4 cloves, 8 black peppercorns, 1 bay leaf, and*
*   6 sprigs fresh parsley wrapped in cheesecloth)*

Place the hen, neck, giblets, and liver in a large stockpot and add the water. Bring to a boil, skimming scum from the surface, reduce the heat to a low simmer, and cook for 30 minutes, skimming off any scum. Add the remaining ingredients, return the heat to the simmer, cover partly, and simmer 3 to 3½ hours longer, adding more water if necessary to keep the solids barely covered. Strain the stock through a double thickness of cheesecloth into a large bowl, let cool, chill (preferably overnight), and remove the solidified fat from the top. (Remove the meat from the hen and reserve for chicken salad or hash.) Covered, the stock keeps 1 week in the refrigerator and, stored in freezer containers filled to within ½ inch of the top, up to 6 months in the freezer.

Makes about 2 quarts

OLD-FASHIONED
CHICKEN AND DUMPLINGS

ONE OF THE TRAGEDIES of trendy modern American cooking (what is called New American Cuisine) has been the virtual disappearance of such homey, soul-warming, traditional dishes like the flavor-packed chicken and dumplings that my grandmother prided herself on making for a large family on winter weekends—the victim often being a testy old hen from the back yard. It's almost pointless to make this particular stew with blander, young fryer or broiler chickens (plump capons or a large roaster will suffice if you can't find a stewing hen), since a rich broth is needed to give the dumplings full flavor. And be sure to cook the dumplings *before* thickening the stew so that their texture will be right.

FOR THE STEW

One 5-pound stewing hen, cut into serving pieces
1 large onion, quartered
2 celery ribs (leaves included), chopped
4 carrots, scraped and cut into thick rounds
Salt and freshly ground black pepper to taste
1 quart water
1 cup milk
¼ cup all-purpose flour blended with ¼ cup water

FOR THE DUMPLINGS

1 cup all-purpose flour
1 teaspoon baking powder
½ teaspoon salt
2 tablespoons chilled vegetable shortening
½ cup milk

continued

In a large, heavy pot over moderately high heat, combine all the ingredients for the stew except the flour-and-water mixture. Bring to a slow boil and skim the surface of any froth. Reduce the heat to a simmer, cover, and cook till the chicken is very tender, 2 to 2½ hours.

Meanwhile, to make the dumplings, sift the flour, baking powder, and salt together in a bowl, then cut in the shortening with a pastry blade or heavy fork till the mixture is mealy. Add the milk and mix lightly till the dough just holds together (do not overmix).

With the stew gently bubbling, drop the dough by rounded tablespoons into the liquid and simmer, uncovered, for 10 minutes. Cover, simmer the dumplings 10 minutes longer, transfer with a slotted spoon to a plate, and keep warm.

To finish the stew, drain the cooking liquid into a bowl, skim off the fat, and pour 3 cups of the liquid into a saucepan, adding a little water if necessary. Add the flour-and-water mixture and stir over moderately high heat till the sauce is thickened. Pour the sauce over the chicken and vegetables and reheat the stew about 10 minutes.

Serve the stew and dumplings together on heated plates.

❧ *Makes 6 servings* ❧

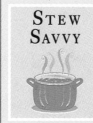

STEW SAVVY

*T*o add more flavor to meat and poultry stews, toss a few large bones in the pot, adding more liquid as necessary, and discarding the bones when the stew has finished cooking.

SOUTHWEST CHICKEN STEW
WITH ALMONDS

My old friend (and perhaps the world's greatest expert on Mexican cuisine) Diana Kennedy would probably balk at this rather tame Southwest American rendition of the classic *pipían* seasoned with fiery piquín peppers and thickened with ground pumpkin seeds. But chicken stew with almonds has, in its own right, become something of a classic throughout Arizona and New Mexico and as far north as Colorado. In southern California, I've sampled even more interesting versions made with turkey legs and duck, but if you try either of these fowl, the cooking time should be reduced by about 45 minutes, till the meat is just tender. Do feel free to experiment with various spices in this dish.

4 fresh ancho peppers
½ cup hot water
One 4- to 5-pound stewing hen, cut into serving pieces
2 medium-size onions, quartered
½ green bell pepper, seeded and cut into thin strips
2 carrots, scraped and cut into ½-inch-thick rounds
5 black peppercorns
Salt to taste
3 cups chicken stock (page 120)
2 garlic cloves, crushed
2 tablespoons vegetable oil
¼ teaspoon ground cinnamon
¼ teaspoon ground cumin
1 cup blanched almonds, toasted (see Note on page 127)

Wearing thin plastic gloves, stem and seed the anchos, tear the flesh into pieces, soak for 1 hour in the water, and drain.

continued

In a large, heavy pot, combine the chicken, onions, bell pepper, carrots, peppercorns, salt, and stock, adding a little water if necessary to cover. Bring to a boil, reduce the heat to low, cover, and simmer till the chicken is just tender, about 1 hour. With a slotted spoon, transfer the chicken to a plate, strain the stock into a bowl, and set aside. Return the chicken to the pot.

Place the soaked anchos and the garlic in a blender or food processor and reduce to a paste. In a medium-size skillet, heat the oil over low heat, scrape the paste into the skillet, and stir for about 4 minutes. Add 2 cups of the reserved stock plus the cinnamon and cumin, stir, and bring to a boil. Pour the sauce over the chicken and vegetables, add the almonds, cover, and simmer till the chicken is very tender, about 30 minutes, then serve.

Makes 6 servings

STEW SAVVY

*T*he hottest parts of the peppers used in many Southwestern stews and chilis are the seeds and membranes. When removing these, wear thin rubber gloves and, should you accidentally rub your eyes, splash them with plenty of cold water.

MAUI PAPAYA
CHICKEN STEW

Hawaiians are experts at incorporating all sorts of tropical fruits and nuts into meat and poultry stews, and none has been so sapid as this curried simmer of chicken and papaya shared with friends at the oceanfront Bay Club in Maui's Kapalua Bay Hotel at Lahaina. I personally find Hawaiian papayas (the fruit has been cultivated there since around 1920) to be much more flavorful than those from Florida, Texas, and California, so if you're not satisfied with whatever variety is available in your market, you might want to substitute (as I've done more than once) fairly ripe mangoes, guavas, or even fresh pineapple. And if you can lay hands on some Kukui nuts . . . !

¼ cup all-purpose flour

3 tablespoons medium-hot curry powder

Salt and freshly ground black pepper to taste

One 3½-pound chicken, cut into serving pieces

¼ cup peanut oil

3 scallions (whites and part of the green leaves included),
    chopped

2 cups chicken stock (page 120)

3 tablespoons peeled and chopped fresh ginger

2 tablespoons firmly packed light brown sugar

2 tablespoons fresh lemon juice

2 ripe papayas, peeled, seeded, and cut into chunks

½ cup crushed macadamia nuts

On a plate, combine the flour, curry powder, and salt and pepper and dredge the chicken pieces in the mixture, tapping off any excess flour. In a large, heavy pot, heat the oil over moderately high heat, then add the chicken and brown lightly on all sides. Add the scallions and stir till softened. Add the stock, ginger, brown sugar, and lemon juice and stir. Bring the liquid to a boil, reduce the heat to low, cover, and simmer till the chicken is tender, about 45 minutes. Add the papaya chunks and nuts, stir, and simmer about 10 minutes longer.

Makes 4 servings

THE ORIGINAL
VIRGINIA COUNTRY CAPTAIN

OVER THE YEARS, no stew has been more bastardized than this delectable Virginia classic that traces its mysterious roots to India and helped to nourish the first colonial settlers. It has been suggested that the term "captain" evolved as a distortion of "capon," but whatever the origins of the name, authentic Country Captain is a slow-simmered, savory stew and *not* one of the quickly sautéed (and usually bland) imitations found on so many menus. This particular recipe comes from Roanoke, Virginia, where my old friend Alan's mother learned it from her mother who learned it from her mother. Unfortunately, the wonderful fresh red and black currants I so relish in England (and that would be so good in this stew) are very rarely found in our markets, so most likely you'll have to settle for the imported dried variety.

¼ cup all-purpose flour
Salt and freshly ground black pepper to taste
Pinch of ground allspice
One 3-pound chicken, cut into serving pieces
2 tablespoons butter
2 tablespoons peanut oil
2 medium-size onions, finely chopped
1 small green bell pepper, seeded and finely chopped

1 garlic clove, minced

2 teaspoons medium-hot curry powder

4 medium-size, ripe tomatoes, chopped and juices retained

1 cup chicken stock (page 120)

3 tablespoons dried currants or golden raisins

1 cup blanched almonds, toasted (see Note)

Chutney

On a plate, combine the flour, salt and pepper, and allspice and dredge the chicken pieces in the mixture, tapping off any excess flour. In a large, heavy pot, heat the butter and oil together over moderately high heat. Add the chicken, brown on all sides, and transfer to a plate. Add the onions, bell pepper, garlic, and curry powder to the pot and stir till the vegetables are softened. Add the tomatoes and stock and return the chicken to the pot. Bring the liquid to a simmer, cover, and cook till the chicken is tender, about 45 minutes. Add the currants, stir, and cook 5 minutes longer.

Serve the chicken with the almonds sprinkled over the top and chutney on the side.

N O T E : *To toast the almonds, scatter them on a baking sheet and roast uncovered, in a 350°F. oven till golden brown, about 10 minutes, stirring once or twice.*

Makes 4 servings

MY CHICKEN SUCCOTASH

I'VE OFTEN SAID that there's virtually no dish on earth that couldn't be prepared in a large, deep skillet, and this unorthodox version of Indian succotash is a good example. Traditionally throughout the Eastern coastal states, the creamy mixture of lima beans, corn, and bacon is used simply as a side dish to outdoor barbecued items. So much do I love succotash that some years ago I decided to add chicken to the stew and serve it as a main course with sliced cured ham, a composed salad, and hot cornbread. Any leftover chicken is fine, but what I prefer is the tender, sweet meat of boiled chicken wings. To add further dimension to the dish, sprinkle on a tablespoon of chopped fresh tarragon.

2 cups fresh or frozen lima beans
5 slices bacon
2 medium-size onions, finely chopped
1½ cups shredded cooked chicken
2½ cups milk
Salt and freshly ground black pepper to taste
Tabasco sauce to taste
2 cups fresh or frozen (and thawed) corn kernels
½ cup heavy cream

Place the lima beans in a saucepan with enough salted water to cover. Bring to a boil, reduce the heat to moderate, cover, cook for 10 minutes, and drain.

Meanwhile, fry the bacon over moderately high heat in a large, deep skillet till crisp, drain on paper towels, crumble, and set aside. Drain off all but 2 tablespoons of fat from the skillet, add the onions, and stir till softened. Add the lima beans, chicken, milk, salt and pepper, and Tabasco, stir, and simmer till the milk is reduced, about 10 minutes. Add the corn and cream, stir, return to a simmer, and cook till the mixture has thickened but is not dry, watching carefully. Sprinkle on the reserved bacon and stir.

Makes 4 to 6 servings

PHILIP'S CHICKEN CACCIATORE WITH WILD MUSHROOMS AND BLACK OLIVES

WHILE CHICKEN CACCIATORE has become a culinary cliché among food snobs in most areas of the country, the dish is curiously still respected and very popular on the West Coast—and especially around Los Angeles where my old friend Philip McKimmey devised this notable version utilizing not only a little bacon fat but also the fresh wild mushrooms and black olives so readily abundant in the region. This stew couldn't be more American!

2 tablespoons olive oil

1 tablespoon bacon grease

One 3-pound chicken, cut into serving pieces and patted dry
    with paper towels

1 medium-size red onion, chopped

1 garlic clove, finely chopped

3 large fresh porcini or other wild mushrooms, stems removed
    and caps chopped

2 teaspoons dried oregano, crumbled

1 cup dry white wine

One 16-ounce can Italian plum tomatoes with their juices

Salt and freshly ground black pepper to taste

1 cup pitted black olives

2 tablespoons chopped fresh parsley leaves

2 tablespoons freshly grated Parmesan cheese

In a large, heavy pot, heat the olive oil and bacon grease together over moderately high heat, then add the chicken pieces and brown on all sides. Add the onion, garlic, mushrooms, and oregano and stir till softened. Add the wine, increase the heat to high, and boil till the wine cooks down slightly. Add the tomatoes plus their juices and salt and pepper and cook for 2 minutes. Reduce the heat to low, cover, and simmer till the chicken is tender, about 45 minutes.

Uncover the stew, return to a boil, and cook till the sauce is the desired consistency. Reduce the heat to moderate, add the olives, and cook for 2 minutes. Transfer the contents of the pot to a large heated platter and sprinkle the parsley and cheese on top.

Makes 4 servings

CLASSIC AMERICAN CHICKEN FRICASSEE

ALTHOUGH LINGUISTICALLY there is a fine line between what constitutes a stew, ragout, fricassee, and braise (and with all the innovations of the freewheeling New American style of cooking, that line virtually disappears), technically a fricassee or braise implies fowl that is browned initially in fat, then simmered slowly in less liquid than that used in a stew or ragout (and often with little more liquid than that produced by the vegetables or fruits with which it's simmered). Further, a true fricassee like this chicken classic usually has a little cream added to the cooking liquid, giving the dish a smoother, silkier, more elegant texture than a stew. Since a fricassee involves maintaining just enough liquid to ensure moistness, keep a close eye on the simmering, adding just a little more stock or water if the chicken appears to be drying out. This same recipe is also good for turkey or duck parts.

¼ cup (½ stick) butter
One 4- to 5-pound roasting chicken, cut into serving pieces and
*   patted dry with paper towels*
1 large onion, finely chopped

1 large celery rib, finely chopped
1 garlic clove, minced
Pinch of dried thyme, crumbled
Pinch of dried marjoram, crumbled
Salt and freshly ground black pepper to taste
1½ cups chicken stock (page 120)
½ cup heavy cream

In a large, heavy pot, heat the butter over moderately high heat, then add the chicken and brown evenly on all sides. Reduce the heat to moderate, add the onion, celery, garlic, thyme, marjoram, and salt and pepper, stir well, and cook till the onion is softened. Add the stock, bring to a simmer, cover, and cook gently over low heat till the chicken is tender, about 45 minutes. Add the cream, increase the heat slightly, and cook till the sauce is thickened, about 3 minutes.

Makes 4 to 6 servings

CHICKEN GUMBO
YA YA

I'M NOT SURE whether the famous Cajun chef Paul Prudhomme actually created this delightful gumbo, but I do recall that the first time I ever heard of or tasted it was when I traveled to New Orleans to do a feature on Paul when he was head chef at Commander's Palace and still relatively unknown. Today, the gumbo is a signature dish at another restaurant in New Orleans called Mister B's—and a delicious version it is. As Paul taught me, the real secret to the gumbo is the long, slow, patient stirring of the roux—a full 45 minutes—which, if necessary, can be made in advance and chilled overnight.

Filé, a powder made from dried sassafras leaves and used as both a flavoring and thickening agent in all gumbos, is generally available in specialty food shops.

¼ cup vegetable oil

¼ cup all-purpose flour

2 tablespoons butter

½ pound smoked sausage (such as kielbasa), cut into
1-inch-thick slices

2 medium-size onions, chopped

1 small green bell pepper, seeded and chopped

2 cups chicken stock (page 120)

1½ cups diced cooked chicken

2 teaspoons filé powder dissolved in ½ cup water

Salt and freshly ground black pepper to taste

4 cups boiled rice

In a small cast-iron skillet, heat the oil over moderate heat and begin adding the flour slowly, stirring steadily. Reduce the heat to low and continue to stir constantly and patiently till the roux is a dark brown, 35 to 45 minutes. Remove the skillet from the heat and allow the roux to cool to room temperature.

Meanwhile, in a large, heavy pot, heat the butter over moderately high heat, add the sausage, and cook till slightly browned on both sides. Add the onions and bell pepper and stir till the vegetables are very soft, about 8 minutes. Add the stock, stir, and simmer for about 10 minutes. Bring the liquid to a boil, scrape in the roux, and stir. Reduce the heat slightly and cook for 20 minutes, stirring occasionally. Add the chicken, filé powder mixture, and salt and pepper, stir, reduce the heat to moderate, and simmer the gumbo briskly 10 minutes longer, making sure that the liquid never boils.

Serve the gumbo over the rice in deep bowls.

Makes 4 to 6 servings

PLANTATION CHICKEN, SAUSAGE, AND HOMINY GUMBO

THIS IS BUT ONE of literally dozens of varieties of the aromatic Creole stew that has been a veritable staple for centuries in New Orleans and the Louisiana bayou country. As always with classic gumbo, the tricky part is the slow cooking of the roux—which must be just medium brown, never dark (and certainly never burnt). Although cooks in New Orleans use delectable Creole smoked sausage, both Polish sausage and French garlic sausage make excellent substitutes. The canned hominy (which is dried hulled corn kernels) is generally available in specialty food shops and some supermarkets, as is the filé powder.

One 2½- to 3-pound chicken, cut up
½ cup vegetable oil
⅓ cup all-purpose flour
2 onions, chopped
½ green bell pepper, seeded and chopped
1 garlic clove, finely chopped
½ pound smoked sausage, thinly sliced
¼ pound baked or boiled ham, cubed
2 bay leaves
½ teaspoon dried oregano, crumbled
½ teaspoon dried thyme, crumbled
Salt and freshly ground black pepper to taste
Cayenne pepper to taste
2 tablespoons filé powder
1 cup canned hominy, drained
3 cups boiled rice

Place the chicken in a large, heavy pot with enough water to cover, and bring to a boil. Reduce the heat to low, cover, and simmer till just tender, about 35 minutes. Remove the chicken and, when cool enough to handle, skin, bone, and shred the meat. Strain the cooking broth into another large pot, set aside, and wash out the pot.

Heat the oil in the pot over moderate heat, then add the flour gradually, stirring constantly with a whisk. Reduce the heat to low and cook the roux, stirring constantly, till medium brown but not dark in color, 35 to 45 minutes.

Add the onions, bell pepper, garlic, sausage, and ham, mix thoroughly, and cook another 10 minutes. Add 2 cups of the reserved broth, the shredded chicken, bay leaves, oregano, thyme, salt and pepper, and cayenne and stir thoroughly. Add 2 cups more of the broth and bring the liquid to a boil. Reduce the heat to low and simmer the mixture for 1 hour. Remove the pot from the heat, add the filé powder and hominy, stir, and let stand for 10 minutes to thicken.

Distribute the rice evenly in the bottom of 6 soup bowls and ladle gumbo on top.

Makes 6 servings

STEW SAVVY *L*earning to cut up whole chickens for stews can usually save up to 50 percent on the cost of precut packaged products.

GEORGIA BRUNSWICK STEW

I STOPPED YEARS AGO DEBATING the provenance of this sumptuous Southern stew on which I was raised and which I still prepare regularly (especially in the summertime as the obligatory accompaniment to the pork barbecue I laboriously pit-cook once a year for a huge crowd). Of course, in the old days we went out of our way to find traditional squirrel for the stew, but now I'm fully accustomed to the acceptable substitute of chicken (ideally, an old flavorful hen should be used, in which case you should cook and prepare it exactly like the ham hock). Since Brunswick stew freezes well, by all means double the recipe so you'll have plenty on hand for simple cold-weather lunches. Quite frankly, I consider this to be the unchallenged aristocrat of American stews—and, contrary to my above proclamation, nobody will ever convince me that the stew was not first concocted in Brunswick, Georgia.

8 slices bacon

*Two 3-pound chickens, cut into serving pieces and patted dry
    with paper towels*

*1½ pounds boneless beef (round or chuck), trimmed of excess fat,
    cut into 1-inch pieces, and patted dry with paper towels*

3 large onions, chopped

3 celery ribs (leaves included), chopped

1 large green bell pepper, seeded and chopped

Vegetable oil if needed

1 large smoked ham hock, trimmed of skin

4 large, ripe tomatoes, chopped and juices retained

3 sprigs fresh parsley, chopped

2 small fresh hot red peppers, seeded and minced

1 teaspoon dried thyme, crumbled

1 teaspoon dried basil, crumbled

Salt and freshly ground black pepper to taste

6 cups beef or chicken stock (pages 6, 120)
10 cups water
2½ cups fresh or frozen corn kernels
2½ cups fresh or frozen lima beans
2 cups fresh or frozen sliced okra
2½ cups mashed boiled potatoes

In a large, heavy pot, fry the bacon over moderately high heat till crisp, then drain on paper towels, crumble, and set aside. Add the chicken pieces to the pot in batches, brown on all sides over moderately high heat, and transfer to a platter. Add the beef to the pot, brown on all sides, and transfer to the platter. Add the onions, celery, and green pepper and stir till softened, adding a little oil if there appears not to be enough fat in the pot. Return the chicken and beef to the pot, then add the ham hock, tomatoes, parsley, hot peppers, thyme, basil, salt and pepper, stock, and water, and stir well. Bring the liquid to a boil, reduce the heat to low, cover, and simmer until the chicken is tender, about 1 hour, skimming the surface from time to time.

With a slotted spoon, transfer the chicken back to the platter and continue to simmer the stew 1½ hours longer. When the chicken is cool enough to handle, remove and discard the skin and bones, shred the meat, and set aside.

Add the corn, lima beans, and okra to the pot, reduce the heat to low, and let simmer for 30 minutes. Remove the ham hock with a slotted spoon, pick the meat from the bone, shred, and return to the pot. Add the reserved crumbled bacon and shredded chicken and stir well. Add the mashed potatoes, stir well, and cook for another 15 minutes. Taste the stew for salt and pepper and serve.

Makes 8 servings

TRADITIONAL KENTUCKY BURGOO

A CLOSE RELATIVE TO THE South's Brunswick stew, Kentucky burgoo was originally prepared in a huge iron pot over an open fire and included anything from wild game to squirrel to mutton. Still a ritual dish served all around Louisville during Kentucky Derby week, burgoo today is almost always made with chicken, beef, and lamb; some cooks sweeten the pot even more by adding such vegetables as cabbage, celery, okra, and even parsnips. Burgoo is simply not burgoo without plenty of hot cornbread or biscuits to dip into the stew, and since it freezes well, I usually double this recipe.

One 4- to 5-pound stewing hen, cut into serving pieces
2 pounds beef shank, trimmed of excess fat
1½ pounds boneless lamb shoulder or shank, trimmed of excess fat
1 medium-size fresh hot red pepper, seeded
Salt and freshly ground black pepper to taste
3 quarts water
3 medium-size onions, chopped
3 medium-size carrots, scraped and cut into rounds
1 medium-size green bell pepper, seeded and cut into thin slices
5 medium-size, ripe tomatoes, chopped and juices retained
2 medium-size potatoes, peeled and diced
½ pound green beans, strings removed and cut in half
3 cups fresh or frozen corn kernels
2 garlic cloves, chopped

In a large, heavy pot, combine the chicken, beef shank, lamb, hot pepper, salt and pepper, and water and bring to the boil, skimming any foam from the top. Reduce the heat to low, cover, and simmer till the meats are almost tender, 2 to 2½ hours.

With a slotted spoon, transfer the meats to a cutting board and discard the pepper. Add the remaining ingredients to the pot and stir. Bring to a boil, reduce the heat to low, cover, and simmer for 1 hour, adding a little more water if the liquid looks too thick.

Remove and discard the skin and bones from the chicken and cut the meat into bite-size pieces. Remove the beef from the bone, discard the bone, and cut the meat into bite-size pieces. Cut the lamb into bite-size pieces. Return all the meats to the pot and stir well. Return the stew to a simmer, cover, and cook till the meats are very tender, 30 to 45 minutes.

Makes 6 to 8 servings

STEW SAVVY *If* you don't have enough leftover meat stew to make another meal, dump it into a food processor with a little extra liquid, blend to a thick consistency, and use as a tasty sauce for pasta.

CRAIG'S RAGOUT
OF CHICKEN GIBLETS
AND ROOT VEGETABLES

OF THE THOUSANDS OF original dishes that my celebrated friend and neighbor Craig Claiborne has introduced to the American public over the past decades, perhaps none impressed me more than this lusty ragout he served over rice for lunch one bleak winter day. Here is still another example of a simple, long-simmering stew done in a deep skillet. If you and/or your guests are among those squeamish souls who've always balked at eating chicken giblets and hearts, I guarantee you'll be converted by this delicious concoction that's so easy to prepare. What I do is collect giblets from all the chickens I cook, freeze them, and eventually use them to make this dish—or an earthy country pâté.

1½ pounds combined chicken giblets and hearts

2 tablespoons butter

Salt and freshly ground black pepper to taste

1 large onion, finely chopped

1 garlic clove, minced

1½ tablespoons all-purpose flour

½ cup dry white wine

2 cups water

1½ tablespoons tomato paste

½ teaspoon dried thyme, crumbled

1 small bay leaf

1 large turnip, peeled and cut into 8 pieces

2 celery ribs, cut into 1½-inch pieces

2 carrots, scraped and cut into 1½-inch-thick rounds

*1 large potato, peeled and cut into 1½-inch-wide pieces like
    french fries*

Cut away the excess gristle from the giblets and hearts, rinse well, and dry with paper towels. In a large, heavy, deep skillet, heat the butter over moderate heat, then add the giblets and salt and pepper, and cook for 10 minutes, stirring. Add the onion and garlic and stir till softened. Sprinkle on the flour and stir for 1 minute. Add the wine, water, tomato paste, thyme, and bay leaf, bring to a simmer, cover, and cook for 10 minutes, stirring. Add the remaining ingredients, return to a simmer, cover, and cook till the giblets and vegetables are very tender, about 1 hour.

Makes 6 servings

STEW SAVVY

*T*o remove fat from the surface of a stew without patiently skimming or waiting for it to chill and congeal in the refrigerator, wipe a piece of soft bread back and forth across the top to soak up the grease. You can also fill a self-sealing plastic bag with ice cubes and draw it back and forth across the surface; the fat will to cling to the cold bag.

ADOBE CHICKEN AND BLACK BEAN CHILI

My REASONING WAS SIMPLE as I struggled to pile moist shredded chicken and black beans atop the Indian fried bread at the popular ranch-style restaurant called The Hacienda in Las Cruces, New Mexico. If the chicken and beans by themselves tasted so good, why not go a few steps further and incorporate them into a spicy chili, thus avoiding all the mess. Here is the result, and, hopeless chili-head that I am, I love the dish.

One 3-pound chicken, cut up
1 large onion, quartered
1 celery rib, cracked into thirds
Salt and freshly ground black pepper to taste
3 tablespoons corn oil
1 large onion, chopped
1 medium-size green bell pepper, seeded and chopped
1 garlic clove, minced
1 large, ripe tomato, chopped and juices retained
2 cups cooked black beans or two 15¼-ounce cans, drained
1 fresh jalapeño pepper, seeded and finely chopped
2 teaspoons ground cumin
1 tablespoon fresh lime juice

Place the chicken, quartered onion, celery, and salt and pepper in a large pot and add enough water to cover. Bring to a boil, then reduce the heat to low, cover, and cook till the chicken is just tender, about 35 minutes. Transfer the chicken to a plate, and when cool enough to handle, remove and discard the skin and bones and cut the meat into small pieces. Strain the stock into a bowl and set aside.

In a large, heavy pot, heat the oil over moderately high heat, then add the chopped onion, bell pepper, and garlic and stir till softened. Add the tomato plus its juices, the chicken, black beans, jalapeño, cumin, and salt and pepper to taste and stir well. Add 2 cups of the reserved stock plus the lime juice, and bring to a boil. Reduce the heat to low and simmer, uncovered, till the chili is nicely thickened and the flavors well blended, about 30 minutes.

Makes 4 to 6 servings

SQUAB AND MUSHROOM STEW

Generally, the only way squab (domesticated pigeon) is ever served is roasted, but given the rich, slightly gamy savor of the fowl, nothing makes more sense than to utilize it in stews—the way the French often prepare such exotic birds as woodcock, guinea hen, and black grouse. I've also used meaty quail in this dish (with a slightly shorter stewing time), and if you want a really earthy stew, substitute fresh (or dried and soaked) wild mushrooms for the more bland button variety. Here's also the perfect opportunity to play around with all sorts of fresh or dried herbs.

3 squabs or Cornish hens (about 1 pound each)
3 tablespoons butter
3 tablespoons vegetable oil
3 medium-size carrots, scraped and cut into thin rounds
1 medium-size onion, finely chopped
1 celery rib, finely chopped
1 garlic clove, minced
5 tablespoons all-purpose flour
3 cups chicken stock (page 120)
1 cup dry red wine
½ pound mushrooms, quartered
¼ teaspoon dried tarragon, crumbled
¼ teaspoon dried thyme, crumbled
Salt and freshly ground black pepper to taste

Wash the squabs, cut each in half down the center of the breast, and dry the portions with paper towels. In a large, heavy pot, heat the butter and oil together over moderately high heat, then add the squabs, brown on all sides, and transfer to a plate. Add the carrots, onion, celery, and garlic to the pot and stir till softened. Add the flour and stir well. Gradually add the stock and wine, stirring, and cook till the sauce begins to thicken. Add the mushrooms, tarragon, thyme, and salt and pepper and stir well. Return the squabs to the pot and stir to coat them with the sauce. Reduce the heat to a simmer, cover, and cook till the squabs are very tender, about 1 hour.

❧ *Makes 3 to 4 servings* ❧

TURKEY, CORN, AND LIMA BEAN MULL

ONE OF THE EASIEST and most practical ways I know to deal with leftover turkey and the stock obtained from boiling giblets, this might well be considered a turkey succotash. A more flavorful mull can be made by starting from scratch with fresh turkey wings and drumsticks found on sale, browning the meat, and simmering it slowly with the vegetables, but when confronted with a mound of turkey after Thanksgiving or Christmas dinner, this is a quick and very respectable alternative to sandwiches and hash.

4 slices bacon
1 medium-size onion, finely chopped
1 celery rib, finely chopped
½ green bell pepper, seeded and finely chopped
3 cups turkey or chicken stock (page 120)
One 10-ounce package frozen corn kernels, thawed
One 10-ounce package frozen lima beans, thawed
2 medium-size potatoes, peeled and cut into small cubes
2 cups diced cooked turkey (preferably dark meat)
½ teaspoon dried tarragon, crumbled
Salt and freshly ground black pepper to taste

continued

In a large, heavy pot, fry the bacon over moderately high heat till crisp, then drain on paper towels, crumble, and set aside. Reduce the heat to moderate, add the onion, celery, and bell pepper, and stir till softened. Add the remaining ingredients plus the reserved bacon and bring to a boil. Reduce the heat to low, cover, and simmer gently till the beans and potatoes are tender, about 20 minutes.

❧ *Makes 4 servings* ❧

TURKEY WING, HAM, AND PEA BOG

WHEN I'M NOT USING inexpensive turkey wings to make gumbo and have extra baked ham on hand, this is the bog that always comes to mind. You can, of course, buy turkey wings by themselves in most supermarkets, but what I've found myself doing lately is removing the wings from a turkey breast intended for roasting and freezing them till I'm ready to make a big stew. Generally I use green peas in this bog, but when I'm lucky enough to have fresh lima beans—well, now *that's* a bog really to rave about.

4 large turkey wings (about 5 pounds)
¼ cup vegetable oil
2 medium-size onions, coarsely chopped
2 medium-size carrots, scraped and coarsely chopped
2 garlic cloves, minced
2 large, ripe tomatoes, coarsely chopped
2 bay leaves
½ teaspoon dried tarragon, crumbled
Salt and freshly ground black pepper to taste
5 cups water

2 ounces cooked ham, cut into thin strips
2 cups fresh or frozen green peas
3 to 4 cups boiled rice (slightly wet)

Cut off and set aside the turkey wing tips and cut the wings in half at the joint. In a large, heavy pot, heat the oil over moderately high heat, add the wings including the tips, and brown lightly on all sides. Add the onions, carrots, and garlic and cook, stirring, till the onions are soft. Add the tomatoes and stir for 1 minute. Add the bay leaves, tarragon, salt and pepper, and water and bring to a boil. Reduce the heat to moderately low, cover, and simmer till the wings are tender, about 2 hours.

Discard the wing tips and bay leaves, transfer the wings to a bowl, remove and discard the skin and bones, and cut the turkey meat into 1½-inch strips. Pour off all but about 2 cups of the stewing liquid, add the turkey strips, ham, and peas to the pot, return the stew to a simmer, and cook till the peas are tender, about 10 minutes. Add the rice and stir till well blended.

Makes 4 to 6 servings

TURKEY GUMBO

WHEN I SEE TURKEY drumsticks and wings on sale in the supermarket, I
automatically think of gumbo—and in particular this zesty concoction inspired by
a complex poultry gumbo I once had at The Olde Pink House in Savannah, Georgia. For this gumbo to work, you simply must have the rich, spicy stock that comes
from simmering the turkey. If, therefore, time is a problem and you think you can
cheat by using leftover turkey and chicken stock, my advice is to choose another
recipe.

1 large turkey drumstick (about 1½ pounds)

2 large turkey wings (about 1 pound)

1 onion, quartered

1 celery rib, cracked in half

1 carrot, scraped and cut in half

1 bay leaf

4 black peppercorns

2 cloves

Salt to taste

3 tablespoons vegetable oil

1 medium-size onion, chopped

1 medium-size celery rib, chopped

1 small green bell pepper, seeded and chopped

2 tablespoons all-purpose flour

3 medium-size, ripe tomatoes, chopped and juices retained

Half of a 10-ounce package frozen corn kernels, thawed

*Half of a 10-ounce package frozen whole okra, thawed and
    cut in half*

¼ cup uncooked rice

1 tablespoon Worcestershire sauce

¼ teaspoon cayenne pepper

Few dashes of Tabasco sauce

*1½ teaspoons filé powder (available in specialty food shops
and some supermarkets)*

In a large, heavy pot, combine the turkey parts, quartered onion, cracked celery rib, carrot halves bay leaf, peppercorns, cloves, and salt and add enough water to cover. Bring to a boil and skim off the froth. Reduce the heat to low, cover, and simmer till the meat is very tender, about 2½ hours, adding water as necessary to keep the ingredients just covered. Transfer the turkey to a cutting board, remove and discard the bones and skin, and cut the meat into 1-inch pieces. Strain the stock through a fine sieve into a bowl and set aside. Wash out the pot.

Heat the oil in the pot over moderate heat, then add the chopped onion, celery, and bell pepper and stir till the vegetables begin to soften. Sprinkle the flour over the top, stir, and cook for 3 minutes. Add 4 cups of the reserved stock and stir. Add the tomatoes plus their juices, the corn, and okra and bring to a boil. Add the rice, stir, reduce the heat to moderately low, and simmer for 20 minutes. Add the turkey, Worcestershire, cayenne, and Tabasco, return to a simmer, and cook 10 minutes longer. Stir in the filé powder.

Makes 6 servings

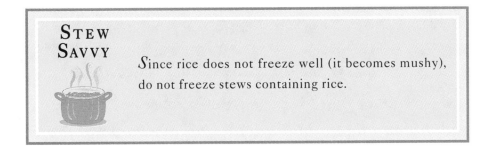

STEW SAVVY

*S*ince rice does not freeze well (it becomes mushy), do not freeze stews containing rice.

KEY WEST TURKEY, SWEET POTATO, AND MANGO POT

ALTHOUGH MOST RESTAURANTS IN Key West specialize primarily in various preparations of that tough mollusk indigenous to the Florida Keys known as conch, if you go somewhere like El Cacique, chances are they might also be serving a Caribbean-style stew like this unusual turkey, sweet potato, and mango pot enhanced by a little coconut. If you can find a small papaya that's not too ripe, adding it gives the stew an even more exotic flavor.

¼ cup vegetable oil

2 pounds turkey breast, skin removed, meat cut into
1-inch pieces, and patted dry with paper towels

1 cup dry white wine

2 tablespoons all-purpose flour mixed with 2 tablespoons
orange juice

4 scallions (whites and part of the greens included), chopped

1 garlic clove, minced

4 medium-size sweet potatoes, peeled and cut into small chunks

1 large, ripe mango, peeled, seeded, and cut into small chunks

1 cup chicken stock (page 120)

Salt and freshly ground black pepper to taste

½ cup fresh or canned unsweetened shredded coconut

In a large, heavy pot, heat half the oil over moderate heat, then add the turkey pieces, brown lightly on all sides, and transfer to a bowl. Add the wine to the pot and stir for 3 minutes, scraping up any browned bits off the bottom. Add the flour-and-orange-juice mixture, stir, and pour over the turkey pieces.

Heat the remaining 2 tablespoons oil in the pot over moderately high heat, add the scallions, garlic, and sweet potatoes, and stir for about 3 minutes.

Return the turkey and juices to the pot, add the mango, stock, and salt and pepper and stir. Bring to a simmer, reduce the heat to low, cover, and cook till the turkey and potatoes are tender, about 40 minutes. Stir in the shredded coconut and serve.

Makes 4 to 6 servings

TEX-MEX
TURKEY CHILI

CONTRARY TO POPULAR NOTIONS, Texans make chili with everything from goat to snake to antelope, so it was certainly no surprise when an old chum in Houston announced one cold weekend that, in my honor (!), he and his wife were planning to serve this turkey chili to no less than twenty guests at their impressive River Oaks home. While the dried ancho chiles have wonderful flavor, they are mild, so if you want more zing, add a couple of small chopped jalapeños—with or without the seeds, depending on how hot you like your chili. Serve boiled pinto beans on the side, as well as crusty corn sticks.

¼ pound dried ancho peppers

2 cups warm water

2 tablespoons corn oil

6 to 7 pounds turkey legs, skin and bones removed and cut into small pieces (about 6 cups)

½ cup chili powder

2 teaspoons ground cumin

2 cups canned tomato puree

2 medium-size onions, finely chopped

2 garlic cloves, minced

Salt and freshly ground black pepper to taste

¼ cup yellow cornmeal

continued

Wearing thin plastic gloves, stem and seed the anchos, tear them into small bits, place in a bowl, and pour on the warm water. Let soak for 1 hour, then strain the soaking liquid into a bowl. Place the anchos plus 1 cup of the soaking liquid into a blender or food processor and reduce to a puree, reserving the other cup of liquid.

In a large, heavy pot, heat the oil over moderate heat, add the turkey pieces, and stir till golden on all sides. Add the chili powder and cumin and continue to stir for 2 minutes. Stir in the pureed anchos, the reserved soaking liquid, the tomato puree, onions, garlic, and salt and pepper. Bring to a boil, then reduce the heat to low, cover, and simmer till the turkey is tender, about 40 minutes. Stirring constantly, add the cornmeal slowly, increase heat, and cook till the chili comes to a boil and begins to thicken. Serve immediately.

Makes 6 to 8 servings

MINNESOTA DUCK AND ONION STEW

SADLY, AND DESPITE ITS rich Scandinavian heritage, it's virtually impossible today to find authentic Swedish or Norwegian food in Minnesota. What you do find in fairly ample abundance, however, is wild fowl and, of course, wild rice—more often than not prepared in the Germanic fashion as it is farther south in Michigan and Illinois. The stew I discovered in St. Croix, Minnesota, was made with two sumptuous, relatively lean, rich wild ducks, but since wild ducks are not exactly in steady supply in our markets, I substituted one of our famous (if tamer) commercial Long Island birds when I returned to East Hampton to reproduce it. Since the proportion of meat to fat and bone can vary dramatically in commercial ducks, you might have to use two 3½- to 4-pound birds to be assured enough lean meat for four people—depending on appetites. I like to serve this stew with spiced apple slices and plenty of boiled wild rice.

One 5-pound duck, skin pricked with a fork and cut into
    serving pieces
¼ cup all-purpose flour
2 tablespoons butter
2 medium-size onions, chopped
1 small green bell pepper, seeded and chopped
1 garlic clove, minced
3 cups full-bodied ale or beer
¼ teaspoon dried thyme, crumbled
1 bay leaf
Salt and freshly ground black pepper to taste
12 small white onions, peeled and scored on the root ends
1 tablespoon cornstarch dissolved in ¼ cup water

Dredge the duck pieces in the flour, tapping off any excess. In a large, heavy pot, heat the butter over moderately high heat, then add the duck pieces, brown on all sides, and transfer to a plate. Pour off all but about 2 tablespoons of the fat, then add the chopped onions, bell pepper, and garlic and stir till softened. Return the duck to the pot, add the ale, thyme, bay leaf, and salt and pepper, and bring to a boil. Reduce the heat to moderately low, cover, and simmer for 1 hour. Add the small white onions and continue to simmer till the onions and duck are tender, about 30 minutes. Stir in the cornstarch mixture and stir over moderate heat till the liquid has thickened. Taste for salt and pepper, and serve.

Makes 3 to 4 servings

STEW SAVVY *Y*ou can turn almost any leftover meat or poultry stew into a sapid curry to be spooned over rice by adding a light- to medium-strength curry powder, a minced hot red pepper, and maybe a little chutney.

JAMES BEARD'S
DUCK AND
PINTO BEAN STEW

Jᴀᴍᴇꜱ Bᴇᴀʀᴅ ᴡᴀꜱ ᴀ dear friend, and this was but one of the many intriguing stews we shared at his Greenwich Village town house in New York. When he gave me the recipe, however, I questioned why he discarded the seasoning ingredients from the beans' soaking liquid, as well as why he overcooked the pintos initially (1½ hours!). "Because that's the way I like the stew," he huffed jovially. Jim and I argued a lot (about food, cooking, restaurants, and . . . opera), so I don't think he'd mind much that I've modified his all-American recipe just slightly.

> *2 cups dried pinto beans, rinsed and picked over*
> *1 medium-size onion, peeled and stuck with 2 cloves*
> *2 garlic cloves, peeled*
> *1 bay leaf*
> *Two 4-pound ducks*
> *5 tablespoons all-purpose flour*
> *Salt and freshly ground black pepper to taste*
> *2 tablespoons butter*
> *2 ounces salt pork, rind discarded and diced*
> *2 medium-size onions, finely chopped*
> *Pinch of dried basil, crumbled*
> *½ teaspoon dry mustard*
> *2 tablespoons vegetable oil*

Place the beans in a large saucepan with enough water to cover and let soak overnight. Drain the beans, add the clove-stuck onion, garlic, and bay leaf, and cover with salted water. Bring to a boil, then reduce the heat to moderately low and simmer for 30 minutes. Drain the beans and seasonings, reserving the soaking liquid.

Skin and cut the ducks into serving pieces, removing as much fat as possible. Slice the skin into thin strips and set aside. On a plate, combine the flour and salt and pepper and dredge the duck pieces in the mixture, tapping off any excess flour. In a large, heavy skillet, heat the butter and salt pork together over moderately high heat till the pork renders most of its fat, then add the chopped onions and stir till softened. Transfer the pork cracklings and onions to a large, heavy pot. In batches, brown the duck pieces evenly in the rendered fat and transfer to the pot. Add the beans plus their seasonings, the basil, mustard, and salt and pepper to taste and stir. Add the reserved bean liquid plus, if necessary, enough water to cover. Bring to a simmer, cover, and cook till the duck and beans are very tender, about 2 hours.

In a skillet, heat the oil over moderately high heat, add the reserved strips of duck skin, and fry till crisp. Drain the strips on paper towels and use to garnish the duck and beans.

Makes 6 servings

DUCK BRAISED
WITH FRESH FIGS

"**I** SUPPOSE THE DUCKS in this stew could simply be initially cut up and browned in the traditional manner," explains my friend Marion Gorman, a Michigan native, "but I find that roasting them first gives the dish so much more flavor." When Marion really wants to impress, she adds a chopped black truffle to the sauce, and her preferred way of serving this stew is over a mound of steamed fresh vegetables.

Two 4-pound ducks
Salt and freshly ground black pepper to taste
2 small oranges, quartered
2 small onions, quartered
2 garlic cloves, peeled
½ cup water
¼ cup (½ stick) butter
1 cup mixed chopped onions, celery, and carrots
1 tablespoon cornstarch
2 teaspoons tomato paste
½ cup chopped mushrooms
1 medium-size, ripe tomato, cut into 8 pieces
2 cups chicken stock (page 120)
24 fresh figs, quartered

Preheat the oven to 375°F.

Wash the ducks, then dry them inside and out with paper towels. Season their cavities with salt and pepper, and insert equal amounts of the oranges, onions, and garlic into the cavities. Tie the ducks' legs together snugly with kitchen string, prick the skin all over with a fork, and place on a rack in a large roasting pan. Pour the water into the pan and roast the ducks for 20 minutes.

Reduce the heat to 350°F., roast another 30 minutes, remove from the oven, and let cool slightly.

In a saucepan, heat the butter over moderate heat, add the mixed vegetables, and stir till softened. Add the cornstarch, tomato paste, mushrooms, and tomato, and stir. Add the stock, increase the heat to moderately high, and stir till the sauce comes almost to a boil. Reduce the heat to low and let simmer for 5 minutes.

Cut the ducks into serving pieces, slicing the breasts in half lengthwise. In a large, heavy pot, arrange half the duck pieces, scatter the figs over the top, and arrange the remaining duck pieces over the figs. Strain the sauce through a fine sieve over the top, bring to a simmer, cover, and cook till the duck meat is very tender, about 45 minutes.

Makes 6 servings

MIDDLEBURY DUCK AND RUTABAGA RAGOUT

F ew of my fellow students at Middlebury College in Vermont would touch the duck stewed with rutabagas that Mrs. Harris would occasionally put on the menu at her modest downtown restaurant, but I loved the pungent, earthy casserole and loved equally listening to the short, rather stern lady tell how she prepared it with apple cider. Rutabaga is in the turnip family, and why it's not more widely used and appreciated (especially as a component in hearty stews) is beyond me. Available all winter, yellow rutabagas are usually coated with wax and must be carefully peeled. The really huge ones are often too pithy, so be sure to choose those that are small or medium sized.

4 slices bacon

One 5-pound duck, cut into serving pieces, as much fat scraped
    from under skin as possible, and patted dry with paper
    towels

2 medium-size onions, chopped

2 celery ribs, chopped

½ teaspoon dried thyme, crumbled

1 bay leaf

6 black peppercorns

Salt to taste

1½ cups chicken stock (page 120)

1 cup apple cider

1 medium-size rutabaga, carefully peeled and cut into
    small cubes

1 tablespoon all-purpose flour mixed with 1 tablespoon water

In a large, heavy pot, fry the bacon over moderately high heat till almost crisp, then drain on paper towels, crumble, and set aside. Add the duck pieces to the pot and brown on all sides. Add the onions and celery, stir, and cook till the vegetables are softened. Add the thyme, bay leaf, peppercorns, salt, stock, and cider, bring to a simmer, reduce the heat to moderately low, cover, and cook for 1 hour, adding a little more stock or cider if necessary. Add the rutabaga plus the flour-and-water mixture and stir well. Return to a simmer, cover, and cook till the rutabaga and duck are tender, about 25 minutes. Serve topped with the crumbled bacon.

Makes 4 servings

EAST HAMPTON
GOOSE, SAUSAGE,
AND CHESTNUT STEW

"HONEY, THE REVEREND JEFFREY has invited me to his house in East Hampton for the weekend," drawled my beloved mentor, Pearl Byrd Foster, on the phone at her tiny New York restaurant, Mr. & Mrs. Foster's Place. "And since I've heard so much about the geese they raise out there, I've decided to try making a goose stew with sausage and chestnuts—perfect for this cold weather." Eventually, I bought a house in East Hampton and got to know Jim Jeffrey, and eventually, Pearl included the stew on the menu of her quintessential American restaurant. Without doubt, it was one of her finest creations. To prepare the chestnuts, cut a deep X on the flat side of the nuts with a very sharp paring knife, toss them into boiling water for about fifteen minutes, and remove both the shell and inner skin.

One 8- to 9-pound goose
3 slices bacon, diced
1 onion, sliced
1 carrot, scraped and sliced
1 garlic clove, crushed
1 cup dry red wine
3 cups chicken stock (page 120)
1 cup prepared tomato sauce
½ teaspoon dried thyme, crumbled
⅛ teaspoon ground fennel seeds
1 bay leaf
Salt and freshly ground black pepper to taste
30 chestnuts, shelled and peeled
6 sweet Italian sausages

12 medium-size carrots, scraped and cut in half
12 small white onions, peeled and scored on the root ends
2 tablespoons softened butter kneaded with 2 tablespoons
    all-purpose flour

Rinse the goose well under cold running water and remove as much fat from it as possible, reserving about 3 ounces of it. Cut the goose into 8 to 10 serving pieces and pat dry with paper towels.

In a large, heavy pot, heat the reserved goose fat and the bacon over moderately high heat, and when most of the fat is rendered, add the goose pieces and brown on all sides. Reduce the heat to moderate, add the sliced onion, sliced carrot, and the garlic, and stir till softened. Pour off all the fat from the pot, increase the heat to moderately high, add the wine, and boil till the wine is almost a glaze. Add the chicken stock, tomato sauce, thyme, fennel, bay leaf, and salt and pepper and stir, scraping the bottom of the pot with a wooden spoon to gather up any browned bits. Bring the liquid back to a boil, reduce the heat to moderately low, cover, and simmer till the goose is tender, about 1½ hours.

Meanwhile, place the chestnuts in a saucepan with enough water to cover, bring to a low boil, cook for 30 minutes, and drain. Arrange the sausages in a medium-size skillet and prick all over with a fork. Add enough water to come halfway up sides of the sausages, bring the water to a low boil, cook for 10 minutes, and drain (draining with it all of the fat). Place the carrot halves in a saucepan with enough water to cover, bring to a low boil, cook for 10 minutes, and drain. Place the white onions in a saucepan with enough water to cover, bring to a low boil, cook for 5 minutes, and drain.

Remove the goose from the pot, strain the cooking liquid through a fine sieve into a bowl, and skim off as much fat as possible. Return the liquid to the pot, add the kneaded butter, and stir with a whisk till well blended. Return the goose to the pot, add the chestnuts, sausages, carrots, and onions, bring to a simmer, cover, and cook till the goose is very tender, 20 to 30 minutes.

Makes 6 to 8 servings

Game and Variety Meat Stews

Ann Arbor Venison and Bing Cherry Stew

Southwestern Venison Sausage Stew

Georgia Venison Ragout with Root Vegetables

San Antonio Venison and Corn Chili

Great Northern Reindeer Mulligan

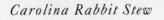

Carolina Rabbit Stew

Low Country Stewed Rabbit Smothered with Onions

Western Jugged Hare

Minnesota Braised Pheasant with Wild Rice

Pheasant, Wild Mushroom, and Walnut Stew

Tennessee Quail Burgoo

Beef Liver and Raisin Braise

Beef Kidney and Mushroom Stew

Kansas City Veal Kidney Braise

Menudo

Philadelphia Pepper Pot

Braised Beef Tongue with Mustard-Raisin Sauce

Game and Variety Meats
for Stewing

Although game remains a mysterious victual to most American cooks, nothing lends itself more to successful stewing than a full-flavored shoulder or round of venison, a couple of mature rabbits, a brace of pheasants, and even tiny quail. Once was the time in this country when wild duck from Lake Erie, Vermont ruffed grouse, New England wild turkey, Southern rabbits, Midwestern woodcock, desert hares, and Northern reindeer were as prized in plush big-city restaurants and aboard luxury crack trains as diamondback terrapin stew. Then, for any number of culinary and conservationist reasons, the popularity of wild game gradually diminished to the point where only hunters who shot their own animals and birds could enjoy the privilege of savoring some of the best food known to man. Today, rabbit, quail, and venison seem to be making a strong comeback, and a small amount of buffalo is being raised for the table; but other than that, it's still not that easy to find game even on a seasonal basis or frozen.

That said, in major cities, reputable butchers who sell federally inspected, high-quality fresh game in season and frozen game year-round do exist, and throughout the country there are markets that will butcher, package, and even label (for a price) any game that you've bagged yourself or received as a gift. (Never forget, however, that game is not automatically wholesome and that you take your chances with animals and birds that have not been officially inspected.)

Ideally, what you're looking for is venison (the meat of deer and other antlered animals) that has been aged long enough to allow its natural enzymes to partially tenderize the meat and develop a certain gamy character, and most that is sold legally in markets has these qualities. As for wild game birds, small, young, tender pheasants, wild ducks, geese, and quail might be perfect for roasting or grilling, but for stewing purposes, nothing is better than a moderate-size, mature bird. No matter what game you're buying, it should always be moist, display good color, and have a clean odor—fresh from the meat counter or when thawed and inspected. Never do I find the services and advice of a friendly butcher more valuable than when dealing with any type of game.

Variety meats (or offal) are such other edible parts (organs) of cows, calves, pigs, sheep, and lambs as the liver, kidneys, sweetbreads (thymus glands), tongue, brains, and tripe (the stomach lining of cows, sheep, and pigs), and while Europeans have always prized these cuts over other parts of the animal, only calf's liver and possibly sweetbreads have found even a modicum of favor with most Americans. Which is sad since, when correctly prepared, variety meats are both tender and delicious.

Sweetbreads, brains, and calf's liver are simply too fragile for stewing, but with these exceptions, all organ meats lend themselves beautifully to slow simmering. It's true that since lamb and veal kidneys are fairly delicate, they should never be cooked too long. Beef and pork kidneys from more mature, muscular animals, by contrast, are ideal for lengthy stewing (up to 45 minutes or an hour), as are the firm, reddish brown livers of these same animals, so long as the membranes and any large vessels are cut away. Just ten years ago, it was rare to find fresh honeycomb tripe anywhere but at the finest butcher shops; today it's available in most supermarkets, often partially cooked and needing only to be trimmed of fat. Although they can be a mess to work with, fresh beef, pork, and smaller veal tongues make exceptional stews. Beef tongue, by far the most available (and cheapest), is also marketed smoked, corned, and pickled, but for stewing I much prefer it fresh. Do remember that all variety meats are highly perishable, that they should be carefully studied and sniffed for freshness, and that the sooner they're cooked, the better.

ANN ARBOR VENISON
AND BING CHERRY STEW

"**W**HAT IN HELL ARE we going to do with this?" bellowed my old friend who was teaching at the University of Michigan in Ann Arbor, staring down at a heroic shoulder of fresh venison that a neighbor had just had butchered. Bill knows a lot about computer science and is not a bad cook, but faced with that big slab of venison, it was up to me to get the meat into a marinade and eventually turn it into a hefty stew. I guess it's pretty common knowledge that Michiganders are blessed with a superabundance of prime venison, but few people realize that, along with the Pacific Coast states, Michigan also produces most of the country's crop of Bing cherries. The combination of venison and cherries therefore couldn't have made more sense. We invited two couples to join us for dinner, and if I say so myself, it was one of the best stews I've ever tasted. It's illegal in this country to sell fresh venison that hasn't been government-inspected, but if you know any hunters, you have every right to accept the friendly gift of a shoulder (the ideal venison cut for stewing). To tame the meat, just make sure to marinate it first. Frozen venison, which is more and more available in our markets, is also perfectly acceptable for this stew.

1 cup dry red wine

3 tablespoons vegetable oil

1 medium-size onion, sliced

½ teaspoon dried thyme, crumbled

2 bay leaves

*2 pounds boneless venison shoulder, trimmed of excess fat and
cut into 1½-inch cubes*

½ cup all-purpose flour

5 slices bacon, cut into small dice

1 medium-size onion, chopped

2 garlic cloves, minced

One 16-ounce can pitted Bing cherries with their syrup

1 cup beef broth (page 6)
¼ teaspoon dried rosemary, crumbled
Salt and freshly ground black pepper to taste

In a large bowl, combine the wine, oil, sliced onion, thyme, and 1 of the bay leaves and stir to blend well. Add the venison cubes, cover with plastic wrap, and let marinate 24 hours in the refrigerator, turning the meat several times. Pat the meat dry with paper towels, strain the marinade into a bowl, and set aside.

Dredge the venison in the flour, tapping off any excess. In a large, heavy pot, fry the bacon over moderate heat till almost crisp, then add the venison and brown on all sides. Add the chopped onion and garlic and stir till softened, about 3 minutes. Pour the juice from the cherries over the meat and add 1 cup of the reserved marinade, the broth, rosemary, the remaining bay leaf, and salt and pepper. Bring to a low simmer, cover, and cook till the venison is very tender, about 2 hours. Add the cherries and cook about 10 minutes longer.

Makes 4 to 6 servings

SOUTHWESTERN VENISON SAUSAGE STEW

From Texas westward to California, some of the world's best venison preparations are the result of deer that have fed on the region's wild grasses, juniper, herbs, and piñon, and nothing has richer flavor than the spicy venison sausages that fill the display cases of meat markets and delis from Houston to Sante Fe to Alta, Utah. Most often, venison sausage is simply grilled at big barbecues, but when it's used to make a thick stew such as this, then you've really got something special. Most all fine delis around the country now carry at least one type of slightly gamy venison sausage, but if you're unable to find any, 1½-inch chunks of venison itself (preferably marinated and cooked about 15 minutes longer before adding the mushrooms) also work well in this stew.

continued

4 slices bacon, cut into small dice

1½ pounds venison sausage links, cut into thirds

2 medium-size onions, chopped

1 garlic clove, minced

Two 12-ounce bottles beer

2 medium-size potatoes, peeled and cut into cubes

1 tablespoon juniper berries, crushed

1 teaspoon dried thyme, crumbled

2 bay leaves

Salt and freshly ground black pepper to taste

½ pound mushrooms, quartered

1 tablespoon all-purpose flour

2 tablespoons butter, softened

1 teaspoon prepared mustard

In a large, heavy pot, fry the bacon over moderate heat till crisp, drain on paper towels, and set aside. Add the sausage to the hot bacon fat, brown evenly on all sides, and transfer to a plate. Add the onions and garlic to the pot and stir until softened, about 5 minutes. Return the sausages to the pot, add the bacon, beer, potatoes, juniper berries, thyme, bay leaves, and salt and pepper, bring to a low simmer, cover, and cook for 30 minutes. Add the mushrooms, stir, return to a simmer, and cook for 20 minutes. In a bowl, combine the flour, butter, and mustard, mixing well to form a paste. Stir the paste thoroughly into the stew to thicken, and heat for 5 minutes.

Makes 4 servings

GEORGIA VENISON RAGOUT
WITH ROOT VEGETABLES

WHEN A RELATIVE IN Macon, Georgia, used to make this heady ragout, he of course used fairly mature fresh venison that first had to be marinated to tenderize the meat and tame the gaminess. My version assumes that you'll be using readily available frozen meat that is much younger and therefore needs no initial marination. It certainly never hurts to marinate any venison intended for stewing (shoulder, round, rump, or shank), but here at least you have the option since the long simmering in itself should be enough to produce tender, succulent meat. My uncle used some type of questionable sweet wine made from berries in his ragout; I prefer sweet vermouth.

1 cup all-purpose flour

Salt and freshly ground black pepper to taste

Cayenne pepper to taste

2 pounds boneless venison shoulder, trimmed of excess fat and
    cut into 1½-inch pieces

¼ cup (½ stick) butter

1 cup sweet vermouth

2 celery ribs (leaves included), chopped

½ teaspoon dried thyme, crumbled

½ teaspoon dried rosemary, crumbled

1 bay leaf

3 cloves

2 cups beef broth (page 6)

12 tiny new potatoes, scrubbed but not peeled

6 small white onions, peeled and scored on the root ends

3 medium-size carrots, scraped and cut into rounds

2 medium-size parsnips, peeled and cut into 1-inch cubes

continued

Combine the flour, salt, pepper, and cayenne and dredge the venison in the mixture, tapping off any excess flour. In a large, heavy pot, heat the butter over moderately high heat, then add the venison and brown on all sides. Add the vermouth and stir well, scraping up any browned bits off the bottom of the pot. Add the celery, thyme, rosemary, bay leaf, cloves, and broth, reduce the heat to a low simmer, cover, and cook for 1 hour. Add the potatoes, onions, carrots, parsnips, and salt and pepper to taste, return to a simmer, cover, and cook till the venison is very tender, about another hour, adding more broth if necessary.

Makes 6 servings

STEW SAVVY

*C*arrots are a natural component of many different stews, but since they can be deceptively sweet when simmered, be extremely careful with the number you add—depending on your tolerance for sweetness.

SAN ANTONIO VENISON
AND CORN CHILI

I'M NOT ABOUT TO participate in the heated, never-ending argument about who makes the greatest traditional beef chili con carne in Texas, but I will insist that the best and most authentic venison chili is this one (with no tomatoes!) that a team of Tex-Mexicans in San Antonio cooked up one morning for me and a few colleagues who were in town to judge the food at a March of Dimes Gourmet Gala. What's nice about using venison to make chili is not only the unusual taste but the fact that, since the meat simmers so long, it requires no initial marination to assure tenderness. Our stew was made with Mexican beer, which does have a distinctive flavor.

6 tablespoons peanut oil

2 large onions, chopped

2 garlic cloves, minced

2 pounds boneless venison (preferably shoulder), trimmed of excess fat and cut into small dice

3 tablespoons chili powder

1 tablespoon cumin seeds

½ teaspoon ground coriander

1 tablespoon salt

Tabasco sauce to taste

Three 12-ounce bottles beer

One 10-ounce package frozen corn kernels

In a large, heavy pot, heat the oil over moderate heat, then add the onions and garlic and stir till softened, about 2 minutes. Add the venison and stir till slightly browned with the onions. Add the chili powder, cumin seeds, coriander, salt, and Tabasco and stir for 1 minute. Add the beer, stir, bring to a low simmer, cover, and cook for 2 hours. Add the corn, return to a simmer, cover, and cook till the chili is the desired consistency, about 30 minutes longer.

Makes 6 servings

GREAT NORTHERN
REINDEER MULLIGAN

IMPRACTICAL AS IT IS today given the virtual nonexistence of American reindeer meat except in Alaska, I simply can't resist including this stew found in an old
booklet from the early part of the century that introduced experimental reindeer
dishes to passengers aboard trains on the Great Northern Line—the recipe "fur-
nished by an old hunter." The text notes that the meat "is finer in texture than
beef and decidedly more tender—this explained by the fact that the reindeer is a
docile animal, seldom exerting itself to the extent of providing ordinary exercise—
therefore he grows fat and soft." Well, I don't know just how tender that reindeer
meat really was without being marinated (I've eaten lots of reindeer in Scandi-
navia and love it), but I did substitute unmarinated venison shoulder with surpris-
ingly delicious results. And the most fascinating taste sensation is the added
tanginess of dill pickles—not unlike that in beef solianka. My guess is that some-
body could make a fortune (and add a whole new dimension to American cooking)
by marketing reindeer from Alaska and Canada. Though the term is almost
archaic, a mulligan is indeed a meat and vegetable stew—just like a mull.

*2 pounds boneless reindeer meat or venison shoulder, trimmed
    of excess fat and cut into 2-inch cubes*

*1 medium-size rutabaga, carefully peeled and cut into 2-inch
    cubes*

2 large onions, peeled and quartered

2 carrots, scraped and cut into 2-inch chunks

2 potatoes, peeled and cut into 1-inch cubes

2 dill pickles, chopped

Salt and freshly ground black pepper to taste

*1 herb bouquet (6 black peppercorns and 4 bay leaves wrapped
    in cheesecloth)*

Place the reindeer meat or venison in a large, heavy pot and add enough water to cover. Bring to a boil, skim the surface of any scum, reduce the heat to a moderate simmer, cover, and cook for 30 minutes. Add the rutabaga and continue to simmer for 15 minutes. Add the remaining ingredients, return to a low simmer, cover, and cook till the meat is tender, about 2½ hours.

Makes 6 to 8 servings

STEW SAVVY *I*nstead of using cheesecloth (often difficult to find) to wrap an herb bouquet, substitute a square of heavy aluminum foil and prick it all over with a fork to release the seasonings.

CAROLINA
RABBIT STEW

I STILL CRINGE WHEN REMEMBERING the sight of our neighbor in North Carolina, Mr. Nunn, deftly skinning rabbits he caught in traps, but then I think of the wonderful stew my granddaddy made with those rabbits and the negative vision fades. Paw Paw didn't do much more than throw a rabbit or so into a big iron pot with cooking meat, a few vegetables, and some seasoning, but to a hungry youngster, there was really no stew like it—except maybe his Brunswick stew. Later on, Mother refined the stew considerably, and this is the way we still prepare it today.

9 slices bacon, finely chopped

*One 4- to 5-pound rabbit or two 2-pound rabbits, dressed and
    each cut into 8 serving pieces*

Salt and freshly ground black pepper to taste

½ cup all-purpose flour

2 medium-size onions, finely chopped

1 garlic clove, finely chopped

1 cup dry red wine

1 cup chicken stock (page 120)

2 tablespoons brandy

1 teaspoon currant jelly

1 bay leaf

¼ teaspoon dried rosemary, crumbled

¼ teaspoon dried thyme, crumbled

In a large, heavy pot over moderate heat, fry the bacon till crisp, then drain on paper towels. Set the pot aside.

Wash the rabbit, pat dry, season with salt and pepper, and dust lightly with the flour. Over moderate heat, brown the rabbit on all sides in the bacon fat, then transfer the pieces to a plate and pour off all but 2 tablespoons of the fat. Reduce the heat slightly, add the onions and garlic, and cook, stirring, for 2 minutes. Add the wine and stock. Stir in the brandy, jelly, and herbs, and return the rabbit to the pot. Add the crumbled bacon, cover, and simmer over low heat till the rabbit is fork-tender, about 1½ hours.

Makes 4 to 6 servings

STEW SAVVY *L*eftover meat, poultry, and game stews are not only delicious when allowed to sit a day or so in the refrigerator and reheated but also can be turned into fillings for savory pies.

LOW COUNTRY
STEWED RABBIT
SMOTHERED WITH ONIONS

IT'S BEEN AT LEAST ten years since I first met Louis Osteen when he was chef at Pawley's Island Inn in the South Carolina Low Country. He was a good Southern cook then, and now he's a truly expert one at his own Charleston Grill farther down the coast. Louis specializes in rather complex but utterly distinctive stews, ragouts, and braises that utilize all sorts of local meats, game, seafood, and vegetables. Over the years, he has come up with some remarkable concoctions, but none has impressed me more than his herby rabbit stew smothered with onions.

Three 2½-pound rabbits, dressed and each cut into
   8 serving pieces
8 medium-size onions, thinly sliced
1 carrot, scraped and sliced into thin 2-inch-long julienne
3 garlic cloves, smashed
4 sprigs fresh thyme, or 2 teaspoons dried, crumbled
2 small sprigs fresh rosemary, or 1 teaspoon dried, crumbled
3 tablespoons crushed black peppercorns
Three 12-ounce bottles dark beer
3 tablespoons sugar
6 tablespoons (¾ stick) butter
6 tablespoons peanut oil
4½ cups chicken stock (page 120)
Salt and freshly ground black pepper to taste
4½ tablespoons all-purpose flour
1½ tablespoons minced garlic
1 herb bouquet (2 bay leaves and 6 sprigs fresh parsley
   wrapped in cheesecloth)

Place the rabbits in a large glass or ceramic baking dish and add 1 of the sliced onions plus the carrot. In a jar, combine the smashed garlic, thyme, rosemary, peppercorns, beer, and sugar, shake vigorously, and pour over the rabbit, turning the pieces to coat. Cover the dish with plastic wrap and refrigerate 1 to 2 days, turning the rabbit pieces several times. Remove the rabbits from the marinade and pat dry with paper towels. Strain the marinade into a large bowl, discard the solids, and set the pan aside.

In a large, heavy skillet, heat the butter and oil together over moderately high heat, add the rabbit pieces in batches, brown on all sides, and transfer to a plate. Add the remaining 7 onions to the skillet, stir till they begin to brown, and transfer to another plate.

Add the stock to the marinade in the saucepan and stir well. Meanwhile, season the rabbits with salt and pepper, arrange the pieces in a large, heavy pot, and sprinkle the flour over the top. Distribute the cooked onions and minced garlic evenly over the rabbit pieces, pour on the liquid, and add the herb bouquet. Bring to a moderate simmer, cover, and cook till the rabbit meat is tender, about 1 hour. Taste for salt and pepper and discard the herb bouquet. Transfer the rabbit pieces to a large, heated serving platter, smother with the onions, and pour a little sauce over the top.

Makes 6 to 8 servings

WESTERN JUGGED HARE

THE ONE TIME I drove through part of Idaho on the way to Nevada (never once seeing, by the way, a distinctive potato preparation at any restaurant!), a woman at a motel told me with some pride about the state's pygmy rabbits that are often fried for breakfast. Well, I didn't taste any Idaho pygmy rabbit, but when I finally arrived in Reno after traveling through American-Basque sheep country, the special stew on the menu at Louis' Basque Corner (where a different stew is featured every night) was a rich, gamy jugged jackrabbit concoction that might well have been found in San Sebastián near the border of Spain and France. The hares found in the desert states are really no more than mature jackrabbits or blacktail rabbits, and while this variety of game is rarely suitable for roasting, grilling, or frying, it is delectable when marinated and simmered slowly in stews— and it must be marinated at least twenty-four hours. Needless to say, very little genuine hare is marketed outside the Great Basin of the United States, so when shopping, simply try to find the largest rabbits possible.

2 cups dry red wine

1 teaspoon salt

1 teaspoon freshly ground black pepper

½ teaspoon dried thyme, crumbled

½ teaspoon powdered bay leaf

1 medium-size onion, minced

*One 4- to 5-pound hare or 2 large rabbits, dressed and cut into
    8 serving pieces*

6 slices meaty bacon, cut into pieces

2 medium-size onions, chopped

3 tablespoons all-purpose flour

*1 herb bouquet (½ teaspoon dried thyme, 1 bay leaf, 1 peeled
    garlic clove, and 2 sprigs fresh parsley wrapped in
    cheesecloth)*

18 small white onions, peeled and scored on the root ends

18 small mushrooms, halved

¼ cup heavy cream

To make the marinade, combine the wine, salt, pepper, thyme, bay leaf, and minced onion in a large glass baking dish and stir till well blended. Add the hare to the marinade, spooning liquid over the pieces, cover with plastic wrap, and let marinate in the refrigerator at least 1 day, turning frequently. Remove the hare from the marinade and pat dry. Strain the marinade into a bowl.

In a large, heavy pot, fry the bacon over moderate heat till almost crisp, then add the chopped onions and stir till golden, about 3 minutes. Add the flour and stir till golden brown, about 5 minutes. Add the hare to the pot. Increase the heat to moderately high, stir, and brown the pieces on all sides. Add the strained marinade and the herb bouquet, reduce the heat to a low simmer, and cook for 1 hour. Add the white onions and mushrooms, return the heat to a simmer, cover, and cook till the hare is tender, about 45 minutes longer. Remove and discard the herb bouquet, skim off any fat from the surface of the stew, add the cream, and stir till thickened.

❧ Makes 6 servings ❧

MINNESOTA BRAISED PHEASANT WITH WILD RICE

Up in Wabasha, Minnesota, there is a delightful hotel called Anderson House (no relation to my old food-loving friend Curt Anderson, who happens to come from that unspoiled state), where, only on weekends, the specialty is this creamy braised pheasant on wild rice—both bird and rice indigenous to Minnesota. Normally roasted, pheasant (both wild and domesticated) tends to become stringy as it cooks, but when it is simmered slowly in stock and wine, then enriched with a little cream, the moist result is ambrosial.

continued

Two 2-pound pheasants, dressed and each cut into 6 serving pieces

1 cup all-purpose flour

¼ cup (½ stick) butter

*1 medium-size leek (white part only), thoroughly washed and
    chopped*

1 carrot, scraped and chopped

1 garlic clove, minced

½ pound mushrooms, quartered

½ teaspoon dried rosemary, crumbled

Salt and freshly ground black pepper to taste

1 cup dry red wine

1 cup chicken stock (page 120)

½ cup heavy cream

Boiled wild rice

Dredge the pheasant pieces in the flour, tapping off any excess. In a large, heavy pot, heat the butter over moderately high heat, add the pheasant, and brown lightly on all sides. Add the leek, carrot, and garlic, and cook, stirring, for 3 minutes. Add the mushrooms, rosemary, salt and pepper, wine, and stock, bring to a low simmer, cover, and cook till the pheasant is tender, about 1¼ hours. Stir in the cream and simmer 10 minutes longer. Serve with wild rice.

Makes 4 servings

PHEASANT, WILD MUSHROOM, AND WALNUT STEW

I**T MAY BE TRUE THAT** the pheasant was introduced to America in the late nineteenth century, when a consul brought back to his Oregon farm a few Shanghai birds; it is true that virtually all walnuts (the "English walnut") in the United States come from California; and it's said that the finest chanterelles, shiitakes, and other wild mushrooms are found in the state of Washington. Combine these ingredients, in any case, in a stew such as this, and American cooking just doesn't get any better. For a slightly richer stew, you might want to substitute a full-bodied red wine like Cabernet or Merlot for the white.

Two 2-pound pheasants, dressed and each cut into 6 serving pieces
12 slices bacon
6 tablespoons (³/₄ stick) butter
1 medium-size onion, chopped
1 carrot, scraped and chopped
2 garlic cloves, minced
1 tablespoon chopped fresh rosemary leaves, or ¹/₂ teaspoon
    dried, crumbled
1 tablespoon chopped fresh thyme leaves, or ¹/₂ teaspoon dried,
    crumbled
1¹/₂ cups chicken stock (page 120)
1¹/₂ cups dry white wine
Salt and freshly ground black pepper to taste
1 pound fresh wild mushrooms (cèpes, chanterelles, or
    shiitakes), stems removed and caps chopped, or 2 ounces
    dried wild mushrooms, soaked in warm water for
    20 minutes, drained, and chopped
1 cup crushed walnuts

continued

Wrap each piece of pheasant with a slice of bacon and secure with a toothpick. In a large, heavy pot, heat the butter over moderately high heat, add the pheasant pieces, and brown on all sides. Add the onion, carrot, and garlic and cook, stirring, about 2 minutes. Add the rosemary, thyme, stock, wine, and salt and pepper, bring to a low simmer, cover, and cook till the pheasant is tender, about 1¼ hours. Transfer the pheasant to a platter and remove and discard the bacon.

Skim the excess fat from the surface of the cooking liquid, bring to a low boil, and cook till slightly reduced. Add the mushrooms and walnuts, return the pheasant to the pot, cover, and simmer till the mushrooms are tender, about 20 minutes.

Makes 4 servings

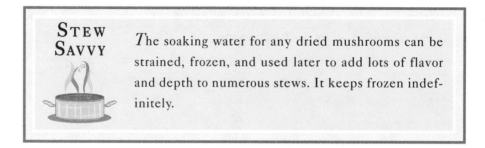

STEW SAVVY *T*he soaking water for any dried mushrooms can be strained, frozen, and used later to add lots of flavor and depth to numerous stews. It keeps frozen indefinitely.

TENNESSEE QUAIL BURGOO

THOUGH NONE IS DIRECTLY related to Old World quail, several types of quail can be found in much of the United States—the mountain quail of the West, the Gambels and Montezumas of the Southwest, and the abundant bobwhites of the Plains and the South. Elsewhere, farm-raised quail are just as popular (if less tasty) with professional and home cooks alike; and if most still think that all quail must be roasted or grilled, at least one old friend in Memphis (who shoots his own birds) still knows that nothing makes for better eating than a traditional quail burgoo simmered long and slowly Southern style, with all sorts of vegetables and seasonings. Henry just throws everything into the pot at the same time and lets the burgoo cook away, but if you want a little more texture to the corn and limas, add them only after the first hour of simmering.

8 quail, dressed

2 cups all-purpose flour

4 slices bacon, cut into bits

2 tablespoons vegetable oil

2 large onions, finely chopped

1 carrot, scraped and finely chopped

3 ripe tomatoes, chopped

2 large potatoes, peeled and cut into small cubes

2 cups fresh or frozen lima beans

2 cups fresh or frozen corn kernels

½ teaspoon dried thyme, crumbled

1 bay leaf

Salt and freshly ground black pepper to taste

Cayenne pepper to taste

3 quarts water

continued

Dredge the quail in the flour, tapping off any excess. In a large, heavy pot, fry the bacon over moderate heat till crisp, drain on paper towels, and set aside. Add the oil to the pot, still over moderate heat, then add the onions and carrot and cook, stirring, for 2 minutes. Add the reserved bacon plus the remaining ingredients, bring to a low simmer, cover, and cook for 2 hours, adding a little more water if the burgoo thickens too much.

Makes 4 to 6 servings

BEEF LIVER
AND RAISIN BRAISE

LIKE BEEF KIDNEY, BEEF liver is a relatively inexpensive variety meat with an assertive edge that almost demands slow simmering to bring out its savory succulence. Add any number of herbs and spices, plus the sweet counterbalance of something like raisins, and the delicate, much more expensive calf's liver you've been accustomed to simply sautéing quickly with onions will seem almost boring. Remember when shopping to buy liver that is firm and reddish brown, and since it is so perishable, make sure to cook it within twenty-four hours.

½ cup all-purpose flour
Salt and freshly ground black pepper to taste
2 pounds beef liver, trimmed of membranes and cut into
  medium-size strips
3 slices bacon, cut into small dice
1 medium-size onion, chopped
¼ teaspoon dried marjoram, crumbled
⅛ teaspoon ground mace
1 cup seedless golden raisins
2 cups beef broth (page 6)
Boiled rice

Combine the flour and salt and pepper and dredge the liver strips in the mixture, tapping off any excess flour. In a large, heavy pot, fry the bacon over moderate heat till almost crisp, then add the onion and cook, stirring, for 2 minutes. Add the liver and brown on both sides, stirring. Add the marjoram, mace, raisins, and broth and stir well, scraping up any browned bits off the bottom. Bring to a low simmer, cover, and cook till the liver is tender, about 45 minutes. Serve the stew over rice.

Makes 4 to 6 servings

BEEF KIDNEY
AND MUSHROOM STEW

WHILE NOTHING IS MORE relished in Britain and France than a savory beef kidney stew, it's taken decades for most Americans to even approach an appreciation of this variety meat that can be so utterly delicious if it's handled and cooked correctly. James Beard loved a good kidney stew and served it often over noodles, as I do, especially when the kidneys are on sale dirt cheap. I must admit that I still find beef kidneys a bit too strong for my taste when they're merely broiled or sautéed, but I think that you'll agree it's an altogether different matter when they're simmered slowly in beef broth with mushrooms and their savor is allowed to mellow.

> 2 pounds beef kidneys
> 3 slices bacon, cut into small dice
> 1 medium-size onion, finely chopped
> ½ cup all-purpose flour
> Salt and freshly ground black pepper to taste
> 2 cups beef broth (page 6)
> ½ pound mushrooms, quartered
> ¼ teaspoon dried rosemary, crumbled
> 1 bay leaf, crumbled
> 1 tablespoon all-purpose flour mixed with 1 tablespoon water
> 1 tablespoon minced fresh parsley leaves

Place the kidneys in a bowl, add enough salted water to cover, and soak for 1 hour at room temperature. Meanwhile, in a large, heavy pot, fry the bacon over moderate heat till almost crisp, add the onion, cook, stirring for 2 minutes, and set the pot aside.

Drain the kidneys, pat dry with paper towels, trim off and discard any fat and tubes, and cut into 1-inch cubes. Combine the flour and salt and pepper and dredge the kidneys in the mixture, tapping off any excess flour. Add the kidneys to the pot and brown over moderate heat, stirring. Add the broth, mushrooms, rosemary, and bay leaf, bring to a moderate simmer, scraping any browned bits off the bottom, cover, and cook till the kidneys are tender, 35 to 40 minutes. Add the flour paste and stir till the liquid has thickened. Taste for salt and pepper and sprinkle the parsley on top.

Makes 4 to 6 servings

KANSAS CITY
VEAL KIDNEY BRAISE

WHEN I LIVED IN Columbia, Missouri, every year friends in the Mission Hills section of Kansas City would invite me to drive over the week before Christmas to partake of an elaborate holiday breakfast buffet that had become something of a social ritual. There must have been twenty-five dishes on that vast mahogany table, but it was the braised veal kidneys spooned over rice (in the South, I've often had them over buttered grits) that eventually sent me back to the kitchen to beg the family cook for the recipe. The stew is also delicious made with small lamb kidneys (about nine), but these must first be soaked about an hour in milk before trimming off the membranes and cutting out the hard cores.

> *3 veal kidneys*
> *2 tablespoons all-purpose flour*
> *¼ cup (½ stick) butter*
> *2 tablespoons vegetable oil*
> *2 medium-size onions, finely chopped*
> *1 large green bell pepper, seeded and finely chopped*
> *¼ teaspoon dried rosemary, crumbled*
> *2 tablespoons fresh lemon juice*
> *2 cups chicken stock (page 120)*
> *Salt and freshly ground black pepper to taste*
> *Cayenne pepper to taste*
> *⅓ cup medium-dry sherry*
> *Boiled rice*

With a sharp knife, trim the membranes from the kidneys, then, with a pair of scissors, cut out and discard the hard cores. Slice the kidneys thinly and toss with the flour. In a large, heavy pot, heat the butter and oil together over moderate heat, then add the kidneys and brown lightly on both sides. Add the onions and bell pepper and stir till softened, about 3 minutes. Add the rosemary, lemon juice, stock, salt and pepper, and cayenne, bring to a low simmer, cover, and cook till the kidneys are tender, 20 to 25 minutes. Stir in the sherry, bring to a boil, and remove from the heat. Serve over rice.

Makes 4 servings

MENUDO

IT'S BEEN SAID THAT, given Americans' aversion to eating something like cow's stomach, the only important tripe dish ever developed in this country was a broiled preparation at Boston's old Parker House hotel. Wrong! Besides Philadelphia's famous pepper pot, menudo has been one of the most popular staples in Texas, New Mexico, and Arizona ever since the dish crossed the Mexican border and was Americanized decades ago. It's a savory stew you really should try making, and the next time you're in Tucson, head for a restaurant called El Dorado for possibly the best menudo of the region.

2 pounds honeycomb tripe, cut into 1-inch pieces
2 pig's feet
2 onions, quartered
6 black peppercorns
Salt to taste
4 dried ancho peppers
2 dried hot red peppers about 2 inches long
3 garlic cloves, peeled
½ teaspoon dried oregano, crumbled
2 cups canned hominy, drained
1 tablespoon fresh lime juice

continued

In a large, heavy pot, combine the tripe and pig's feet, add enough water to cover, bring to a boil, and skim the scum from the surface. Add the onions, peppercorns, and salt, reduce heat to a low simmer, cover, and cook till the tripe and pig's feet are tender, about 3½ hours.

Meanwhile, remove the stems and seeds from the anchos and other hot peppers, tear them into pieces, and crumble into a bowl. Add enough warm water to just cover, soak for 1 hour, drain, and set aside.

Drain the tripe and pig's feet in a large colander set over a large bowl. Discard the onions and peppercorns, and measure and set aside about 4 cups of the cooking liquid. Return the tripe to the pot. Remove and discard the skin, gristle, and fat from the pig's feet, cut the meat into small pieces, and add to the tripe.

In a blender or food processor, combine the hot peppers, garlic, oregano, and 1 cup of the reserved cooking liquid and process into a paste. Add the paste and remaining cooking liquid to the pot, stir in the hominy, lime juice, and salt to taste, bring to a low simmer, cover, and cook for 30 minutes.

❧ Makes 6 servings ❧

PHILADELPHIA
PEPPER POT

Sᴘɪᴄʏ Pʜɪʟᴀᴅᴇʟᴘʜɪᴀ ᴘᴇᴘᴘᴇʀ ᴘᴏᴛ may not be as popular today as the city's herby scrapple made with all sorts of variety meats, but once was the time when the soupy tripe stew was hawked in the streets by women cooks and dispensed from pushcarts. Some think that the immigrant origins of the stew are Dutch, others English, but given its similarity to *tripes à la mode de Caen* (and the cosmopolitan nature of Philadelphia in the early days), James Beard always said it was essentially French—and I agree. In any case, the pepper pot is a unique regional dish and one that I love to serve (often with sautéed wild mushrooms) on a cold winter night with plenty of biscuits and sturdy red wine. If you've never dealt with tripe, this stew is the most appetizing starting point.

2 pounds honeycomb tripe

1 small veal knuckle

1 herb bouquet (½ teaspoon dried thyme, 2 sprigs fresh parsley, and 1 bay leaf wrapped in cheesecloth)

1½ quarts water

1 large onion, chopped

Salt and freshly ground black pepper to taste

1 small fresh hot red pepper, chopped

2 large potatoes, peeled and diced

¼ pound beef suet, finely chopped

1 cup all-purpose flour

Place the tripe in a saucepan with enough water to cover, bring to a boil, remove from the heat, and set aside.

In a large, heavy pot, combine the veal knuckle, herb bouquet, and water, bring to a boil, and skim the surface for scum. Reduce the heat to a low simmer, cover, and cook for 2½ hours. Strain the broth into a bowl and set aside. When cool enough to handle, remove the meat from the bone, cut into small cubes, and wash out the pot. Rinse the tripe and cut into small cubes.

In the pot, combine the veal meat, tripe, onion, salt and black pepper, hot pepper, and about 3 cups of the reserved broth. Bring to a low simmer, cover, and cook for 2 hours. Add the potatoes. In a bowl, mix the suet and flour, add just enough water to make a thick paste, add to the stew, and stir well. Return the stew to a simmer, cover, and cook till the tripe is tender, about 1 hour longer. Taste for salt and pepper and serve.

Makes 4 to 6 servings

BRAISED
BEEF TONGUE WITH
MUSTARD-RAISIN SAUCE

Tongue, probably the most muscular of the variety meats, is not only ideal for slow stewing but utterly delicious when cooked patiently and served with a sweet-sour sauce. I use mainly beef tongue for the simple reason that it is cheap and much more available than pork, veal, or lamb tongue. The latter is equally delectable if you can find it, but do remember that it cooks in less time than the beef. This dish is also very good spooned over rice or noodles.

One 2½- to 3-pound fresh beef tongue
1 large onion, peeled and studded with 3 cloves
1 large carrot, cut in half
1 celery rib (leaves included), cracked in half
1 bay leaf
4 black peppercorns
Salt to taste
3 slices bacon, cut into small dice
3 scallions, cut in half lengthwise and thinly sliced
1 garlic clove, peeled and crushed
1 celery rib, diced
1 cup beef broth (page 6)
1 cup water
Salt and freshly ground black pepper to taste
3 tablespoons Dijon mustard
½ cup seedless golden raisins

In a large, heavy pot, combine the tongue, onion, carrot, cracked celery, bay leaf, peppercorns, salt, and enough water to cover. Bring to the boil and skim the scum off the surface. Reduce the heat to a low simmer, cover, and cook about 2 hours. Plunge the tongue into another pot of cold water and discard the contents of the first pot. Lift the tongue from the water, remove the skin, cut away the root, gristle, and small bones, cut the meat into ½-inch-thick slices, and set aside.

To prepare the sauce, fry the bacon in a heavy skillet over moderate heat till almost crisp, then add the scallions, garlic, and diced celery and stir till lightly browned, about 7 minutes. Add the broth, water, salt and pepper, and mustard, stir till the mustard is well incorporated, bring to a low simmer, and cook for 30 minutes. Let the mixture cool slightly, then transfer to a blender or food processor and reduce to a puree.

Pour the puree into a large, heavy pot, add the tongue slices and raisins, bring to a low simmer, cover, and cook till the tongue is fork-tender, about 1 hour. Serve the tongue topped with the sauce.

Makes 6 servings

Seafood Stews

Fish Stock

Cape Girardeau Catfish Stew

Galveston Grouper and Pecan Mull

Northwest Salmon Solianka

Tampa Bay Snapper Stew

Curried Fish Kettle

Oregon Fish Chili

Lake Superior Whitefish and Shrimp Stew

Old Stone Fish Stew

Cioppino

Neal Myers's Seafood Stew

Down East Mixed Shellfish Stew

Commander's Seafood Gumbo

Carolina Gumbo

Maine Red Shrimp and Scallop Stew

Savannah Shrimp Pilau

Classic Shrimp Creole

Sullivan's Island Shrimp Bog

Cajun Crawfish Étouffée

Crawfish Stew

Jasper White's Chunky Lobster Stew

Montauk Lobster and Leek Stew

Florida Conch Stew

Mother's Old-Fashioned Oyster Stew

Seattle Oyster and Spinach Stew

Monterey Mussel Stew

Pacific Squid and Artichoke Stew

Maryland Terrapin Stew

Fish and Seafood for Stewing

Who says that America can't pride itself on seafood stews the same way that the French boast their *bourride* and *bouillabaisse*, the Italians their *zuppa di pesce*, and the Spanish their *paella*? Needless to say, I'm hardly referring to those modernized, contrived, anemic concoctions of undercooked fish and shellfish and baby veggies in light, tasteless broths touted as "stews" in fashionable New American restaurants and trendy cookbooks. Rather, I'm talking about the great pilaus, étouffées, and gumbos of the South, the lusty cioppino and solianka of California and the Pacific Northwest, the elegant shellfish stews of New England, and the various muddles, bogs, mulls, and kettles found from the coasts of Long Island to the Gulf inlets of Texas to the shores of Lake Superior and the vast Mississippi River. The stewing, braising, and gentle simmering of seafood is as much a culinary art in most areas of this country as the barbecuing of meat and poultry, and to witness the tradition being corrupted by pretentious big-city chefs more interested in abstract innovation than in regional authenticity is nothing less than depressing.

The main difference between seafood stews and all others is that, generally, the main ingredients are not cooked nearly as long as meat, poultry, and vegetables for the simple reason that long simmering tends to disintegrate most fish and toughen most shellfish. As a result, integral flavor must usually be derived from good, fresh stock, as well as from secondary ingredients that are allowed to simmer in the stock. To be sure, there are stews like Florida conch, some cioppino, and certain gumbos that only benefit from a relatively lengthy cooking, and both squid and octopus simply must be simmered long enough to be transformed into melting tenderness and succulence. But for the most part, seafood suffers from overcooking and should remain in the liquid base no more than a few minutes.

When shopping for seafood, never forget that it must be fresh, fresh, fresh when at all possible; that it is highly perishable; and that the sooner it goes into the pot the better. Of course, there's nothing like having a reliable fishmonger, but when you're on your own, always look for the signs of quality: fish that has no off-smell whatsoever, with clear, glassy eyes, bright red or pink gills, and firm texture; shrimp and crawfish (even when previously frozen, which most are these days) that are shiny, firm, and almost odorless; scallops that are moist and glistening; mussels, clams, and oysters with tightly closed shells; squid that is not flaccid and has a gray, not purplish, outer membrane; and lobsters that are alive and kicking.

Virtually all seafood can make good stews, but some are better than others. In the way of fish and mollusks, I prefer lean, meaty types like snapper, sea bass, pike, cod, halibut, and squid (usually interchangeable with octopus), using oily varieties such as salmon, tuna, bluefish, and even swordfish only when I know they will not totally overwhelm other important ingredients in the stew. Much as I love sole, flounder, and pompano, I do shy away from these thin, delicate fish that flake away so easily when exposed to bubbling liquid. All bivalves are wonderful in stews so long as they're not overcooked, but I'm very partial to clams and mussels since their juices add lots of extra flavor to the stew base.

Since most seafood is simmered in stews far too short a time to impart their savors to the base liquid, I can't overemphasize the importance of using fresh fish stock whenever possible. Sometimes, water will suffice (especially when the seafood is bold and wine, herbs, and spices are added), but in the long run, there's really no substitute (including bottled clam juice or those fish bouillon cubes) for a full-flavored, honest, homemade stock.

FISH STOCK

¼ cup (½ stick) butter

2 medium-size onions, sliced

2 carrots, sliced

4 celery ribs (leaves included), chopped

Salt to taste

4 cups dry white wine

6 cups water

¼ cup fresh lemon juice

4 pounds lean fish bones, heads, and tails (from bass, scrod,
    cod, or snapper), well rinsed

10 sprigs fresh parsley

2 bay leaves

5 cloves

10 black peppercorns

In a large, heavy pot, heat the butter over moderate heat, then add the onions, carrots, and celery, and cook, stirring 2 to 3 minutes. Add the remaining ingredients and stir well. Bring to a boil and skim any scum from the surface. Reduce the heat to a low simmer and cook for 30 minutes. Skim off any additional scum and strain the stock through a double thickness of cheesecloth into a large bowl. Covered, the stock keeps in the refrigerator 3 to 4 days, and stored in freezer containers filled to within ½ inch of the top, up to 3 months in the freezer.

Makes 2 quarts

CAPE GIRARDEAU
CATFISH STEW

THE ONLY REAL DIFFERENCE between this catfish stew that friends throw together at their weekend retreat near Cape Girardeau, Missouri, and the one that my granddaddy used to make at our cabin on the Catawba River in North Carolina is the enormous size of the Mississippi blue catfish—which can weigh up to sixty pounds! No doubt a younger, smaller catfish is one of the sweetest fish on earth when correctly baked or broiled, but when it comes to making a stew, I'll opt for a full-flavored seven- or eight-pound critter any day. (Use only freshwater catfish, not saltwater.) You can throw just about anything into catfish stew (potatoes, rutabagas, parsnips, acorn squash, etc.) and cook accordingly, but do remember that this should be a fairly thick stew. Also, if you want a really great stew (and can abide dressing the hideous creatures), buy the whole fish and use the head, tail, and bones to make a rich catfish stock. Double or triple this recipe and you have the perfect stew for a crowd—served with salad, hot biscuits, and ice-cold beer. I do love catfish stew, but I draw the line at cooking it in washtubs the way they sometimes do down in Texas.

5 slices meaty bacon, cut into tiny cubes

2 medium-size onions, finely chopped

3 medium-size, ripe tomatoes, chopped and juices retained

2 large potatoes, peeled and cut into 1-inch cubes

2 cups fish stock (page 198)

¼ teaspoon ground cloves

2 tablespoons Worcestershire sauce

Tabasco sauce to taste

Salt and freshly ground black pepper to taste

2 pounds catfish fillets, cut into 1½-inch pieces

In a large, heavy pot, fry the bacon over moderate heat till crisp, drain on paper towels, and set aside. Add the onions to the pot and cook, stirring, till very soft, about 4 minutes. Add the tomatoes, potatoes, stock, cloves, Worcestershire, Tabasco, and salt and pepper and bring to a boil. Reduce the heat to a low simmer, cover, and cook for 30 minutes. Add the catfish and reserved bacon, stir, cover, and continue to simmer till the fish flakes, 10 to 12 minutes.

Makes 4 to 6 servings

STEW SAVVY

*F*ish in stews should be cooked just till it almost flakes; if it flakes fully, it's probably overdone.

GALVESTON GROUPER AND PECAN MULL

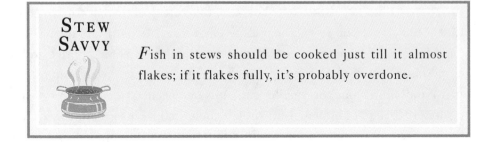

FOR SOME STRANGE REASON, people don't think of Texas as a seafood-producing state when, actually, the Gulf waters around Galveston, Port Arthur, and Corpus Christi, as well as the estuaries all along the coast, are teeming with fat snapper, grouper, shrimp, and buster crab. Nor is it remembered that the pecans harvested every fall in eastern Texas and across the border in Louisiana are every bit as sweet and luscious as those grown in Georgia, which is probably explanation enough for this down-to-earth, unusual mull (or my interpretation of it) that Houston friends and I sampled one weekend in Galveston at some colorful joint near the beach. "There ain't nothing like cracker crumbs to thicken fish stew," insisted the jolly, buxom waitress whom I took to also be the owner and cook.

¼ cup (½ stick) butter

1 large leek (white part only), thoroughly washed and diced

2 celery ribs, diced

1 small red bell pepper, seeded and diced

2 garlic cloves, minced

3 medium-size, ripe tomatoes, diced

2 cups water

2 teaspoons fresh lemon juice

1 teaspoon Worcestershire sauce

Tabasco sauce to taste

Salt and freshly ground black pepper to taste

1½ pounds grouper fillets (or other firm white fish), cut into 1½-inch pieces

1 cup pecan halves

½ cup fine cracker crumbs

In a large, heavy pot, heat the butter over moderate heat, then add the leek, celery, bell pepper, and garlic, and cook, stirring till soft, about 5 minutes. Add the tomatoes, water, lemon juice, Worcestershire, Tabasco, and salt and pepper, bring to a low simmer, cover, and cook for 1 hour. Add the grouper and pecans and simmer till the fish begins to flake, about 8 minutes. Add the cracker crumbs and bring to a boil, stirring constantly till the mull thickens to the desired consistency.

Makes 4 to 6 servings

STEW SAVVY

To neatly chop pecans and walnuts needed for stews, place them in a strong plastic bag on a counter, flatten the bag and fold over the open end to secure, and whack the nuts with a hammer or cleaver.

NORTHWEST
SALMON SOLIANKA

WHILE THE SOLIANKA FOUND in the upper Midwest tends to involve various cuts of beef, the one originated by Russian immigrants in the Pacific Northwest around the turn of the century is still always made with the region's delectable salmon from the Columbia River. (Which version is authentically Russian I've yet to determine, but I love them both.) Since the oily salmon carcass yields a stock that contributes lots to the stew's distinctive savor, you almost have to make it from scratch. I like to serve this solianka with boiled small new potatoes sprinkled with chopped fresh dill.

One 3- to 3½-pound fresh salmon
1 small onion, peeled and studded with 2 cloves
1 celery rib, cracked into thirds
6 black peppercorns
Salt to taste
1½ quarts water
¼ cup (½ stick) butter
1 medium-size onion, chopped
3 large, ripe tomatoes, chopped
2 tablespoons chopped green olives
4 medium-size dill pickles, chopped
2 teaspoons capers, drained
1 bay leaf
Freshly ground black pepper to taste

Either dress the salmon yourself or have the fishmonger do it, reserving the head and bones and cutting the fillets into 1½-inch chunks. Place the fish head and bones in a large pot and add the studded onion, celery, peppercorns, salt, and water. Bring to a boil, skimming the froth, then reduce heat to a low simmer, cover, and cook for 1½ hours. Strain the broth through a double thickness of cheesecloth into a bowl and reserve, discarding the solids. Wash out the pot.

Heat the butter in the pot over moderate heat, then add the chopped onion and tomatoes, and cook, stirring, to reduce the tomato juices slightly, about 10 minutes. Add the salmon chunks, olives, pickles, capers, bay leaf, and salt and pepper, and just enough of the reserved stock to cover the ingredients. Bring to a low simmer, cover, and cook till the salmon flakes, 13 to 15 minutes.

Makes 4 servings

STEW SAVVY

*T*o pit olives easily and quickly for a stew, loosen the meats by rolling them under the blade of a heavy knife, then remove the pits.

TAMPA BAY SNAPPER STEW

WHEN IN FLORIDA, ORDER snapper stew at finer restaurants in Tampa or St. Petersburg, and if you're lucky, it will be made solely with one of the area's greatest delicacies: red snapper cheeks. Tampa Bay locals would probably balk at my adding vegetables to what they consider to be a pristine dish, but since few people have steady access to tender, delectable snapper cheeks, I find this combination works very well. You can substitute red mullet, sea bass, perch, or cod in this stew.

continued

3 tablespoons vegetable oil

2 medium-size onions, chopped

2 celery ribs, chopped

1 garlic clove, minced

2 medium-size, ripe tomatoes, chopped

1 cup fish stock (page 198) or bottled clam juice

1 cup water

One 10-ounce package frozen cut-up okra, thawed

One 10-ounce package frozen corn kernels, thawed

1/4 teaspoon dried summer savory, crumbled

1 bay leaf

Salt and freshly ground black pepper to taste

1 tablespoon Worcestershire sauce

Tabasco sauce to taste

1 1/2 pounds red snapper fillets, cut into 1 1/2-inch cubes

In a large, heavy pot, heat the oil over moderate heat, then add the onions, celery, and garlic, and cook, stirring till soft, about 3 minutes. Add everything but the fish. Bring to a boil, reduce the heat to moderate, and cook for 20 minutes. Add the snapper, return the heat to a simmer, and cook until the fish just flakes, about 8 minutes.

Makes 4 to 6 servings

CURRIED FISH KETTLE

I DON'T KNOW WHEN I acquired my passion for curried seafood stews, but show me a restaurant menu with a lobster, shrimp, crab, or fish stew to which curry has been added and all other options are out of the question. This particular creamy fish kettle seems to demand a fun group of guests, so more often than not I invite eight or ten to indulge, bake up plenty of buttermilk biscuits, and, yes, serve the stew in a big copper kettle. If you prefer a soupier stew, omit the mashed potato.

3 tablespoons olive oil
1 onion, finely chopped
1 celery rib, finely chopped
1 garlic clove, minced
2 tablespoons mild curry powder
3 tablespoons all-purpose flour
1 large, ripe tomato, chopped and juices retained
1 quart fish stock (page 198)
⅛ teaspoon chopped saffron threads
1 small potato, peeled, boiled in water to cover until tender, and mashed
Salt and freshly ground black pepper to taste
2 pounds firm fish fillets (such as striped bass, haddock, or cod), cut into 1-inch pieces
1 cup half-and-half

In a large pot, heat the oil over moderate heat, then add the onion, celery, and garlic, and cook, stirring, for 3 minutes. Add the curry powder and flour and continue to stir 2 minutes longer. Add the tomato and its juices, stock, saffron, mashed potato, and salt and pepper and stir till well blended. Bring to a low simmer, cover, and cook for 20 minutes. Add the fish, return to a simmer, and cook just till the fish flakes, about 8 minutes. Stir in the half-and-half and heat the kettle till piping hot.

Makes 6 servings

OREGON FISH CHILI

IN HIS HOME STATE of Oregon, James Beard had a talented colleague named John Carroll who often assisted him in cooking classes, and this is the unusual seafood chili that the two created after class one afternoon when confronted with lots of leftover fish from the local waters. What I find impressive (and important) is not only the way the onions are almost caramelized by slow, long simmering but also how the hot peppers transform what might have been a bland concoction into a zesty, full-flavored stew with lots of sophistication. One note: If you do use flounder, test the fish for flakiness after about 8 minutes to make sure it doesn't disintegrate.

6 slices meaty bacon

2 large onions, thinly sliced

4 garlic cloves, minced

1 small fresh jalapeño pepper, seeded and chopped

3 tablespoons chili powder

One 28-ounce can whole tomatoes with their juices, chopped

1 teaspoon dried oregano, crumbled

1 teaspoon ground cumin

1 tablespoon white wine vinegar

Salt to taste

*One 4-ounce can green chiles, seeded, deribbed, and cut into
    thin strips*

*2½ pounds, firm fish fillets (such as sea bass,
    red snapper, or flounder), cut into 1-inch cubes*

In a large, heavy pot, fry the bacon over moderate heat till just crisp, drain on paper towels, and set aside. Add the onions to the pot, reduce the heat to very low, and cook, stirring occasionally, till very soft and almost caramelized, about 30 minutes. Add the garlic, jalapeño, and chili powder, stir well, and cook 10 minutes longer.

Stir in the tomatoes and their juices, oregano, cumin, vinegar, and salt, bring the mixture to a simmer, and cook, uncovered, until it thickens slightly, about 20 minutes. Crumble and add the reserved bacon, the green chiles, and fish and simmer till the fish is cooked through and flaky, about 10 minutes.

✌ Makes 6 to 8 servings ✌

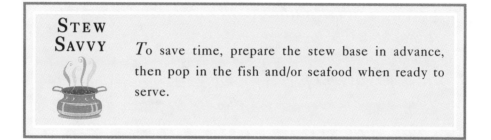

STEW SAVVY

*T*o save time, prepare the stew base in advance, then pop in the fish and/or seafood when ready to serve.

LAKE SUPERIOR WHITEFISH AND SHRIMP STEW

OF ALL THE DELECTABLE species of fish indigenous to various regions in the United States, none do I search out with greater vigilance than the large, sweet, sumptuous (and increasingly rare) whitefish (or cisco) pulled from the icy waters of Lake Superior (and, to an extent, Lake Michigan) and shipped to the better markets and seafood houses of Milwaukee, Detroit, and Chicago. You might spot broiled or grilled whitefish on the menus of such respectable venues in Chicago as Chestnut Street Grill, the venerable Cape Cod Room in the Drake Hotel, and Shaw's, but nowhere will you find this sublime whitefish and shrimp stew—almost a chowder—that was featured at the Windy City's much lamented Wrigley Building Restaurant up until just a couple of years ago. The flavor and texture of fresh lake whitefish are inimitable, but if a substitution must be made, the best options are pike, salmon trout, or even saltwater bass.

continued

6 tablespoons (¾ stick) butter

3 medium-size onions, finely chopped

6 medium-size red potatoes, peeled and cut into 1-inch cubes

3 cups fish stock (page 198)

1 cup milk

½ teaspoon dried thyme, crumbled

¼ teaspoon ground fennel seeds

1 bay leaf

Salt and freshly ground black pepper to taste

1½ pounds whitefish fillets, cut into 1½-inch cubes

1 pound medium-size shrimp, shelled and deveined

In a large, heavy pot, heat the butter over moderate heat, then add the onions and cook, stirring till golden, about 5 minutes. Add the potatoes and stir. Add the stock, milk, thyme, fennel, bay leaf, and salt and pepper, bring to a gentle simmer, and cook till the potatoes are tender, about 20 minutes. Add the whitefish and shrimp, return to a simmer, and cook just till the shrimp are fully pink and the fish begins to flake, about 8 minutes. Discard the bay leaf and taste the stew for salt and pepper.

Makes 6 servings

STEW SAVVY *T*o devein uncooked shrimp used in many stews, simply grasp the vein at the head end and steadily pull it out.

OLD STONE FISH STEW

"Do you want to come over for some fish stew tonight?" was Pierre Franey's last-minute invitation to my mother, aunt, and me to join him and others at his waterfront cottage in the Springs section of East Hampton on Long Island. (He'd been out fishing most of the day.) Over the years, I savored some remarkable food produced by the hands of this famous French master, who is now sadly missed, but I don't think I ever raved over anything like this sumptuous all-American seafood stew consumed with nothing but fresh country sourdough bread and bottle after bottle of chilled California Chardonnay. The name of the stew is explained by the fact that Pierre lived on Old Stone Highway.

1¼ pounds skinless tilefish, monkfish, or cod fillets
1 pound halibut or red snapper fillets
¼ cup olive oil
2 large onions, finely chopped
2 celery ribs, finely chopped
1 medium-size green bell pepper, seeded and finely chopped
2 garlic cloves, minced
1 cup dry white wine
1 bay leaf
1 teaspoon dried thyme, crumbled
4 cups canned crushed tomatoes with their juices
¼ teaspoon red pepper flakes
Salt and freshly ground black pepper to taste
1 pound mussels, scrubbed, beards removed, and soaked in cold
 water (see Monterey Mussel Stew, page 236)
½ pound medium-size shrimp, shelled and deveined
¼ cup chopped fresh parsley leaves

Cut all the fish into 1½-inch cubes and set aside. In a large, heavy pot, heat the oil over moderate heat, then add the onions, celery, bell pepper, and garlic, and cook, stirring, for 5 minutes. Add the wine, bay leaf, and thyme and cook for 1 minute. Stir in the tomatoes and their juices, red pepper flakes, and salt and pepper and simmer for 10 minutes. Increase the heat to moderately high, add the fish and mussels, stir, and cook till the mussels open, about 3 minutes (discard any that do not open). Add the shrimp and parsley and cook till the shrimp are just cooked through, about 3 minutes longer.

Makes 6 servings

CIOPPINO

Anyone who remembers Bernstein's Fish Grotto on Powell Street in San Francisco with its massive bow of a ship as the entrance remembers that the landmark restaurant served the best cioppino in history—a highly aromatic, robust stew with an ever-changing variety of fish, shellfish, and whatever other fresh seafood that was available. Some say that cioppino (which means "chopped a little") originated in Sicily, others that the dish was created by Italian fishermen from Genoa who settled in San Francisco at the turn of the century. Whatever, the spectacular stew has evolved as one of the great specialities of the City by the Bay (especially when made with the region's incomparable fresh Dungeness crab from December to May), each rendition different from the one before. Bernstein's is no more, but this is basically the recipe for that particular incredible stew that demanded to be eaten with loaves of hot sourdough bread.

2 tablespoons butter
1 large Spanish onion, chopped
2 garlic cloves, minced
1/4 cup olive oil
6 medium-size, ripe tomatoes, chopped and juices retained
24 small mushrooms, halved
One 6-ounce can tomato paste

2 teaspoons dried basil, crumbled

1 teaspoon dried oregano, crumbled

2 teaspoons celery seeds

Salt and freshly ground black pepper to taste

½ cup fresh lemon juice

1½ cups dry red wine

½ cup red wine vinegar

¼ cup dry vermouth

1½ pounds firm fish fillets (such as bass, red snapper, or halibut), cut into chunks

1½ pounds medium-size shrimp, shelled and deveined

½ pound fresh claw crabmeat, picked over for shells and cartilage

12 fresh clams, scrubbed and well rinsed

In a large, heavy pot, heat the butter over moderate heat, then add the onion and garlic, and cook, stirring, for 3 minutes. Add the olive oil, tomatoes, and mushrooms and cook, stirring, for 3 minutes. Stir in the tomato paste, then add the basil, oregano, celery seeds, salt and pepper, lemon juice, wine, vinegar, and vermouth. Bring to a boil, reduce the heat to low, cover, and simmer for 1 hour, stirring occasionally and adding a little more red wine if the liquid gets too thick. Add the fish, shrimp, and crabmeat and simmer for 10 minutes. Add the clams and cook till the shells open (discard any that do not), about 10 minutes.

Makes 6 to 8 servings

STEW SAVVY When you find shrimp on sale (even those that have been flash-frozen and thawed) but are not ready to make a stew, cover them completely with water in plastic containers and freeze. When thawed under cold running water, they taste like fresh.

NEAL MYERS'S SEAFOOD STEW

Neal Myers, executive chef at Ben Benson's Steak House in New York City, is as proud of his elaborate seafood stew as his T-bones and doesn't mince words when discussing the subject. "The idea that the rarer and more expensive the seafood, the better the stew is a bad misconception. We often forget how these stews came into being in the first place: commercial fishermen blessed with an overabundance of ordinary seafood that ended up on their own tables as stews." Neal's stew is rather complex, but believe me when I say it's worth the effort. During the winter months, fresh Pacific Coast Dungeness crabs can sometimes be found in the finer seafood markets of large cities, so keep an eye open for these huge crustaceans. Although Neal's recipe makes four servings, I had no trouble stretching it to feed six people—served with lots of hot garlic bread. Do try to use the fresh herbs where indicated.

¼ cup extra-virgin olive oil

1 small onion, chopped

2 garlic cloves, chopped

2 dozen littleneck clams, scrubbed and well rinsed

12 mussels, scrubbed, beards removed, and well rinsed

2 whole Dungeness crabs or 4 blue crabs

1 cup dry white wine

1 celery rib, chopped

1 large green bell pepper, seeded and diced

4 mushrooms, quartered

1 teaspoon dried marjoram, crumbled

1 teaspoon dried rosemary, crumbled

Pinch of Old Bay Seasoning (available in most supermarkets)

1 tablespoon fresh thyme leaves

1 tablespoon chopped fresh basil leaves

6 medium-size, ripe tomatoes, peeled, chopped, and juices retained

1 cup dry red wine

8 large shrimp in their shells

8 sea scallops

½ pound monkfish fillets, cut into 4 pieces

½ pound cod fillets, cut into 4 pieces

½ pound spinach, thoroughly washed, tough stems discarded, and coarsely chopped

¼ cup chopped fresh parsley leaves

To make the fish stock, heat 2 tablespoons of the oil over moderately high heat in a pot large enough to hold the clams, mussels, and crabs, then add the onion and garlic, cook, and stirring, for 2 minutes. Add the clams, mussels, crabs, white wine, and just enough water to cover, bring to a simmer, cover, and cook till the clams and mussels open, about 3 minutes (discard any that do not). Transfer to a large bowl and reserve. Strain the stock through cheesecloth into a bowl and reserve. Wash out the pot.

In the pot, heat the remaining 2 tablespoons of oil over moderate heat, then add the celery, bell pepper, and mushrooms, and cook, stirring, for 5 minutes. Add the marjoram, rosemary, Old Bay Seasoning, thyme, and basil and stir for 1 minute. Add 1 quart of the reserved fish stock, the tomatoes with their juices, and red wine, bring to a simmer, and cook for 5 minutes. Add the shrimp and cook for 2 minutes. Add the scallops and monkfish and cook till the flesh just turns opaque, about 3 minutes. Remove the seafood, shell and devein the shrimp when cool enough to handle, pick the meat from the crabs, and keep warm. Keep the liquid in the pot hot.

In each of 4 large serving bowls, place a cod fillet on the bottom. Divide the clams, mussels, scallops, monkfish, and shrimp among the bowls and sprinkle a quarter of the spinach over each. Top with equal amounts of crabmeat. Pour a quarter of the hot liquid over each (this will cook the cod and spinach) and sprinkle with the parsley.

❦ *Makes 4 servings* ❧

STEW SAVVY

*T*o seed and devein peppers neatly and safely, cut off thick strips along the length of the pepper, leaving a core with seeds to discard.

DOWN EAST
MIXED SHELLFISH STEW

AN ELABORATE SCANDINAVIAN-STYLE BUFFET might be what primarily attracts tourists to the stylish Country Way Restaurant in South Paris, Maine, but the dish that my companions and I raved most about was this simple but flavor-packed American shellfish stew served in an elegant casserole. "We cook a lot of lobster here," explained chef Henry Paradis, "so the stew is a good way to utilize any that we don't put on the buffet." The trick, of course, is not to overcook the seafood, so watch carefully once it's added to the pot.

3 tablespoons olive oil

2 medium-size onions, chopped

2 celery ribs, chopped

1 medium-size green bell pepper, seeded and chopped

½ pound mushrooms, sliced

One 28-ounce can crushed tomatoes

Salt and freshly ground black pepper to taste

¼ teaspoon dried oregano, crumbled

¼ cup dry sherry

1 cup uncooked rice

1 pound small shrimp, shelled and deveined

1 pound small fresh scallops (preferably bay)

½ pound fresh-cooked lobster meat, cut into small chunks

In a large, heavy casserole, heat the oil over moderate heat, then add the onions, celery, bell pepper, and mushrooms, and cook, stirring, for about 5 minutes. Add the tomatoes, salt and pepper, oregano, sherry, and rice, stir, and bring to a boil. Reduce the heat to low and cook for 15 minutes. Add the seafood, stir, and cook till the seafood and rice are just tender, about 10 minutes. Serve the stew directly from the casserole.

Makes 6 servings

COMMANDER'S
SEAFOOD GUMBO

ACCUSTOMED MY WHOLE LIFE to seafood gumbos made with a traditional roux, I balked when Ella Brennan, part-owner of the redoubtable Commander's Palace in New Orleans, told me that the restaurant had perfected a much lighter, rouxless, fatless gumbo that I simply had to sample. Yes, the gumbo was distinctive and delicious, and, no, I did not necessarily miss the rich quality imparted by a long-simmering roux. On the other hand, after executing the renegade recipe a couple of times, the balance of flavors just didn't seem exactly right to my taste—something was missing. As a result, I decided simply to cook the onions, bell pepper, and garlic in forbidden butter before adding the other ingredients, and this did the trick. Try making the gumbo with and without the butter, then you decide—but don't tell Miss Ella that I suggested the option.

¼ cup (½ stick) butter

3 medium-size onions, diced

1 medium-size green bell pepper, seeded and diced

1 garlic clove, minced

3 medium-size, ripe tomatoes, diced

½ cup canned tomato puree

1 teaspoon dried thyme, crumbled

2 bay leaves

Salt and freshly ground black pepper to taste

¾ pound fresh or frozen (and thawed) okra, stems removed and chopped

1 quart fish stock (page 198)

2 pounds medium-size shrimp, shelled and deveined

12 fresh oysters, shucked and drained

½ *pound fresh lump crabmeat, picked over for shells and*
  cartilage
1 *tablespoon filé powder (found in specialty food shops and*
  some supermarkets)

In a large, heavy pot, heat the butter over moderate heat, then add the onions, bell pepper, and garlic and cook, stirring, for 5 minutes. Add the tomatoes, tomato puree, thyme, bay leaves, and salt and pepper, stir well, and let simmer about 10 minutes. Add the okra and cook 5 minutes longer. Add the stock, bring to a rolling boil, then reduce the heat to moderate. Add the shrimp, oysters, and crabmeat, stir, and simmer for 15 minutes. In a bowl, mix the filé powder with 1 cup of the gumbo, remove the pot from the heat, and stir in the filé powder until thickened. Taste the gumbo carefully for salt and pepper and serve.

Makes 4 to 6 servings

CAROLINA GUMBO

EVER SINCE THE DAYS of the great Carolina rice plantations, gumbo has been as much a staple in the coastal Low Country as in Louisiana. The big difference between this gumbo and the Creole version is that it's not conceived on a roux base and therefore has a totally different flavor. Also, the shrimp and oysters are purposefully overcooked so that they almost disintegrate, imparting all their savor and enriching the gumbo's texture.

4 slices bacon

4 chicken legs or thighs, boned and patted dry with paper towels

2 onions, diced

½ green bell pepper, seeded and diced

2 garlic cloves, minced

⅛ teaspoon dried thyme, crumbled

Salt and freshly ground black pepper to taste

Tabasco sauce to taste

One 10-ounce package frozen okra, thawed

4 ripe tomatoes, chopped

2 pounds medium-size shrimp, shelled and deveined

1 pint shucked oysters, with their liquor

2 quarts fish stock (page 198)

2 bay leaves

1 lemon, halved and seeded

Buttered boiled rice

In a large, heavy pot, fry the bacon over moderate heat until crisp, drain on paper towels, and when cool enough to handle, crumble. Add the chicken to the pot, cook on all sides till golden, then drain on paper towels. When cool enough to handle, shred the meat. Add the onions, bell pepper, garlic, thyme, salt, pepper, and Tabasco to the pot, reduce the heat slightly, and cook, stirring for 3 minutes. Add the okra, stir, and cook another 3 to 4 minutes. Add the bacon, chicken, tomatoes, shrimp, and oysters with the liquor and stir. Add the stock, bay leaves, and lemon halves, plus, if necessary, enough water to just cover. Bring to a low simmer, cover, and cook for 2 hours, stirring occasionally. Remove the lemon halves and serve the gumbo over rice.

Makes 6 servings

MAINE RED SHRIMP AND SCALLOP STEW

W HEN VISITING MAINE, MOST people think of one thing and one thing only: lobster. Yes, Maine lobsters are equaled only by the large purple and black-shelled critters trapped in the deep, ice-cold waters around Nova Scotia, but what I look for mostly when wandering the docks of Port Clyde or Cape Elizabeth are the tiny, incredibly sweet red shrimp (hardly two inches long) that remind me of those fished in Europe's North Sea, as well as the small local scallops, both of which are often incorporated (edible shrimp shells and all) in all sorts of wonderful stews and chowders. Do buy the smallest shrimp you can find, try to use bay scallops, and by no means overcook either.

3 tablespoons butter
1 medium-size onion, chopped
1 medium-size celery rib (leaves included), chopped
2 cups milk
1 cup half-and-half
¼ teaspoon dillweed, crumbled
¼ teaspoon ground fennel seeds
Salt and freshly ground black pepper to taste
Tabasco sauce to taste
1 pound small shrimp, shelled and deveined
½ pound small fresh scallops

continued

In a large, heavy saucepan, heat the butter over moderate heat, then add the onion and celery and cook, stirring, till very soft, about 4 minutes. Add the milk, half-and-half, dillweed, and fennel, bring to a boil, reduce the heat to a low simmer, and cook for 5 minutes. Season with the salt, pepper, and Tabasco and stir. Add the shrimp and scallops, stir, return to a simmer, and cook till the shrimp and scallops are just cooked through, about 5 minutes.

Makes 4 servings

SAVANNAH SHRIMP PILAU

WHO KNOWS EXACTLY WHEN, how, and why pilau (or pilaw, or piloo, or pilaff) emigrated from Turkey or Persia or India to the rice-producing Carolina Low Country, but for two centuries, what evolved into a delectable fluffy rice and meat, fish, or poultry stew has been a veritable staple along the Carolina, Georgia, and even northern Florida coasts. Today, pilau is almost always made with seafood, chicken, or a combination of both; some are spicy, some not; some are curried, others spiked with hot red bird's-eye peppers. I've eaten pilaus from Wilmington, North Carolina, down to Jacksonville, Florida, but none remains etched in memory like the simple shrimp pilau at Mrs. Wilkes' Boarding House in Savannah, Georgia—still going strong after decades. (Notice that shrimp pilau is not unlike shrimp creole, the major difference being that in the latter the rice is not cooked in the stew itself.)

6 slices bacon, cut into small dice
3 medium-size onions, chopped
2 cups uncooked rice
3 cups chicken broth (page 120)
5 medium-size, ripe tomatoes, chopped

2 teaspoons Worcestershire sauce

1 teaspoon ground nutmeg

1 bay leaf

Salt and freshly ground black pepper to taste

½ teaspoon cayenne pepper

1½ pounds large shrimp, shelled and deveined

In a large, heavy pot, fry the bacon over moderate heat till crisp, drain on paper towels, and set aside. Pour off all but about 3 tablespoons of the fat from the pot, add the onions, and cook, stirring, until just soft, about 3 minutes. Add the rice and stir till the grains glisten with fat. Add the broth, tomatoes, Worcestershire, nutmeg, bay leaf, salt and pepper, and cayenne and stir. Bring to a low simmer, cover, and cook for 30 minutes. Add the shrimp and reserved bacon and toss well. Return to a simmer, cover, and cook till most of the liquid has been absorbed and the shrimp are pink and curled, about 8 minutes. Fluff the pilau with a fork and serve.

Makes 6 servings

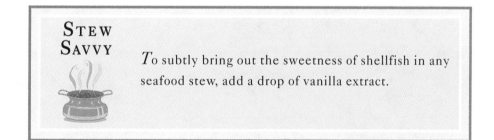

STEW SAVVY

*T*o subtly bring out the sweetness of shellfish in any seafood stew, add a drop of vanilla extract.

CLASSIC
SHRIMP CREOLE

I WISH I COULD say that I got this incomparable recipe from some exotic Creole cook in some colorful cafe on Dumaine or Burgundy Street in New Orleans. The truth is that this was my Georgia grandmother's "receipt," and no doubt she inherited it from her mother. Maw Maw used to always overcook the shrimp and serve much too much rice, but that didn't matter to a hungry youngster: the stew was always (and still is) a special treat. The only change I've made in the recipe (besides the cooking of the shrimp) is from fresh tomatoes to canned ones. Maw Maw would have used three or four chopped home-grown tomatoes (plus the juices), but given the seasonal scarcity of really good tomatoes, I find myself more often using the canned ones in stews.

2 slices bacon, cut into tiny bits
2 medium-size onions, chopped
2 medium-size celery ribs, chopped
1 large green bell pepper, seeded and chopped
1 garlic clove, minced
One 28-ounce can whole tomatoes with their juices, chopped
¼ teaspoon dried basil, crumbled
1 bay leaf
Salt and freshly ground black pepper to taste
2 teaspoons Worcestershire sauce
Tabasco sauce to taste
1 pound medium-size shrimp, shelled and deveined
Boiled rice

In a large, heavy pot, fry the bacon over moderate heat till crisp, drain on paper towels, and set aside. Add the onions, celery, bell pepper, and garlic to the pot and cook, stirring, for 4 minutes. Add the tomatoes and their juices, the basil, bay leaf, salt and pepper, and Worcestershire, and Tabasco and stir well. Bring to a low simmer, cover, and cook till the mixture thickens, 25 to 30 minutes. Add the shrimp and reserved bacon and stir. Return the stew to a simmer and cook, uncovered, just till the shrimp turn pink and curl, about 8 minutes.

To serve, place the desired amount of rice on serving plates, make wide wells in the rice, and spoon the stew into the wells.

❧ Makes 4 servings ☙

STEW SAVVY

Simmered slowly in water with onions, celery, and various herbs and spices, shrimp shells make a delectable broth that can be used to make seafood gumbos, cioppino, and other fish stews.

SULLIVAN'S ISLAND SHRIMP BOG

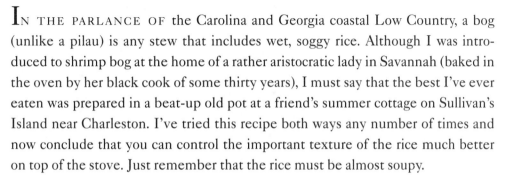

IN THE PARLANCE OF the Carolina and Georgia coastal Low Country, a bog (unlike a pilau) is any stew that includes wet, soggy rice. Although I was introduced to shrimp bog at the home of a rather aristocratic lady in Savannah (baked in the oven by her black cook of some thirty years), I must say that the best I've ever eaten was prepared in a beat-up old pot at a friend's summer cottage on Sullivan's Island near Charleston. I've tried this recipe both ways any number of times and now conclude that you can control the important texture of the rice much better on top of the stove. Just remember that the rice must be almost soupy.

continued

1½ cups uncooked rice

½ pound sliced bacon, finely diced

2 medium-size onions, finely chopped

2¼ cups chicken stock (page 120)

2 medium-size, ripe tomatoes, peeled, finely chopped, and juices
retained

2 teaspoons fresh lemon juice

1½ teaspoons Worcestershire sauce

1 teaspoon salt

¾ teaspoon ground nutmeg

¼ teaspoon freshly ground black pepper

¼ teaspoon cayenne pepper

2 pounds medium-size shrimp, shelled and deveined

¼ cup minced fresh parsley leaves

In a fine sieve, rinse the rice well under cold running water and drain. In a large, heavy pot, fry the bacon over moderate heat, drain on paper towels, and set aside. Pour off all but 3 tablespoons of the grease, add the onions to the pot, and cook for 3 minutes over moderate heat, stirring. Add the rice and stir well. Add the stock, tomatoes with their juices, lemon juice, Worcestershire, salt, nutmeg, and black and cayenne peppers, bring to a low simmer, cover, and cook for 20 minutes. Stir in the crumbled bacon and the shrimp and continue cooking, uncovered, for 10 minutes, adding a little more stock if the rice seems to be drying out. Stir the bog with a fork, taste for seasoning, and sprinkle the parsley on top.

Makes 6 servings

CAJUN
CRAWFISH ÉTOUFFÉE

Over the years, I guess I've cooked and eaten as many Cajun seafood étouffées as Creole gumbos, but none has topped this classic crawfish étouffée served at the Bon Ton Cafe in New Orleans. An étouffée (any combination of ingredients "smothered" in a tightly covered pot) can be made with or without a roux base, but it's almost pointless to bother preparing one unless you use a good, fresh stock. Nothing equals fresh crawfish in this dish, but since they are highly perishable and therefore rarely available outside their native Gulf region, you'll probably have to settle for frozen peeled tails marketed in 1-pound bags. (The delectable fat in crawfish heads does not freeze at all well, so wonderful as the fresh substance is in an étouffée, I usually discard it when frozen if it's lost its rich, yellowish color.) If you can't find any crawfish at all, small shrimp make an acceptable substitute in this dish.

¹⁄₄ cup vegetable oil
¹⁄₄ cup all-purpose flour
1 medium-size onion, finely chopped
1 large celery rib, finely chopped
1 small green bell pepper, seeded and finely chopped
1 garlic clove, minced
1 teaspoon dried basil, crumbled
¹⁄₂ teaspoon dried thyme, crumbled
Cayenne pepper to taste
1³⁄₄ cups fish stock (page 198)
7 tablespoons butter
6 scallions, finely chopped
1¹⁄₂ pounds fresh or frozen (and thawed), crawfish tails, shelled
Salt and freshly ground black pepper to taste
Boiled rice

continued

In a large, heavy pot, heat the oil over moderately high heat, then add the flour and whisk constantly (watching carefully) till the roux is reddish brown, about 20 minutes. Add the onion, celery, bell pepper, garlic, basil, thyme, and cayenne and continue whisking till the vegetables are softened, about 5 minutes. Add the stock, whisk till well blended, and remove the pot from the heat.

In a large saucepan, heat the butter over moderate heat, add the scallions and crawfish, and stir for 1 minute. Scrape the contents of the pan into the large pot, add salt and pepper, and stir well. Bring to a simmer and cook, stirring often, till the crawfish are fully pink and curled, about 8 minutes.

To serve, place a small mound of rice in the center of each serving plate and spoon equal amounts of étouffée around the sides.

Makes 4 to 6 servings

CRAWFISH STEW

THIS SOUPY, SPICY STEW, one of the glories of Cajun cooking, is always served over mounds of boiled rice and requires no accompaniments other than a tart salad, biscuits or cornbread, and ice-cold beer. For the right flavor, the scallions are imperative, and while the crawfish give the stew an inimitable sweetness, if you can't find them even frozen, substitute small shrimp.

¾ cup vegetable oil
¾ cup all-purpose flour
2 large onions, chopped
1 celery rib (leaves included), chopped
1 medium-size green bell pepper, seeded and chopped
2 garlic cloves, minced
2½ pounds fresh crawfish tails or two 1-pound bags frozen
*   crawfish tails, shelled*
1 quart fish stock (page 198) or water
3 tablespoons prepared tomato sauce
9 scallions, chopped
½ cup chopped fresh parsley leaves
Salt and freshly ground black pepper to taste
Tabasco sauce to taste
Boiled rice

In a large, heavy pot, heat the oil, then add the flour and whisk steadily (watching carefully) over moderately high heat till a dark brown roux forms, about 15 minutes. Add the onions, celery, bell pepper, and garlic and cook, stirring, till the vegetables soften, about 3 minutes. Add the crawfish and stir just till they turn pink. Gradually add the stock, stirring steadily. Add the tomato sauce and stir. Bring the stew to a low simmer, cover, and cook slowly for 30 minutes. Stir in the scallions, parsley, salt and pepper, and Tabasco and simmer 2 minutes longer. Serve over rice.

Makes 6 servings

JASPER WHITE'S
CHUNKY LOBSTER STEW

Jasper White is probably Boston's finest chef, and take my word that his chunky lobster stew is the most distinctive and sumptuous you'll ever taste. Yes, it takes lots of pots, and forget about making the stew if you're not willing to deal with live lobsters and to prepare the stock redolent of fresh chervil. This is one recipe that should be followed to the letter if it's to turn out right.

Five 1-pound live lobsters
1 medium-size onion, chopped
4 bay leaves
2 large, ripe tomatoes
20 sprigs fresh chervil
2 cups heavy cream
½ cup (1 stick) butter
2 large leeks (white parts only), thoroughly washed and cut into
   ½-inch dice
2 medium-size carrots, scraped and very thinly sliced
Salt and freshly ground black pepper to taste
Cayenne pepper to taste

Fill a large canning pot three-quarters full of salted water and bring to a rolling boil. Plunge the lobsters in batches head-first into the water and blanch for 4 minutes. Remove them from the pot, punch a little hole in the top of each head with an ice pick or sharp knife, and allow to drain. When cool enough to handle, break off the claws and tails, shuck the meat, and remove and discard the intestinal veins from the tails. Chop the meat into large bite-size pieces and reserve in the refrigerator.

Place all the lobster shells in a large pot, add enough water to barely cover, and add the onion and bay leaves. Bring to a boil, skim off the scum, and reduce the heat to a simmer. Peel and seed the tomatoes and add the seeds and juices to the stock. Cut the tomatoes into medium-size dice and set aside.

Pick the chervil leaves off the stems, chop them coarsely, and set aside. Add the stems to the stock. Simmer the stock for 1 hour, stir in the cream, and simmer 20 minutes longer.

In another large pot, heat the butter over moderately high heat, then add the leeks and carrots and cook for 5 minutes, stirring. Add the lobster meat and diced tomatoes and simmer for 2 minutes. Strain the hot stock into the pot (about 6 cups), season with salt, pepper, and cayenne, stir well, and sprinkle the chopped chervil leaves over the top.

Makes 6 servings

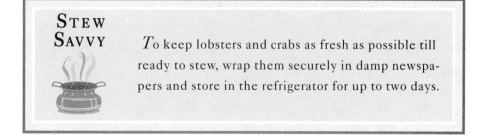

STEW SAVVY *T*o keep lobsters and crabs as fresh as possible till ready to stew, wrap them securely in damp newspapers and store in the refrigerator for up to two days.

MONTAUK LOBSTER
AND LEEK STEW

SOME OF THE LOBSTERS unloaded at the docks of Montauk on the eastern end of Long Island are almost as gigantic and succulent as those trapped in Maine and Nova Scotia, so whenever I want to serve whole boiled or steamed lobsters or prepare this heroic stew, I think nothing of driving thirty minutes from my home in East Hampton out to Gosman's Seafood Market to choose a few prime victims.

Do remember to let this stew rest in the refrigerator a few hours before reheating; it not only allows the flavors to meld but also tenderizes the lobster meat. This is a stew worthy of the most elegant occasion—at the table or (as I usually serve it) on a buffet.

4 medium-size leeks (white parts only)
Two 2-pound lobsters (females with roe, if possible)
½ cup (1 stick) butter
1 medium-size onion, minced
Salt and freshly ground black pepper to taste
Dash of Worcestershire sauce
2 tablespoons dry sherry
1 quart milk

Split the leeks lengthwise, wash thoroughly under running water, and place in a large skillet with ½ inch of water. Bring to a low boil, cover, and steam the leeks till just tender, about 18 minutes (the time will depend on the width of the leeks). Drain, chop coarsely, and set aside.

To steam the lobsters, place a rack in a very large pot or canning kettle, add 2 to 3 inches of salted water (or sea water if possible), and bring to a rolling boil. Place the lobsters head first on the rack, cover, and when the water returns to a boil, steam for 18 minutes. Reserve the cooking liquid. Transfer the lobsters to a work surface and, when cool enough to handle, split in half lengthwise with a large, heavy knife and drain. Remove and discard both the dark intestinal vein running down the tail and the stomach sac in the head part. Remove the meat, tomalley (greenish liver), coral (dark roe), and all the white substance (fat) from inside the shells and set aside. Cut the meat into 1-inch chunks.

In a large pot, heat 2 tablespoons of the butter over moderate heat, then add the onion and cook, stirring, for 3 minutes. Add 2 more tablespoons of the butter along with the tomalley, coral, and white substance, and stir 2 minutes longer. Increase the heat to moderately high, add the remaining 4 tablespoons butter, the lobster chunks, leeks, salt and pepper, Worcestershire, and sherry and cook, stirring, for 5 minutes. Let the mixture cool, then add the milk and 1 cup of the reserved cooking liquid and let the stew sit, covered, in the refrigerator for about 4 hours. When ready to serve, reheat thoroughly and taste for seasoning.

NOTE: *Officially U.S. lobstermen are required by law to throw roe-rich female lobsters back into the sea. Since, however, 50 percent of our lobsters are now imported from Canada, the tender females are often available.*

Makes 4 servings

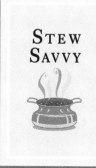

STEW SAVVY

*T*o determine whether a lobster is male or female (the latter containing delectable coral—or greenish black roe—used to enhance some stews), flip the critter on its back and look for the two small spiny "feet" between the head and the body. If they are quite soft and tender to the touch, the lobster is female.

FLORIDA
CONCH STEW

CONCH (PRONOUNCED conk), a very muscular, rather hideous mollusk with a large spiral shell, is indigenous to our tropical Southern waters and one of the glories of Floridian cooking. (Anybody who's ever wandered the beaches of Key West in early morning has probably been startled by one of these weird creatures hopping in leaps and bounds along the sand.) Conch is used to make all sorts of delectable salads, fritters, chowders, and stews, but since the flavorful meat is so tough, it must first be pounded and cut up to be edible. Quite sweet and redolent of the sea, conch tastes somewhat like fresh clams, so if you're unable to find it in the market (some specialty shops carry it frozen), a credible substitute would be about 2 pounds of steamed and shelled quahog, cherrystone, or West Coast razor clams—simmered no more than ten minutes before adding the milk. And don't balk at the evaporated milk; it is a traditional ingredient in conch stew and chowder.

4 slices bacon, cut into bits

1 large onion, chopped

1 celery rib, chopped

1 garlic clove, minced

2 medium-size ripe tomatoes, chopped and juices retained

2 medium-size potatoes, peeled and cut into ¹⁄₂-inch cubes

2 pounds frozen conch meat, thawed, pounded until quite thin,
*   and cut into 1-inch pieces*

2 bay leaves

Salt and freshly ground black pepper to taste

2¹⁄₂ cups water

One 5-ounce can evaporated milk

In a large, heavy pot, fry the bacon over moderate heat till crisp, then add the onion, celery, and garlic, and cook, stirring, till soft, about 3 minutes. Add the tomatoes with their juices, potatoes, conch, bay leaves, salt and pepper, and water and bring to a boil. Reduce the heat to low, cover, and simmer till the conch is tender, about 1 hour. Pour in the evaporated milk and stir till the stew is heated through, never allowing it to boil.

Makes 4 to 6 servings

MOTHER'S OLD-FASHIONED OYSTER STEW

THIS RECIPE HAS BEEN in my family three-quarters of a century, and while my mother serves the stew ritually as the first course of an elaborate Christmas dinner, I also find it perfect for a casual lunch—with a green or fruit salad and hot buttered biscuits or hush puppies. Mother balks at adding sherry to the stew, but I think it gives it real zip. Do remember that to avoid toughness all you want to do is heat the oysters in the liquid.

¼ cup (½ stick) butter
2 tablespoons all-purpose flour
3 cups milk
1 cup half-and-half
1 tablespoon grated onion
Salt and freshly ground black pepper to taste
1 quart shucked oysters, plus their liquor
Imported paprika for garnish
Oyster crackers

continued

In a large saucepan, heat the butter over moderately low heat, then add the flour and stir till blended and smooth. Gradually add the milk, stirring constantly, then add the half-and-half, onion, and salt and pepper, stirring. Place the oysters plus their liquor in another large saucepan and bring to a boil. Reduce the heat to moderate, add the milk mixture, and heat well without boiling till the oysters curl, about 3 minutes. Serve the stew in heated soup bowls, sprinkle each with a little paprika, and pass a bowl of oyster crackers to be sprinkled over the stew.

Makes 4 servings

STEW SAVVY After buying fresh oysters and/or clams that you plan to shell for seafood stews, chill them a while to facilitate shucking.

SEATTLE OYSTER AND SPINACH STEW

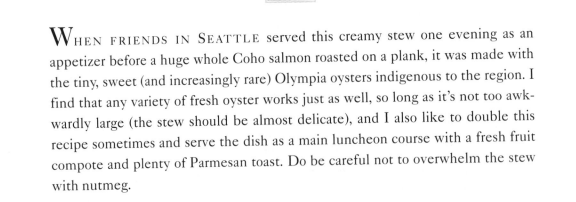

WHEN FRIENDS IN SEATTLE served this creamy stew one evening as an appetizer before a huge whole Coho salmon roasted on a plank, it was made with the tiny, sweet (and increasingly rare) Olympia oysters indigenous to the region. I find that any variety of fresh oyster works just as well, so long as it's not too awkwardly large (the stew should be almost delicate), and I also like to double this recipe sometimes and serve the dish as a main luncheon course with a fresh fruit compote and plenty of Parmesan toast. Do be careful not to overwhelm the stew with nutmeg.

1 quart shucked oysters, plus their liquor

1 tablespoon butter

1 tablespoon finely grated onion

1 cup milk

1/2 cup minced celery

1 cup fresh or frozen (and thawed) chopped spinach, tough stems removed

1 cup heavy cream

1 tablespoon dry sherry

Salt and cayenne pepper to taste

Ground nutmeg to taste

1/4 cup (1/2 stick) butter, softened

Strain the liquor from the oysters into a small saucepan, bring it to a boil, skim off any froth, and set aside. In a large saucepan, heat the 1 tablespoon butter over moderate heat, add the onion, and cook, stirring, for 2 minutes. Add the oysters, simmer till they curl, about 3 minutes, and remove from the heat. Pour the milk into another large saucepan, add the celery and spinach, and cook over moderate heat for 5 minutes. Stir in the cream, bring almost to a boil, and remove the pan from the heat. Add the reserved oyster liquor, sherry, salt and cayenne, and nutmeg, and stir well. Ladle the stew into wide soup bowls and top each serving with a little softened butter.

Makes 4 appetizer servings

MONTEREY
MUSSEL STEW

Unbeknownst to most Easterners familiar only with the blue-black mussels ubiquitous to our Atlantic coastline, one of the most delectable varieties of this bivalve mollusk is the smaller, sweeter, Pacific mussel indigenous to waters from Alaska down to northern California. Because of the threatening red tide, however, West Coast mussels are generally available only from November through April, which made this particularly sapid stew I sampled at a Monterey March of Dimes Gourmet Gala in late spring even more special.

4 pounds mussels

1 medium-size onion, chopped

2 garlic cloves, minced

1 cup dry white wine

½ cup (1 stick) butter

1 tablespoon all-purpose flour mixed with 1 tablespoon milk

1¼ cups heavy cream

2 medium-size leeks (white parts only), thoroughly washed and finely chopped

Salt and freshly ground black pepper to taste

Imported medium-hot paprika to taste

Boiled rice

To prepare the mussels, place in a sink and wash under running water to remove sand. Scrub with a stiff brush, then remove and discard the fibrous beards. Place the mussels in a container of cold water to soak for 30 minutes, swirling them around and changing the water several times till it is clear. Discard any mussels that will not close. Drain.

Put the onion, garlic, and wine in a large pot. Bring to a boil, add the mussels, reduce the heat slightly, cover, and steam until the mussels open, 5 to 6 minutes (discard any that do not). Remove the pot from the heat and transfer the mussels to a large bowl. Strain the broth through cheesecloth into a bowl and set aside. Remove the mussels from their shells and set aside.

In another pot, heat the butter over moderate heat, then add the flour-and-milk mixture and blend till smooth. Slowly add the cream and leeks, stirring constantly, and let simmer for 5 minutes. Add the mussels and reserved broth, season with the salt, pepper, and paprika, stir, and simmer for 1 minute to heat through. Serve the stew over rice.

Makes 6 servings

STEW SAVVY *N*othing is better for removing tiny bones from fish or debearding mussels intended for a stew than a pair of needlenose pliers.

PACIFIC SQUID
AND ARTICHOKE STEW

ALTHOUGH I SUPPOSE IT was Jeremiah Tower (owner/chef at Stars restaurant in San Francisco) who first taught me how to stew the small, delectable Pacific squid found all along the California coast, it was at some seafood shack in Santa Barbara that I was introduced to the remarkable combination of squid and artichokes stewed in red wine. Both squid and octopus are ideal for stewing since each loses its toughness and takes on a melting, rich meatiness when slowly simmered in wine, but I personally prefer the subtle flavor of squid. Cleaned squid is often available in finer fish markets, but I find it ridiculous to pay double the price for a job you can so easily do yourself. Like shrimp, most of the squid sold as fresh has actually been frozen and thawed. No problem, basically, so long as there's no off-smell, the flesh is firm and shiny, and the outer membrane is gray rather than purplish—a sign that the squid has been sitting around too long.

> 3 pounds whole small squid
> ¼ cup olive oil
> 3 medium-size onions, chopped
> 2 garlic cloves, minced
> ½ teaspoon dried oregano, crumbled
> ½ teaspoon dried marjoram, crumbled
> Salt and freshly ground black pepper to taste
> 2 large, ripe tomatoes, chopped and juices retained
> 2 cups dry red wine
> One 9-ounce package frozen artichoke hearts, thawed and
>   (if necessary) leaves and chokes removed

To clean the squid, separate the heads and bodies, cut off the tentacles just below the eyes, and reserve the tentacles and body sacs. Remove and discard the transparent quill inside the body sacs, rinse the sacs well, and peel off and discard the grayish membrane covering them. Gently pull off the flaps from the body sacs and discard. Cut the body sacs into 1-inch pieces and chop the tentacles coarsely.

Place the squid pieces in a large pan and add enough water to cover. Bring to a boil, cook just till opaque, about 1 minute, and drain well.

In a large, heavy pot, heat the oil over moderate heat, add the onions and garlic, and cook, stirring till golden, about 3 minutes. Add the oregano, marjoram, salt and pepper, tomatoes with their juices, wine, and squid, bring to a low simmer, and cook for 45 minutes. Add the artichoke hearts, return to a simmer, cover, and cook until the squid and artichoke hearts are tender, about 30 minutes.

Makes 6 servings

MARYLAND
TERRAPIN STEW

Turtle meat has been part of America's culinary heritage since the seventeenth century, but not till the nineteenth century did diamondback terrapin stew become so popular with connoisseurs in elite East Coast restaurants and social clubs (especially in Baltimore and Philadelphia) that the reptile almost became extinct. I easily recall eating terrapin stew with my parents at Old Bookbinder's in Philadelphia (where it was called "snapper soup"), at the "21" Club in New York City, and at upscale seafood houses along Maryland's Chesapeake Bay, but in the last couple of decades—even though the species has been restored—it's a rare day you encounter this great delicacy, even in Maryland where diamondbacks thrive. Today, fresh terrapin meat is virtually nonexistent on the market, but you can find both canned and frozen varieties in specialty food shops (at a price) that at least approximate the succulent real McCoy used in the stew that grandees like Diamond Jim Brady and Lucius Beebe once consumed with sybaritic abandon.

1½ quarts canned terrapin meat
Chicken stock as needed (page 120)
¾ cup (1½ sticks) butter
1 large onion, finely chopped
½ cup dry sherry
Salt and freshly ground black pepper to taste
Cayenne pepper to taste
2 hard-boiled eggs, peeled and chopped

Drain the terrapin meat, reserving the liquid in a bowl, and mince the meat. Measure the liquid and add enough chicken stock to yield 1¾ cups. In a saucepan, heat the stock mixture.

In a large pot, heat ¼ cup (½ stick) of the butter over moderate heat, add the onion, and cook, stirring, till very soft, about 3 minutes. Add the hot stock, stir in the remaining butter and the sherry, season with salt, pepper, and cayenne, and simmer over low heat for about 5 minutes. Add the terrapin meat and chopped eggs, return to a simmer, and cook to heat through and mingle the flavors, 10 to 15 minutes. Transfer the stew to a large, heated serving tureen and serve.

Makes 4 servings

Vegetable, Bean, and Fruit Stews

Southern Succotash

New Mexican Colache

Leeks, Parsnips, and Potatoes Stewed in Beer

Cajun Maque Choux

Okra and Tomato Stew

Michigan Cabbage Stewed in White Wine

Stewed Red Cabbage and Apples

Brownsville Nopalito

Southern Collard Greens Stewed with Salt Pork

Mrs. Randolph's Stewed Spiced Mushrooms

Jack Czarnecki's Stewed Wild Mushrooms

California Vegetable and Chickpea Chili

Pumpkin, Kidney Bean, and Sausage Pot

Stewed White Beans and Tomatoes

Delta Red Beans and Rice

Colorado Curried Lentil Stew

Stewed Mixed Fruit

Bucks County Stewed Spiced Pears

Stewed Gingered Figs

Cape Cod Stewed Apple and Cranberry Compote

Spicy Stewed Dried Fruit Compote

Vegetables, Beans, and Fruits
for Stewing

E xcept maybe in the South, few people in this country realize that histori-
cally some of our best and easiest-to-prepare stews have revolved around
the rich bounty of vegetables, beans, and fresh fruits with which we're
blessed. Perhaps I'm just naive, but I find it downright incomprehensible (not to
mention sad) that most of our supposedly bright young professional chefs who
boast a keen interest in regional American cookery have never even heard of,
much less prepared, succotash, Southwestern colache, Cajun maque choux, and a
score of other delicious vegetable, bean, mushroom, and fruit stews intended to
highlight or complement a good meal. Likewise, I regret that home cooks no
longer take advantage, as our predecessors did, of all the handsome squash, cab-
bages, tomatoes, leafy greens, root vegetables, legumes, and dried fruits filling the
markets by turning them into interesting stews that are not only different and tasty
but also nutritious. As James Beard once wrote: "If you have never tasted a stewed
or braised vegetable, you'll find it is a revelation, completely different from one
that is eaten raw, plainly cooked, boiled, sautéed, or fried."

While executing a simple white bean stew or lentil braise usually
requires little more than the knowledge of how long each legume should be
cooked, stewing vegetables and fruits is a bit more testy (and considerably more
intriguing), often requiring a good sense of flavor combinations, texture, and timing. Once you're accustomed to stewing one vegetable or fruit, for example, you
can then move on to create a ragout or compote of various different types, first
allowing the sturdier items to become tender, next adding those that need less
simmering, and ultimately determining which combinations and textures suit your
taste. Beans and tomatoes; leeks, potatoes, and parsnips; cabbage, apples, and
raisins; squash, onions, and chickpeas; pears, plums, and grapes—the marriages

are endless, and when you begin experimenting with herbs and spices, the possibilities just get more exciting.

Never do I follow the seasons more than when deciding which vegetable or fruit stew to prepare, and never do I so insist upon the freshest of produce than when it's intended to be stewed. (None of that stewing just as an excuse to use up tired, discolored ingredients that are over the hill.) Sure, there are some vegetable stews that taste just as good with frozen limas or corn, canned tomatoes, or dried wild mushrooms, and in my opinion, no dessert is more elegant than dried fruits that have been gently simmered in a spicy liquid and served warm or chilled. But when fresh pumpkin, tomatoes, corn, lima beans, cranberries, and pears are in season, or when I spy bright collards or meaty chanterelle mushrooms or tiny, smooth parsnips in the market, rest assured that all other options cease to exist.

SOUTHERN SUCCOTASH

I HATE TO DISABUSE my fellow Southerners of the conviction that the origins of succotash are in Dixie, but the truth is that this classic corn and lima bean stew was most probably first concocted by Indians in New England—and, more specifically, by the Narragansetts of Rhode Island, who referred to the ingredients in any stew pot as "succotash." No matter, for today succotash is as closely identified with Southern cooking as burgoo, and what Southerner could imagine eating pit-cooked barbecued pork without a big bowl of thick succotash on the side?

2 cups fresh or frozen lima beans
5 slices bacon, cut into dice
2 medium-size onions, finely chopped
2 cups fresh or frozen corn kernels
2 cups peeled and chopped fresh or canned tomatoes with their juices
Salt and freshly ground black pepper to taste
Tabasco sauce to taste

Place the lima beans in a saucepan with enough salted water to cover, bring to a moderate simmer, and cover. Cook till tender, about 15 minutes, and drain. Meanwhile, in a large, heavy pot, fry the bacon over moderate heat till crisp and pour off all but about 3 tablespoons of grease. Add the onions and stir till softened, about 2 minutes. Add the lima beans, corn, and tomatoes and continue cooking another 5 minutes, stirring. Season with salt, pepper, and Tabasco and continue to cook, stirring, till the mixture has thickened but is not dry. Transfer the succotash to an earthenware tureen or deep serving dish and toss lightly before serving.

Makes 6 to 8 servings

NEW MEXICAN COLACHE

In Mexico, colache has always been a rather lowly preparation of corn and other vegetables fried in bacon fat with a little vinegar and sugar, but it appears that after this distant cousin of succotash crossed the border into Arizona and New Mexico, it evolved into a more sophisticated stew. Today, it's unlikely you'll find colache in Sante Fe's many upscale restaurants, but head for a more modest place like The Shed, or venture outside the city, and there's a good chance the stew will be on the menu. Note that genuine colache is a fairly thick stew.

3 tablespoons peanut oil

2 medium-size onions, chopped

1 garlic clove, minced

1½ pounds medium-size yellow squash (about 4), scrubbed, ends trimmed, and cut into ¼-inch-thick rounds

1 pound fresh green beans, cut in half

1 small fresh jalapeño pepper, seeded and finely chopped

3 medium-size, ripe tomatoes, peeled, chopped, and juices retained

Salt and fresh ground black pepper to taste

½ cup chicken stock (page 120)

1 cup fresh or frozen corn kernels

In a large, heavy pot, heat the oil over moderate heat, then add the onions and garlic and cook, stirring till golden, about 4 minutes. Add the squash, green beans, and jalapeño and stir for 2 minutes. Add the tomatoes and their juices, salt and pepper, and stock, bring to a low simmer, and cook for 20 minutes. Add the corn, stir well, and continue to simmer till the squash and beans are very tender, about 15 minutes.

Makes 6 servings

LEEKS, PARSNIPS, AND POTATOES STEWED IN BEER

Parsnips, which were introduced by Europeans to the Virginia colony in the early seventeenth century and cultivated by both settlers and Indians, seem finally to be regaining popularity after decades of curious neglect. And well they should, given their distinctive, almost buttery savor. Although the wild parsnip of the West is particularly prized, the hearty All-American variety available everywhere is very good for stewing alone or, as in this recipe, with any number of other assertive ingredients. Ditto the noble leek, which is so ideal for stewing and much more available than just twenty years ago. For a nice change of pace, try serving this stew with a charred, juicy steak.

¼ pound salt pork, rind discarded, cut into ½-inch dice

2 medium-size leeks (white part and part of green leaves included), thoroughly washed, split down the middle, and cut into 1-inch pieces

1 garlic clove, minced

5 medium-size parsnips (about 1¼ pounds), peeled and cut into 1-inch cubes

3 medium-size potatoes, peeled and cut into 1-inch cubes

2 tablespoons all-purpose flour

¼ teaspoon dried marjoram, crumbled

Salt and freshly ground black pepper to taste

3 cups dark beer

1 cup half-and-half

In a large, heavy pot, cook the salt pork, stirring, over moderate heat till golden brown, about 10 minutes. Add the leeks and garlic and cook, stirring, until the leeks soften completely, 7 minutes longer. Add the parsnips and potatoes, sprinkle the flour over the top, add the marjoram, salt, and pepper, and stir 2 minutes. Add the beer plus, if necessary to just cover the vegetables, a little water, bring to a low simmer, cover, and cook till the vegetables are tender, 20 to 25 minutes. Add the half-and-half, stir, and cook 5 minutes longer.

Makes 6 servings

CAJUN MAQUE CHOUX

So UTTERLY REGIONAL IS this classic Cajun stew that, while virtually every family in the state of Louisiana has its own distinctive version, you'll rarely find maque choux mentioned in the most comprehensive food dictionaries, certainly not in any all-purpose cookbook, and almost never in Southern "receipt" collections. (Even the origins of the name itself—French, Acadian, Spanish?—are totally obscure.) But down in New Orleans and over in Cajun country, this stew rules supreme on the lowliest to the most sophisticated tables, prepared simply with corn and other vegetables as in this basic recipe or enriched with crawfish (as Paul Prudhomme's mother, Hazel, always did), spicy tasso ham (as renowned chef Emeril Lagasse does), or chicken (as I hope my favorite Cajun hangouts in New Orleans still do). Plain vegetable maque choux is a wonderful accompaniment to roasted or grilled meats and poultry, but if you'd like to transform it into an unusual main-course luncheon dish for four (as I've done more than once), simply add about 2 cups of diced cooked chicken, cured ham, or raw shrimp and adjust the amount of water accordingly. The only cardinal rule about this dish is that you must use fresh corn, since the "milk" obtained from scraping the kernels off the ears gives the stew much of its unique character.

continued

10 ears fresh corn

½ cup (1 stick) butter

1 large onion, finely chopped

½ medium-size green bell pepper, seeded and finely chopped

*2 medium-size, ripe tomatoes, peeled, chopped, and juices
    retained*

½ cup water

Salt and freshly ground black pepper to taste

Cayenne pepper to taste

Holding each ear of corn over a large plate, cut the kernels off with a sharp knife, scraping down the ears a second time to collect as much "milk" from the cobs as possible.

In a large, heavy pot, heat the butter over moderate heat, then add the onion and bell pepper, and cook for 5 minutes, stirring. Add the corn plus its "milk," the tomatoes, and water, cover, and cook for 10 minutes. Season with salt, pepper, and cayenne, stir well, and cook, uncovered, till the liquid is slightly reduced, about 12 minutes.

Makes 6 servings

OKRA AND TOMATO STEW

HISTORY RECORDS THAT OKRA (a tropical and semitropical plant with edible pods) was first brought to America by African slaves, who boiled its fruits as a vegetable and used them to make stews and soups. (The word *gumbo* actually derives from the Bantu word for okra.) Stewed okra and tomatoes remains one of the South's most popular dishes, and every home cook has his or her special version. My mother wouldn't dream of adding brown sugar or herbs to her stew, but I think they both enhance the flavor.

3 strips bacon, diced

1 medium-size onion, finely chopped

1 small green bell pepper, seeded and finely chopped

1 garlic clove, minced

1 pound fresh or frozen (and thawed) okra, stems removed and cut into rounds

1 teaspoon all-purpose flour

2 large, ripe tomatoes, chopped and juices retained

1 tablespoon light brown sugar

1 tablespoon finely chopped fresh basil leaves, or 1/2 teaspoon dried, crumbled

Salt and freshly ground black pepper to taste

In a large pot, fry the bacon over moderate heat till half done, then add the onion, bell pepper, and garlic and cook, stirring, till the vegetables soften, about 3 minutes. Add the okra, reduce the heat to low, and cook, stirring, till the okra is limp, 10 minutes. Sprinkle the flour over the mixture and stir 1 minute. Add the tomatoes and their juices, the brown sugar, basil, and salt and pepper and cook till the okra is limp and the stew thickened, about 10 minutes.

Makes 4 to 6 servings

MICHIGAN CABBAGE
STEWED IN WHITE WINE

THE DUTCH MAY HAVE been the first immigrants to grow cabbage (and, by the way, to chop it into cole slaw) when they settled in the northeast of the United States, but it was the Germans of Michigan and Illinois who, aware of the ideal climate, really cultivated the vegetable as a staple. Stewed cabbage is as popular today in upper Midwest homes with German roots as it was a century ago—usually prepared in this classic Old World manner but often enriched by the addition of chopped apples, raisins, or bits of cooked ham. I like to serve it with virtually any pork dish.

6 slices bacon, cut into small dice

*1 medium-size head green cabbage (about 3 pounds), discolored
    leaves removed, cored, and coarsely chopped*

1 cup dry white wine

½ teaspoon ground caraway seeds

¼ teaspoon dried tarragon, crumbled

Salt and freshly ground black pepper to taste

In a large pot, fry the bacon over moderate heat till almost crisp. Add the cabbage, toss till well coated with grease, and cook, uncovered, until softened, about 10 minutes. Add the remaining ingredients, bring to a low simmer, cover, and cook till the cabbage is very tender, about 15 minutes. With a slotted spoon, transfer the cabbage to a heated platter. Bring the liquid in the pot to a boil, cook till slightly reduced, and pour over the cabbage.

Makes 6 servings

STEWED RED CABBAGE
AND APPLES

I'M NOT AT ALL certain who originally inspired this particular German-style stew, but since the name "Carol" is scribbled on the small piece of paper with the recipe, it simply must be the fellow Fulbright student with whom I studied in France many years ago and whose German family I later visited in Sheboygan, Wisconsin. I don't remember her or her mother preparing the dish, but since I've used the recipe for over three decades, I must have loved the stew, wherever I first tasted it. And yes, of course, it's to be served with almost any form of pork.

3 tablespoons butter

2 medium-size onions, chopped

2 Granny Smith apples, cored and cut into small wedges

2 tablespoons light brown sugar

⅛ teaspoon ground cloves

⅛ teaspoon ground cinnamon

1 medium-size head red cabbage (about 3 pounds), discolored
   leaves removed, cored, and shredded

¼ cup dry red wine

¼ cup water

Salt and freshly ground black pepper to taste

In a large, heavy pot, heat the butter over moderate heat, then add the onions and apples and cook, stirring, till the onions are softened, about 2 minutes. Add the brown sugar, cloves, and cinnamon, stir, and continue to cook, stirring, till the apples are soft, about 4 minutes. Add the cabbage and stir to incorporate. Add the wine and water, season with salt and pepper, and bring to a low simmer. Cover and cook till the cabbage is very tender, about 1 hour.

Makes 4 to 6 servings

BROWNSVILLE NOPALITO

"I JUST CAN'T BELIEVE that you've never tasted nopalito!" exclaimed Mary Yturria as I gawked at the weird casserole of stewed cactus, dried shrimp, and eggs on the elaborate buffet at her large home in Brownsville, Texas. No, I had indeed not ever even heard of this Tex-Mex specialty, but once I sampled the intriguing dish, I couldn't ask Mary for the recipe fast enough. Both packaged cactus leaves and dried shrimp (which have an almost sweet flavor) are now widely available in Mexican and Latin American markets, as well as in better food shops, so you really don't have any excuse not trying the stew. I warn you that it's not the prettiest side dish with those cooked eggs mixed in, but I also promise that it's like nothing you've experienced—even if it's not really a certifiable stew.

2 quarts salted water
1 pound young cactus, washed and cut into strips
2 tablespoons vegetable shortening
1 medium-size onion, chopped
1 small green bell pepper, seeded and chopped
2 tablespoons bottled hot pepper sauce
½ cup dried shrimp, soaked for 30 minutes in hot water to cover
 and drained
3 large eggs, beaten
Salt and freshly ground black pepper to taste

In a large kettle, bring the water to a full boil, then add the cactus, cook till tender, about 20 minutes, and drain. In a large, heavy pot, heat the shortening over moderate heat, then add the onion and bell pepper, and cook, stirring, till softened, about 3 minutes. Add the cactus, pepper sauce, and shrimp and stir thoroughly. Add the eggs, season with salt and pepper, and stir slowly till the eggs have set, 5 to 7 minutes. Serve as a side vegetable.

Makes 4 to 6 servings

SOUTHERN COLLARD GREENS STEWED WITH SALT PORK

Stewed collard greens (a variety of kale) have been a staple on the Southern table for over two centuries, served with fried chicken, barbecued meats, baked short ribs of beef, and numerous other regional specialities. I can still see my Georgia grandmother breaking off pieces of cornbread and dropping them into a bowl of the "pot likker" the collards were stewed in, a custom still observed religiously by everyone in my family. The greens are delicious as they are in this recipe, but if you really want to cook "Southern," add a big chunk of cured country ham to the pot. Fresh cornbread is really a must with this stew, though I've been known to dunk biscuits with equal relish.

> *3 pounds fresh young collard or mustard greens*
> *1 pound salt pork, rind discarded, cut into 1-inch dice*
> *1 large onion, chopped*
> *1½ cups water*
> *1 teaspoon sugar*
> *2 teaspoons red pepper flakes*
> *Salt and freshly ground black pepper to taste*

Remove any blemished spots from the greens and strip the leaves from the stems, discarding the stems. Wash the leaves carefully under cold running water. Shake off the water, but don't dry with paper towels.

In a large, heavy skillet, cook the salt pork, stirring, over moderate heat till almost browned, about 10 minutes. Add the onion and cook, stirring, till softened, about 2 minutes. Transfer the salt pork and onion to a plate and add water to the skillet. Bring to a boil, scraping any browned bits off the bottom of the pan, and set the pan aside.

Place the still-damp greens in a large pot over high heat, cover tightly, and cook till they begin to wilt, about 3 minutes. Add the contents of the skillet and stir in the salt pork, onion, sugar, red pepper flakes, and salt and pepper. Reduce the heat to moderate, cover, and cook till the greens are tender, about 45 minutes. Drain off the cooking liquid ("pot likker"), transfer the greens to a large platter, and serve little bowls of the liquid in which to dunk cornbread.

Makes 6 servings

MRS. RANDOLPH'S STEWED SPICED MUSHROOMS

MARY RANDOLPH'S *The Virginia House-Wife* of 1824 remains a seminal American cookbook, a book that illustrates, in addition to dozens of other factors, the important role that stewing played in the early development of our cookery. In this simple recipe, all that is important is that the lid on the pot be very tight to allow the mushrooms to render all their liquid. This stewing method also works well with fresh wild mushrooms, though they do not yield as much liquid as the ordinary button variety.

1 pound large button mushrooms, stems removed and caps
cut into quarters
1/2 cup dry red wine
1/8 teaspoon ground cloves
1/8 teaspoon ground allspice
Salt and freshly ground black pepper to taste
3 tablespoons butter, softened
1 teaspoon all-purpose flour

In a large, heavy saucepan, combine the mushrooms, wine, cloves, allspice, and salt and pepper. Cover the pan very tightly and cook the mushrooms over moderately low heat till they are tender and have released their liquid, about 20 minutes. Combine the butter and flour, add to the mushrooms, and stir gently till the remaining liquid is nicely thickened. Serve immediately.

Makes 4 to 6 servings

STEW SAVVY

*T*o keep mushrooms firm and spot free till ready to stew, store them in paper rather than plastic containers.

JACK CZARNECKI'S STEWED WILD MUSHROOMS

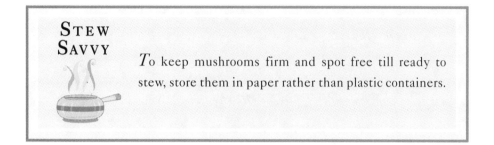

WHEN ONE OF MY MENTORS, Silas Spitzer, first took me to Joe's Restaurant in Reading, Pennsylvania, over twenty years ago, it was probably the only venue in the United States that served any variety of wild mushroom on a regular basis. At that time, Joe Czarnecki collected his own mushrooms, created innumerable dishes featuring the different fungi, and generally waged a campaign to popularize an item that was virtually unknown to most Americans. The restaurant thrived, wild mushrooms have become staples in restaurants and homes throughout the country, and today Jack Czarnecki, owner/chef at Joe's, carries on the culinary innovations of his father as "King of the Mushroom." This is one of Jack's more unadorned recipes, a stew conceived to highlight the distinctive natural savor of fresh wild mushrooms. Normally, I don't give a whit about cooking with overly hyped, brutally expensive extra-virgin olive oil, but for this dish it is fully appropriate.

continued

2 tablespoons extra-virgin olive oil

1 medium-size onion, chopped

½ pound fresh wild mushrooms (cèpes, chanterelles, shiitakes, or morels), stems removed

½ cup water

1 teaspoon salt

1 teaspoon sugar

1 tablespoon soy sauce

½ teaspoon dried summer savory, crumbled

2 teaspoons cornstarch mixed with ¼ cup cold water

In a medium-size pot, heat the oil over moderate heat, then add the onion and cook, stirring, till slightly browned, about 6 minutes. Add the mushrooms and water, bring to a low simmer, cover, and cook till the mushrooms are greatly reduced in size and completely covered with liquid, about 30 minutes. Add the salt, sugar, soy sauce, and summer savory, stir well, and simmer about 5 minutes longer. Add the cornstarch mixture and stir till the stew is thickened.

Makes 4 servings

CALIFORNIA VEGETABLE AND CHICKPEA CHILI

ONLY NATIVE CALIFORNIANS like two wine-making friends of mine in Salinas can regularly throw together a vegetable chili such as this utilizing their almost year-round abundance of fresh vegetables and herbs. For those of us with seasonal gardens, various substitutions often have to be made (canned tomatoes, dried herbs, and the like), but such is the availability almost everywhere today of certain fresh produce even in the coldest months that no imaginative cook should have much trouble concocting a very tasty vegetable and bean chili according to this basic recipe. One advantage, by the way, of using a 28-ounce can of tomatoes with their juices instead of the fresh is that most likely you won't have to add any water to keep the chili slightly soupy.

½ cup vegetable oil

2 medium-size onions, chopped

1 celery rib, chopped

1 small green bell pepper, seeded and chopped

1 garlic clove, minced

2 medium-size yellow squash or zucchini, scrubbed, ends trimmed, and chopped

Two 32-ounce cans chickpeas (garbanzo beans), drained

2 tablespoons chopped fresh coriander (cilantro) leaves

2 tablespoons chili powder

1 tablespoon chopped fresh oregano leaves, or ½ teaspoon dried, crumbled

1 tablespoon chopped fresh basil leaves, or ½ teaspoon dried, crumbled

1 teaspoon ground cumin

Salt and freshly ground black pepper to taste

Cayenne pepper to taste

4 large, ripe tomatoes, chopped and juices retained

1½ cups tomato juice

In a large, heavy pot, heat the oil over moderate heat, then add the onions, celery, bell pepper, and garlic, and cook, stirring, till softened, about 2 minutes. Add the squash and cook, stirring, 3 minutes longer to soften. Add the remaining ingredients and stir well. Reduce the heat to a low simmer, cover, and cook for 1 hour, adding a little water if the stew begins to get too thick.

Makes 4 to 6 servings

PUMPKIN, KIDNEY BEAN, AND SAUSAGE POT

CONFRONTED EVERY FALL WITH literally acre after acre of colorful huge pumpkins that fill the open fields of Bridgehampton and Water Mill on the eastern end of Long Island, I'm forever coming up with ways to utilize the orange gourds that we lug home for any number of purposes. I doubt that the Pilgrims had anything like this savory stew when they served pumpkin at their second Thanksgiving in 1623, but if they had, I can't imagine that they wouldn't have served it right alongside their roasted wild turkey and boiled cranberries. While I always use fresh pumpkin when it's in season, the canned product is fully acceptable and admittedly more practical.

1½ cups dried kidney beans, rinsed and picked over
½ pound breakfast sausage links, pricked with a fork
¼ cup vegetable oil
2 large onions, chopped
1 garlic clove, minced
2 cups beef broth (page 6)
1 cup prepared tomato sauce
Salt and freshly ground black pepper to taste
Cayenne pepper to taste
3½ cups 1-inch peeled fresh or canned pumpkin dice
(about 1 pound)
½ cup finely chopped fresh parsley leaves

Place the beans in a large bowl, add enough cold water to cover by 3 inches, let soak overnight, and drain.

In a large, heavy pot, fry the sausage over moderate heat till browned on all sides, transfer to a plate, and drain off the fat from the pot. Add the oil, onions, and garlic and cook, stirring, till softened, about 3 minutes. Add the beans, sausage, broth, and tomato sauce, season with salt, pepper, and cayenne, bring to a low simmer, cover, and cook till the beans are tender, about 2 hours. Add the pumpkin, stir, and cook till the pumpkin is tender, about 20 minutes. Stir in the parsley and serve.

Makes 6 servings

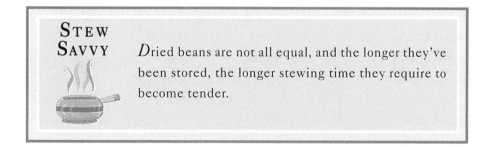

STEW SAVVY *D*ried beans are not all equal, and the longer they've been stored, the longer stewing time they require to become tender.

STEWED WHITE BEANS
AND TOMATOES

Different varieties of white beans are grown in California, New Mexico, Colorado, and Michigan, and I don't suppose there's a bean stew anywhere that I love better (especially served with roast lamb) than this herby combination of white beans and tomatoes. I utterly ignore the silly trend today of cooking beans just till they are crisp to the bite, forever convinced that only long, slow simmering brings out the full flavor of any bean—not to mention an unctuous texture. You don't want them mushy, to be sure, but they should be very tender and succulent.

1 pound dried white navy or pea beans, rinsed and picked over
2 quarts water
1 large onion, peeled and studded with 2 cloves
1 herb bouquet (¹/₂ teaspoon dried thyme, 1 bay leaf, 3 sprigs
    fresh parsley, and 1 peeled garlic clove wrapped in cheese-
    cloth)
Salt and freshly ground black pepper to taste
¹/₄ cup (¹/₂ stick) butter
2 medium-size onions, finely chopped
2 garlic cloves, minced
3 medium-size, ripe tomatoes, peeled, seeded, and chopped
1 tablespoon tomato paste
2 tablespoons chopped fresh parsley leaves

Place the beans in a large, heavy pot, add enough cold water to cover by 3 inches, and let soak overnight. Drain the beans and add the 2 quarts fresh water, the studded onion, herb bouquet, and salt and pepper. Bring the liquid to a boil, reduce the heat to a low simmer, cover, and cook till the beans are just tender, about 1¹/₄ hours. Strain the beans, reserving 1¹/₂ cups of the cooking liquid. Discard the studded onion and herb bouquet. Wash out the pot.

In the pot, heat the butter over moderate heat, then add the chopped onions and garlic, and cook, stirring, till softened, about 2 minutes. Add the tomatoes and tomato paste, stir well, and simmer for 10 minutes. Add the reserved cooking liquid and simmer for 5 minutes, stirring occasionally. Add the beans and taste for salt and pepper. Return to a simmer, cover, and cook till the beans have absorbed most of the liquid but are still moist, about 20 minutes. Stir in the parsley and serve.

Makes 6 to 8 servings

STEW SAVVY

*R*ich in nutrients and flavor, the water used to cook most beans should be saved to mix into and enrich the liquid base of many stews. Ditto potato cooking water, as the starch in it helps to thicken a stew.

DELTA RED BEANS AND RICE

THROUGHOUT THE LOUISIANA DELTA—including virtually every Creole and Cajun restaurant in New Orleans—red beans and rice have always been traditionally served on Mondays. Supposedly introduced into the region by African slaves, the stew—depending on who's cooking—can contain such additional ingredients as ham hocks, diced chicken, and salt pork; and today arguments still rage over whether the beans and rice should be cooked separately and whether a local packaged seasoning called "pickled pork" is obligatory. In any case, the stew is one of America's greatest contributions to gastronomy, and whenever I'm in New Orleans, one of the first restaurants I visit is the funky Mother's just to perch at a formica table with a big bowl of red beans and rice, a half-loaf of hot French bread, and a Dixie beer.

1½ cups dried kidney beans, rinsed and picked over
3 tablespoons vegetable oil
1 medium-size onion, chopped
1 celery rib, chopped
½ small green bell pepper, seeded and chopped
1 garlic clove, minced
½ pound garlic or smoked sausage, thinly sliced
1 small fresh hot red pepper, chopped
¼ teaspoon dried thyme, crumbled
Salt and freshly ground black pepper to taste
1 tablespoon cider vinegar
1 cup uncooked rice
2 cups chicken broth (page 120)
½ cup diced cooked chicken
½ cup finely chopped fresh parsley leaves

Place the kidney beans in a large, heavy pot with enough cold water to cover by 3 inches and let soak overnight. Drain the beans in a colander and dry the pot.

Heat the oil in the pot over moderately high heat, then add the onion, celery, bell pepper, and garlic, and cook, stirring, till softened, about 3 minutes. Return the beans to the pot and add the sausage, hot pepper, thyme, salt and black pepper, vinegar, and enough water to cover by 1 inch. Bring to a low simmer, cover, and cook till the beans are tender and most of the liquid has been absorbed, 35 to 40 minutes.

Meanwhile, in a medium-size saucepan, combine the rice, broth, chicken, and salt to taste and bring to a boil. Reduce the heat to moderate, cover, and cook till all the liquid has been absorbed, about 13 minutes.

In a large serving bowl, combine the beans and rice mixtures, sprinkle over the parsley, and mix well.

Makes 6 servings

STEW SAVVY *To* minimize the natural "gas" in dried beans used in stews and chilis, never use the water in which they were soaked to cook them or to enrich the stew base. Always cook the beans in fresh water.

COLORADO CURRIED
LENTIL STEW

Lentils, one of the first legumes to be cultivated by humans, come in every size and color from India, Africa, Egypt, and France, but the variety that is most readily available to us is the brown American lentil grown in Colorado, Oregon, and Washington State and processed for quick cooking (i.e., no long soaking necessary). While I love nothing more than a simple, hearty lentil stew made with a big ham hock, I must say that this curried version shared with colleagues in Boulder, Colorado, and made with some of the fattest, most beautiful brown lentils I've ever seen, is simply out of this world and perfect for a cold weather lunch. Lentils do absorb a lot of water while simmering, so be sure to watch the pot carefully after about 30 minutes.

4 slices bacon, diced
1 large onion, chopped
½ pound cooked ham, diced
¼ teaspoon ground tumeric
¼ teaspoon ground ginger
⅛ teaspoon ground cloves
2 cups dried lentils, rinsed and picked over
2 large, ripe tomatoes, chopped
3 medium-size carrots, scraped and chopped
7 cups water
Salt to taste
Boiled rice

In a large, heavy pot, fry the bacon over moderate heat till almost crisp, then add the onion and ham, and cook, stirring, till they are slightly browned, about 5 minutes. Add the spices and stir for 30 seconds. Add the lentils, tomatoes, carrots, water, and salt and stir well. Bring to a boil, reduce the heat to a moderate simmer, and cook, uncovered, till the lentils are tender, about 40 minutes. Serve the stew over rice.

Makes 6 servings

STEWED MIXED FRUIT

THIS IS THE TYPE of fruit stew I serve most often in late summer and early fall, when the markets are overflowing with beautiful fresh produce. Feel free to use any combination of fruits and spices, but I do suggest that you stand over the stew with a fork to make sure the fruit doesn't overcook. I think that fruit and almonds make a perfect marriage, but you might also want to play around with other chopped nuts.

2 cups cranberry juice
1 cup water
One 2-inch stick cinnamon
1 small piece fresh ginger, peeled and cut in half
2 tablespoons finely chopped orange peel
2 tablespoons sugar
2 medium-size Granny Smith apples, cored, peeled, and cut into chunks
2 firm pears, peeled, cored, and cut into chunks
4 firm purple plums, pitted and cut into quarters
1 cup seedless white grapes
1 cup dark raisins
½ cup chopped almonds, toasted (see Note on page 127)

continued

In a large pot, combine the cranberry juice, water, cinnamon, ginger, orange peel, and sugar and bring to a low boil. Add the apples, cover, and cook till almost tender, about 12 minutes. Add the pears, cover, and cook for 5 minutes. Add the plums, grapes, and raisins, cover, and cook till the plums are tender, 5 to 10 minutes. Let the stew stand off the heat for about 5 minutes, then remove and discard the cinnamon and ginger. Carefully spoon the fruit and a little liquid into serving bowls and sprinkle the almonds over the top.

❧ Makes 6 servings ❧

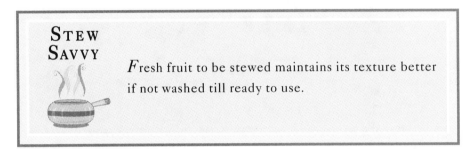

STEW SAVVY

*F*resh fruit to be stewed maintains its texture better if not washed till ready to use.

BUCKS COUNTY
STEWED SPICED PEARS

Wᴏɴᴅᴇʀꜰᴜʟ Bᴀʀᴛʟᴇᴛᴛ, Bᴏsᴄ, Sᴇᴄᴋᴇʟ, and Comice pears are grown in the Pacific Northwest, Illinois, and New York, but the juiciest, most flavorful ones I've ever tasted in this country were the large, tart, thin-necked Boscs from New Jersey and Pennsylvania that friends and I used to stew and serve chilled at our eighteenth-century farmhouse in Bucks County, Pennsylvania. I still prefer russet Boscs for stewing, but so long as they're firm, there's nothing wrong with green-skinned Anjous, ruddy Comices, juicy Clapps, or tiny Seckels. Sugar-sweet Bartletts make for sublime eating, but unless you can find the relatively sturdy

Max Red variety, they're just too fragile for stewing. When stewing any pears, I always poke at them with a fork after about twenty minutes to make sure they're not overcooking.

1 cup dry vermouth
1 cup orange juice
⅔ cup sugar
4 cloves
One 2-inch stick cinnamon
6 firm Bosc pears, peeled, halved, and cored

In a wide, shallow, flameproof casserole, combine the vermouth, orange juice, sugar, cloves, and cinnamon, stir, and simmer over low heat for 5 minutes. Arrange the pears in the liquid and spoon the liquid over them. Bring to a low simmer, cover tightly with a sheet of aluminum foil, and cook till the pears are tender but not too soft, about 35 minutes, basting twice during the stewing. Allow the pears to cool in the liquid, basting from time to time, then chill for 1 hour before serving.

Makes 6 servings

STEW SAVVY

*T*o neatly core apples and pears for stewing, cut the fruit in half lengthwise and remove the core with a melon scooper. Likewise, to pit plums and peaches, make a single cut around the seed, then twist the halves apart.

STEWED
GINGERED FIGS

ALTHOUGH FIGS WERE INTRODUCED to America by the Spaniards on the Caribbean island of Hispaniola in the early sixteenth century, it was not until the 1700s that the missions set up in southern California began cultivating the famous Mission fig so widely available today. All of our figs (the Mission, Kadota, Calimyrna, San Pedro, etc.) come from California, and any can be stewed to produce a delectable dessert, such as this gingered creation.

1 pound firm, ripe, fresh figs, peeled
2 cups water
2 tablespoons fresh lemon juice
1½ cups sugar
One 2-inch piece fresh ginger, peeled
3 tablespoons finely chopped orange peel

In a large saucepan, combine all the ingredients, except the orange peel, bring to a low simmer, and cook, uncovered, till the figs are tender and clear, 20 to 30 minutes. Remove the pan from the heat, cover, and let the figs cool in the liquid. Serve the figs with a little liquid spooned over each portion and sprinkle orange peel on top.

Makes 6 servings

STEW SAVVY *N*ever discard leftover liquid used to stew fruits. Save it to add to the liquid in fruit gelatins or to glaze baked hams and poultry.

CAPE COD
STEWED APPLE
AND CRANBERRY COMPOTE

ONLY IN AMERICA ARE cranberries in wide cultivation, envied by chefs throughout Europe where the berries are still considered somewhat exotic. Good varieties are grown in New Jersey, Wisconsin, and Oregon, but once you've tasted the fat, almost sweet berries of Cape Cod, Massachusetts (where cranberry bogs abound and a gentle old lady once served me this memorable compote topped with fresh vanilla ice cream), others fade by comparison. Frozen cranberries are widely available during the cold months and quite suitable, but be warned that when I was desperately searching for a bag of frozen cranberries last spring, not one was to be found within a twenty-five mile radius of home.

¼ cup (½ stick) butter
5 Granny Smith apples, cored, peeled, and cut into thin wedges
1 cup sugar
1 teaspoon grated orange peel
1 cup apple juice
¼ cup port wine
1 cup fresh cranberries, rinsed and picked over

In a medium-size pot, heat the butter over low heat, then add the apples and cook, stirring, till they begin to soften, about 10 minutes. Add the sugar, orange peel, apple juice, and wine and stir gently. Add the cranberries, bring to a moderate simmer, and cook, uncovered, till the cranberries pop, about 7 minutes. Either serve the compote warm or let cool and then chill.

Makes 6 servings

SPICY STEWED
DRIED FRUIT COMPOTE

So what on earth do you do with the expensive dried pears, figs, apricots, and other fruits included in that enormous holiday gift basket? I simply eat some since I love dried fruits in any form, but more often than not they end up being stewed in a spicy liquid, chilled overnight to amalgamate the flavors, and served as an impressive dessert at a snazzy dinner. Because of the high cost, I don't make a habit of buying any of the luscious dried fruits that are available year-round in deluxe food shops, but when I (and my mother) want to end a fine meal with something really unusual (and not too filling), this compote is ideal.

½ pound dried fruits (combined apricots, figs, pears, peaches, etc.)
3 cups water
1 cup dry white wine
4 thin lemon slices, seeded
One 2-inch stick cinnamon
½ cup honey
¼ cup dark rum
¼ teaspoon ground allspice

In a large, heavy pot, combine the fruits, water, wine, lemon slices, and cinnamon and stir. Bring to a boil, reduce the heat to a low simmer, and cook till the fruits begin to swell, about 20 minutes. Transfer the fruits to a plate. Add the honey, rum, and allspice to the pot, increase the heat to high, and cook, stirring, till the liquid is reduced by half. Return the fruits to the pot, stir well, and let cool. Transfer the fruits and liquid to a serving dish, cover with plastic wrap, and chill overnight. When ready to serve, bring the fruits back to room temperature.

Makes 6 to 8 servings

STEW SAVVY

*T*o keep stewed fruits from darkening while cooking, make sure they are fully submerged in the liquid—even if it means weighting them down with a heavy plate.

Biscuits

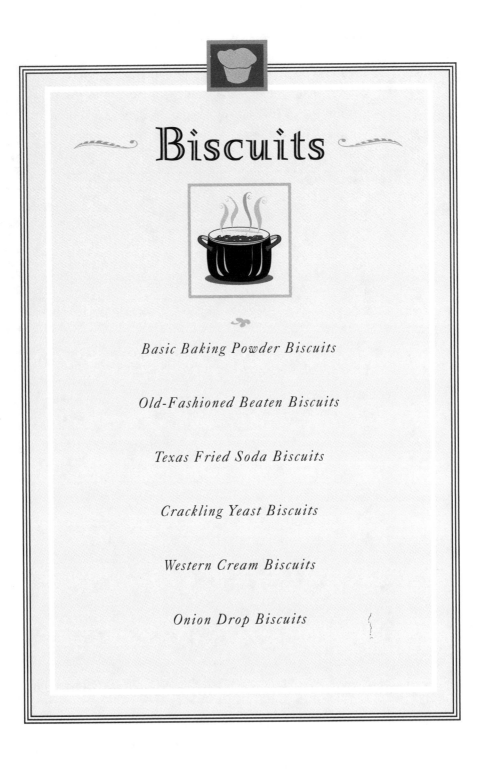

Basic Baking Powder Biscuits

Old-Fashioned Beaten Biscuits

Texas Fried Soda Biscuits

Crackling Yeast Biscuits

Western Cream Biscuits

Onion Drop Biscuits

Herbed Sour Cream Biscuits

Sweet Potato Biscuits

Cheddar Biscuits

Midwestern Bran Biscuits

Bill Neal's Hominy Ham Biscuits

New England Rye Biscuits

Biscuit Muffins

Indian Cornmeal Biscuits

Raisin Scones

Mother's Skillet Cornbread

A good American stew almost demands a good American biscuit, and the variety of baking powder, baking soda, yeast, beaten, fried, cream, and drop biscuits from which the home cook has to choose is almost staggering. Who knows exactly when and how we distorted the British sweet "biscuit" (that is, cookie) and came up with our savory, crusty classics, but it's for sure that biscuits have been a staple of the American diet (especially in the South) ever since the technique for milling fine, smooth white flour was perfected in the nineteenth century, allowing numerous baking alternatives not possible with coarse-grained whole-wheat flour.

Debates rage throughout the country over every facet of biscuit making. Is bleached all-purpose flour better than the coarser unbleached? Southern purists like my mother will use *only* soft, bleached, winter Southern flour like White Lily or Red Band, which are low in gluten. Is it better to sift ingredients for even leavening, or does whisking do just as good a job? What fat produces a better biscuit: shortening, butter, or lard? Should biscuit dough be rolled or gently patted out with the hands for the best texture? Does a genuine American biscuit ever contain sugar? Southerners say absolutely not; Yankees insist by all means; Midwesterners and Westerners play the options. Should the baking sheet for biscuits be greased, and exactly how far apart on the sheet should biscuits be baked for perfect texture and browning? What is the ideal baking temperature and timing, 450°F. for 10 to 12 minutes, or 400°F. for 12 to 14 minutes? Yes, Americans take biscuit making very seriously.

Each argument has its valid points, and the various recipes here illustrate the national spectrum of convictions regarding flours, leavenings, fats and liquid binders, flavorings, and cooking techniques. Since individual tastes vary so radically, I'm not about to advocate which biscuit goes best with which stew. On the other hand, I do have my own strong opinions about biscuits in general:

1. The reason Southern biscuits are the greatest in the world is because of the superior soft, low-gluten, winter wheat flour that is used. The very finest is White Lily, which is all I use and which now can be ordered in five-pound bags by

writing White Lily Kitchens, P.O. Box 871, Knoxville, Tennessee 37901. If this is too inconvenient or impractical, and you're forced to use the more widely available hard summer flour, you can simulate with some success the Southern product by using about one-quarter cake flour to three-quarters regular all-purpose flour (unbleached is okay, too, but it is coarser and darker than bleached). I have made some decent biscuits with self-rising all-purpose flour (to which baking powder and salt have already been added), but for this flour to be effective, it must be strictly fresh.

2. There are three types of fat used to make biscuits: vegetable shortening, lard, and butter. While lard yields the most distinctly crisp layers, I think a good shortening like Crisco produces the tenderest and fluffiest biscuits. Butter certainly has its flavor advantages, but this fat also gives the weakest structure to biscuits. Sometimes I blend two of the fats, and you might try the same for optimum results.

3. A cardinal rule is that, with few exceptions, biscuits must be handled as little as possible to prevent toughness—minimum stirring of ingredients, kneading the dough no more than a few strokes, and gentle rolling or patting it out.

4. Cutting out biscuits is very important, and nobody should be without a sturdy, sharp, metal biscuit cutter. A small juice glass can be used, but remember that since this does not allow air to escape during the cutting, the biscuit can be overly compressed. To avoid jagged edges on biscuits (and uneven baking of the sides), never twist the cutter—simply cut straight down in one quick stroke.

5. You can add virtually any extra ingredients to biscuit dough, but if you do add other solids, just make sure they are finely diced or chopped so that the texture of the biscuit is not adversely affected.

6. If you like your biscuits browned all over, bake them about ½ inch apart on the baking sheet. Personally, I prefer the sides of most biscuits to be rather soft, so to keep the sides from overbrowning, I generally space them about ¼ inch apart.

Finally, since biscuits are just as good when left over, I might also suggest that you double or triple most of these recipes. Leftover biscuits as such are not very good reheated, but when they're split (never cut open with a knife!), buttered, and toasted, they're delicious for breakfast and almost as good with stews as freshly baked ones. Biscuits stored in airtight plastic bags will keep well when refrigerated about four days, and they can be frozen for up to a month without losing much of their moisture.

BASIC BAKING POWDER
BISCUITS

THIS, MY MOTHER'S AGE-OLD "receipt," is not only the quintessential
Southern baking powder biscuit made with buttermilk but the recipe that illustrates more than any other the fine art of biscuit making. Ideally, the biscuits
should be made with soft, low-gluten, Southern winter flour, but since this is not
easily available in most areas of the country, you can simulate it somewhat by using
about one-quarter cake flour to three-quarters regular all-purpose. By no means
should you knead this dough as with other breads, and since the nature of all ovens
can vary dramatically, begin watching the biscuits very carefully after ten minutes
to make sure the tops don't overbrown.

2 cups all-purpose flour
4 teaspoons baking powder
½ teaspoon baking soda
½ teaspoon salt
¼ cup vegetable shortening (preferably Crisco)
1 cup buttermilk

Preheat the oven to 450°F.

Sift together the flour, baking powder, baking soda, and salt in a large
mixing bowl. Add the shortening and cut it in with a pastry cutter or 2 knives till
the mixture resembles coarse meal. Add the buttermilk and mix with a large
wooden spoon just till the dough is soft, adding a little more buttermilk if necessary. Transfer the dough to a floured surface and, using a light touch, turn the
edges toward the middle, pressing with your hands. Press the dough out to a ¼-
inch thickness. Cut straight down into even rounds with a biscuit cutter or small
juice glass and place the rounds no more than ½ inch apart on a large, ungreased

baking sheet. Gather up the scraps of dough and repeat the procedure. Bake the biscuits just till lightly browned on top, about 12 minutes.

⊷ Makes about 16 biscuits ⊷

STEW SAVVY

*N*othing is more indispensable to biscuit making than a genuine metal biscuit cutter, but if you can't find one and want to make your own, the sharp end of a clean, small tomato paste can will work very well.

OLD-FASHIONED BEATEN BISCUITS

Small beaten biscuits (also called Maryland biscuits in that state) have been around for ages and recall the days when the first sound in the morning was the *whack whack whack* of dough being beaten repeatedly with a rolling pin in the kitchen. These biscuits, which are fun to make and by design are dry and hard, are altogether different from their light, fluffy counterparts. This is one biscuit that must be baked at a moderate temperature for at least thirty minutes to attain the right texture.

4 cups all-purpose flour
1 teaspoon salt
3 tablespoons vegetable shortening
1 cup water

Preheat the oven to 350°F.

Sift the flour and salt together into a large mixing bowl. Add the shortening and cut it in with a pastry cutter or 2 knives till the mixture resembles coarse meal. Add the water and stir with a large wooden spoon till the dough is soft. Transfer the dough to a lightly floured surface and begin beating it all over with a floured rolling pin, folding it back on itself as it flattens and beating constantly till very smooth, at least 15 minutes. Pinch off small pieces of dough about the size of a Ping-Pong ball, roll between the palms of your hands, and place on an ungreased baking sheet. Flatten the balls with a fork, then press again to form a crisscross pattern. Bake till the biscuits are lightly golden and quite crisp, about 30 minutes.

Makes about 50 biscuits

TEXAS FRIED SODA BISCUITS

THESE TANGY BISCUITS GO back to the days of early westward expansion, when pioneers may have had plenty of buttermilk (from making fresh butter) and lard but only an open fire over which to cook. Since baking powder was not introduced till 1856, settlers had to depend for leavening on a product called saleratus (i.e., baking soda), sold in a bright red package. The product's main advantage was that it combined quickly with the acid in buttermilk to release the carbon dioxide needed to make the dough rise. Soda biscuits are still a popular staple in Texas—maybe because they go so well with chili.

> 2 cups all-purpose flour
> 1½ teaspoons baking soda
> 1½ teaspoons salt
> ¼ cup lard, cut into small pieces
> 1 cup buttermilk
> Tabasco sauce to taste
> Vegetable oil for deep-frying

In a large mixing bowl, whisk the flour, baking soda, and salt together till well blended. Add the lard and work it into the dry ingredients with your fingertips till the mixture resembles meal. Gradually add the buttermilk, stirring with a large wooden spoon just till the dough is soft. Stir in the Tabasco. Transfer the dough to a floured surface, knead a few seconds, and roll out to a ½-inch thickness. Cut out rounds with a biscuit cutter or small juice glass. Gather up the scraps of dough and repeat the process.

In a large, deep, cast-iron skillet, heat about 1½ inches of oil to 350°F. or till a speck of dough tossed in sputters. Add the biscuits in batches, cover the skillet, and fry for 4 minutes. Turn the biscuits over, cover, and fry till the biscuits are golden and puffy, about 4 minutes longer. Drain on paper towels and keep hot.

Makes at least 20 small biscuits

CRACKLING
YEAST BISCUITS

CRACKLINGS ARE THE CRISP bits that result from frying salt pork rather slowly in its own fat, and they've been used to make biscuits ever since batches were cooked up in the nation's first farmhouses and around chuckwagons. In some areas of the country, these would be called angel or wedding biscuits since they're made with yeast, and in the South buttermilk most likely would be used—in which case ¼ teaspoon baking soda would have to be added to leaven the acid dough. I've also made these biscuits with bits of salty country ham or bacon.

½ package active dry yeast
2 tablespoons warm (not hot) water
¼ cup finely diced salt pork
2 cups unbleached all-purpose flour
1 teaspoon baking powder
½ teaspoon salt
¼ cup vegetable shortening
1 cup milk

In a small bowl, stir together the yeast and water and set aside. (If the mixture does not foam up after a few minutes, it means the yeast is no longer active and the mixture should be discarded.)

In a heavy skillet, fry the salt pork over moderate heat till it is well browned and crisp, about 10 minutes, then drain the cracklings on paper towels.

Sift together the flour, baking powder, and salt in a large mixing bowl. Cut in the shortening with a pastry cutter or 2 knives till the mixture resembles coarse meal, then stir in the cracklings. Make a well in the dry ingredients, pour the yeast mixture and milk into the well, and stir gently with a large wooden spoon just till the dry ingredients are moistened and the dough is soft. Cover with plastic wrap or a clean kitchen towel and let rise about 1 hour in a warm area.

Preheat the oven to 425°F.

Transfer the dough to a floured surface and knead 3 to 4 times. Roll out the dough to a ½-inch thickness and cut out rounds with a biscuit cutter or small juice glass. Gather up the scraps of dough and repeat the procedure. Place the rounds on an ungreased baking sheet and bake till golden brown, about 15 minutes.

Makes at least 1 dozen biscuits

WESTERN CREAM BISCUITS

I CALL THESE CREAM BISCUITS "Western" only because they're the ones James Beard loved to bake in his cooking classes at Seaside, Oregon, and serve with chicken and seafood stews. (I've also had memorable cream biscuits at various restaurants in San Francisco.) Since the biscuits are merely dipped in butter before baking, they remain light, creamy, and utterly delectable.

2 cups bleached all-purpose flour
1 tablespoon baking powder
½ teaspoon baking soda
1 teaspoon salt
1½ teaspoons sugar
1¼ cups heavy cream
¼ cup (½ stick) butter, melted

Preheat the oven to 425°F.

Sift together the flour, baking powder, baking soda, salt, and sugar in a large mixing bowl. Stirring constantly, add the cream till the dough becomes just firm and is no longer sticky. Transfer the dough to a well-floured surface, knead 4 to 5 times, and pat out into a rectangle about ½ inch thick. Cut out 2-inch squares, then gather up the scraps of dough, repat, and cut out more squares. Dip both sides of each square briefly into the melted butter and place on an ungreased baking sheet. Bake till golden, about 14 minutes.

Makes at least 1 dozen biscuits

STEW SAVVY *B*iscuits will not rise properly if the baking soda is too old. To test, sprinkle a teaspoon of baking soda over a tablespoon of vinegar in a tiny bowl. If it bubbles up, it's good.

ONION DROP BISCUITS

DROP BISCUITS (ALSO KNOWN as batter biscuits in the Midwest) are leavened with both baking powder and eggs, and since they contain little fat, the baking sheet must be greased to prevent sticking. These biscuits are also good made with finely chopped fresh chives, parsley, dill, grated Parmesan cheese, or a little prepared horseradish added to the cream.

2 cups unbleached all-purpose flour
2½ teaspoons baking powder
1 teaspoon salt
1 cup heavy cream
2 large eggs, beaten
2 tablespoons minced onion

Preheat the oven to 425°F.

In a large mixing bowl, whisk together the flour, baking powder, and salt till well blended. In another bowl, whisk or beat the cream with an electric mixer till almost stiff and fold into the dry mixture. Add the eggs and onion and stir with a large wooden spoon till well blended. Drop the batter by rounded tablespoons at least 2 inches apart onto a greased baking sheet and bake till golden brown, 13 to 15 minutes.

Makes at least 1 dozen biscuits

HERBED SOUR CREAM BISCUITS

THE COMBINATION OF UNBLEACHED white and whole wheat flours gives these Yankee biscuits a sturdy, slightly dense texture softened subtly by the use of either sour cream or plain yogurt. I make the biscuits with all sorts of dried herbs, but when I plan to serve them with seafood stews, no flavoring is better than about a tablespoon of finely chopped fresh dill.

1 cup unbleached all-purpose flour
1 cup whole wheat flour
1 teaspoon sugar
1 teaspoon salt
2 teaspoons baking powder
½ teaspoon baking soda
1 teaspoon dried thyme, crumbled
1 teaspoon dried rosemary, crumbled
5 tablespoons vegetable shortening
1 cup sour cream or plain yogurt

Preheat the oven to 450°F.

Sift together the flours, sugar, salt, baking powder, and baking soda into a large mixing bowl, then stir in the thyme and rosemary. Cut in the shortening with a pastry cutter or knives till the mixture resembles coarse meal. Add the sour cream and stir with a large wooden spoon till well blended and soft. Transfer the dough to a floured surface and pat out to about ½ inch thick, handling the dough as little as possible. Cut the dough into rounds with a biscuit cutter or small juice glass and place on an ungreased baking sheet. Gather up the scraps of dough and repeat the procedure. Bake till golden brown, 12 to 14 minutes.

Makes about 1 dozen biscuits

SWEET POTATO
BISCUITS

Sweet potato biscuits are heavier in texture and have an altogether different flavor from those made with all flour, and while not really suitable for breakfast, they are delicious with hearty stews. Do not use butter in these biscuits, and when rolling out the dough, apply as light a touch as possible—never overrolling.

> 5 medium-size sweet potatoes
> ⅔ cup vegetable shortening
> 2½ cups all-purpose flour
> 3 teaspoons baking powder
> ½ teaspoon salt
> Milk as needed

Place the potatoes in a large saucepan with enough water to cover, bring to a moderate simmer, cover, and cook till the potatoes are very tender, about 30 minutes. When cool enough to handle, peel the potatoes, place them in a large mixing bowl, and mash with a potato masher or heavy fork. Immediately add the shortening, continue to mash till well blended, and let cool.

Preheat the oven to 425°F.

Add the flour, baking powder, and salt to the potato mixture and mix with a wooden spoon till well blended, adding a little milk if necessary to make a smooth dough. On a lightly floured surface, roll out the dough to a ½-inch thickness with a floured rolling pin. Cut out rounds with a biscuit cutter or small juice glass and place on an ungreased baking sheet. Gather up the scraps of dough and repeat the procedure. Bake the biscuits till golden, about 12 minutes.

Makes about 20 biscuits

CHEDDAR BISCUITS

Bᴇᴄᴀᴜsᴇ ᴏғ ᴛʜᴇ ʙᴜᴛᴛᴇʀ and cheese, these are not the fluffiest biscuits in the world, but, heavens, are they good! And if you want to make them even better, reduce the Cheddar by a quarter and add ¼ cup grated Parmesan cheese. Watch these biscuits carefully to make sure they don't brown too much. Also, this biscuit dough makes an ideal topping for pot pies (with or without the cheese, depending on what type of pie).

2 cups unbleached all-purpose flour
2½ teaspoons baking powder
1 teaspoon salt
6 tablespoons (¾ stick) butter, cut into small pieces
1 cup finely grated extra-sharp Cheddar cheese
Cayenne pepper to taste
1 cup milk

Preheat the oven to 425°F.

In a large mixing bowl, whisk together well the flour, baking powder, and salt. Cut in the butter with a pastry cutter or 2 knives till the mixture resembles coarse meal. Add the cheese and cayenne and stir till well blended. Add the milk and stir with a large wooden spoon till the dough is soft, adding a touch more milk if necessary. Transfer the dough to a floured surface, knead 3 to 4 times, then roll out to a ½-inch thickness, cut out rounds with a biscuit cutter or small juice glass, and place on an ungreased baking sheet. Gather up the scraps of dough and repeat the procedure. Bake till just golden brown, 12 to 13 minutes.

Makes at least 1 dozen biscuits

MIDWESTERN
BRAN BISCUITS

Biscuits made with part wheat bran seems to be a Midwestern specialty—at least according to my experience while living in Missouri. The bran makes the biscuits slightly coarse, a texture I like when they're to be served with a rugged meat or poultry stew. For an even sturdier texture, you might want to substitute cracked wheat for the bran.

1½ cups all-purpose flour
2½ teaspoons baking powder
1 teaspoon salt
5 tablespoons butter, cut into pieces
½ cup wheat bran
⅔ cup milk

Preheat the oven to 450°F.

In a large mixing bowl, whisk together well the flour, baking powder, and salt. Cut in the butter with a pastry cutter or 2 knives till the mixture resembles coarse meal. In another bowl, combine the bran and milk and let stand for 2 minutes. Add the bran mixture to the flour mixture and stir well with a large wooden spoon till well blended and soft. Transfer the dough to a floured surface and knead 3 to 4 times. Roll out the dough to a ½-inch thickness, cut out rounds with a biscuit cutter or small juice glass, and place on an ungreased baking sheet. Gather up the scraps of dough and repeat the procedure. Bake the biscuits till golden brown, 12 to 14 minutes.

Makes at least 1 dozen biscuits

BILL NEAL'S
HOMINY HAM BISCUITS

Until his untimely death a few years ago, Bill Neal, owner/chef of the nationally recognized Crook's Corner restaurant in Chapel Hill, North Carolina, was not only a major proponent of authentic Southern cooking but a passionate and expert biscuit maker. There wasn't a style of biscuit that Bill didn't make, but this unusual one made with hominy grits and country ham became a signature dish.

1½ cups all-purpose flour
½ teaspoon salt
2½ teaspoons baking powder
¼ teaspoon sugar
2 tablespoons lard
6 tablespoons milk
½ cup cold plain grits cooked according to the package directions
¼ cup finely diced cured country ham

Preheat the oven to 400°F.

Sift the flour, salt, baking powder, and sugar into a large mixing bowl, add the lard, and work it in with your fingertips till the mixture resembles coarse meal. Stir in the milk, then beat in the grits and ham till well blended. Transfer the dough to a lightly floured surface, knead briefly, and roll out to a ½-inch thickness. Cut the dough into rounds with a biscuit cutter or small juice glass and place on an ungreased baking sheet. Gather up the scraps of dough and repeat the procedure. Bake till golden, 10 to 12 minutes.

Makes 16 to 18 biscuits

NEW ENGLAND RYE BISCUITS

Rye flourishes in cool climates and poor soil and has been used to make sturdy, slightly sweet biscuits in farmhouses throughout New England. Today, most rye biscuits are leavened with added wheat flour, and while most Southerners would never touch this type of biscuit, I find them perfectly compatible with any full-flavored stew.

2 cups rye flour
1 cup all-purpose flour
4 teaspoons baking powder
1 teaspoon sugar
1 teaspoon salt
6 tablespoons (¾ stick) butter
1½ cups milk

Preheat the oven to 450°F.

In a large mixing bowl, whisk together well the flours, baking powder, sugar, and salt. Cut in the butter with a pastry cutter or 2 knives till the mixture resembles coarse meal. Add the milk and stir with a large wooden spoon till the dough is soft. Transfer the dough to a floured surface, knead 4 to 5 times, then roll out to a ½-inch thickness. Cut out 3-inch rounds with a biscuit cutter or medium-size juice glass and arrange on an ungreased baking sheet. Gather up the scraps of dough and repeat the procedure. Bake till light brown, 13 to 14 minutes.

Makes at least 1 dozen biscuits

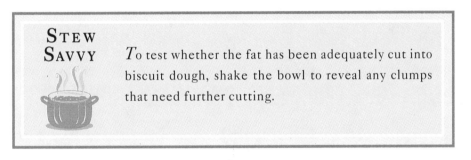

STEW SAVVY *T*o test whether the fat has been adequately cut into biscuit dough, shake the bowl to reveal any clumps that need further cutting.

BISCUIT MUFFINS

I DON'T KNOW WHETHER BISCUIT muffins are as popular today in the Deep South as they were forty or fifty years ago, but I do know that two famous Southern cooks, Craig Claiborne and Paul Prudhomme, still prize their respective recipes for these slightly sweet breads that require lengthy baking.

> 2¼ cups bleached all-purpose flour
> 1 teaspoon salt
> 3 tablespoons sugar
> 1½ teaspoons baking powder
> ¼ teaspoon baking soda
> 10 tablespoons (1¼ sticks) butter, cut into small pieces
> 1 cup buttermilk

Preheat the oven to 350°F.

Sift together the flour, salt, sugar, baking powder, and baking soda in a large mixing bowl. Add the butter and work it into the dry ingredients with your fingers till the mixture resembles coarse meal. Add the buttermilk and stir with a large wooden spoon till just blended. Spoon the mixture into a muffin tin with 12 cups (each about ⅓-cup capacity) and bake till golden brown and crusty, 40 to 45 minutes.

Makes 12 biscuit muffins

INDIAN
CORNMEAL BISCUITS

Travel almost anywhere in America's Southwest (including Texas) and even in some pretty fancy regional restaurants you're bound to come upon rough, crunchy, uneven cornmeal biscuits somewhat like those that Indians have been baking (or frying) for centuries. Of course, heavy biscuits made traditionally with only cornmeal, lard, and water are not the greatest treat in the world, but once they're leavened with wheat flour and eggs and softened with milk, they're truly special—and delicious with Mexican-style stews and chili.

1 cup bleached all-purpose flour
1 cup yellow cornmeal
1 teaspoon salt
½ teaspoon sugar
¼ cup lard, cut into small pieces
2 large eggs, beaten
⅔ cup milk

Preheat the oven to 425°F.

In a large mixing bowl, combine the flour, cornmeal, salt, and sugar. Add the lard and work it in with your fingertips till the mixture resembles coarse meal. Add the eggs and milk and stir with a large wooden spoon till the dough is firm, adding a little more cornmeal if necessary. Transfer the dough to a floured surface and knead with your fingertips for about 15 seconds. Divide the dough into 12 pieces and pat each into a disk about ¾ inch thick and 1½ inches in diameter. Place the disks on an ungreased baking sheet and bake till puffy and golden brown, about 15 minutes.

Makes 1 dozen biscuits

RAISIN SCONES

Despite the curious connection between the British biscuit (sweet cookie) and the American biscuit (savory bread), I have this theory that the true ancestor of our biscuit is the English scone since, basically, both are made the exact same way with the same ingredients. It's true that an English scone might be prepared with milled oats or barley (a rarity with American biscuits) and can now contain any number of sweet ingredients, but generally, plain British scones are very much like our biscuits. I like to serve these raisin scones with any fruit stew.

2 cups bleached all-purpose flour
¼ cup sugar
4 teaspoons baking powder
¼ teaspoon salt
6 tablespoons (¾ stick) butter
½ cup dark seedless raisins
½ cup or more milk
1 large egg white, slightly whisked

Preheat the oven to 425°F.

In a large mixing bowl, whisk together well the flour, sugar, baking powder, and salt. Cut in the butter with a pastry cutter or 2 knives till the mixture resembles coarse meal. Add the raisins and mix well. Add enough milk to make a soft but not wet dough, mixing with a large wooden spoon, then divide the dough in half. Transfer the halves to a floured surface and pat each into a 6-inch round. Place each round on an ungreased baking sheet, brush with the egg white, and with a sharp knife, cut each round into 6 wedges. Separate the wedges and bake till golden brown, 12 to 14 minutes.

Makes 1 dozen scones

MOTHER'S
SKILLET CORNBREAD

Okay, so cornbread doesn't fall into the exact same category as biscuits—though the ingredient concepts for the two are very similar. No matter, for the truth is that some stews (like collard greens with salt pork and any number of Southwestern concoctions) almost beg for wedges of golden, soft but crumbly, full-flavored cornbread to dip into the delectable cooking liquid. Of course, when I was very young, there was never any problem with my grandmother over which bread to serve with stews: she simply put *both* biscuits and cornbread on the table! Alas, Mother doesn't do that much today, but her skillet cornbread remains in a class by itself.

1½ cups white cornmeal
3 tablespoons bleached all-purpose flour
1 teaspoon baking soda
1 teaspoon salt
1¾ cups buttermilk
1 large egg
2 tablespoons vegetable shortening
1 tablespoon bacon grease

Preheat the oven to 475°F.

In a large mixing bowl, whisk together well the cornmeal, flour, baking soda, and salt. In another bowl, whisk together well the buttermilk and egg, then add it to the dry ingredients and mix the batter with a large wooden spoon till well blended. Place the shortening and bacon grease in a 9-inch cast-iron skillet and heat till the shortening melts. Pour the hot fats into the batter, stir well, and pour the batter back into the skillet. Bake till the cornbread is golden brown, about 20 minutes. To serve, turn the skillet upside down onto a big plate, remove, and cut the cornbread into wedges. (To make corn sticks, pour the batter into greased corn stick pans and bake till golden brown, about 10 minutes.)

Makes 4 to 6 servings

Index

hominy:
chicken and sausage gumbo, plantation, 134–135
ham biscuits, Bill Neal's, 290
Santa Fe posole, 58–59
Hoosier pork spareribs and sweet potato stew, 74–75
hot pot, New England, 98
Hungarian goulash, Twentieth Century Limited, 23–24

I

Illinois:
Chicago flank steak and green pea stew, 31–32
Midwestern beef solianka, 17–18
Indiana, Hoosier pork spareribs and sweet potato stew, 74–75
Indian chili, Tigua green, 45–46
Indian cornmeal biscuits, 293
Iowa:
beef stew in ale, Maytag, 11–12
coffee beef stew, Liz Clark's, 13–14
Irish lamb stew with root vegetables, 93–94

J

Jack Czarnecki's stewed wild mushrooms, 257–258
Jack's, 90
jambalaya, Cajun ham, sausage, and shrimp, 80–81
James Beard's duck and pinto bean stew, 154–155
Jasper White's chunky lobster stew, 228–229
Jean Anderson's jugged beef with cranberries and mushrooms, 19–20
Joe's Restaurant, 257
Judy's Bonaker beef stew, 8–9
jugged:
beef with cranberries and mushrooms, Jean Anderson's, 19–20
hare, Western, 178–179

Julia Child's favorite beef stew, 14–15

K

Kafka, Barbara, 107
Kansas City veal kidney braise, 188–189
Kapalua Bay Hotel, 125
Keens Chophouse, 90
Kennedy, Diana, 58–59, 123
Kentucky:
burgoo, traditional, 138–139
stewed ham hocks and lima beans, 86–87
veal, corn, and mushroom burgoo, 111–112
kettle, curried fish, 205
Key West turkey, sweet potato, and mango pot, 150–151
kidney:
beef, and mushroom stew, 186–187
veal, Kansas City braise, 188–189
kidney bean, pumpkin, and sausage pot, 260–261
Kreuz market, 85
Kunz, Gray, 70

L

La Casa de Manuel, 72
Lagasse, Emeril, 249
Lake Superior whitefish and shrimp stew, 207–208
lamb:
and apricot stew, 95–96
curry, an American, 99–100
fricassee with vegetables, minted, 105–106
and leek stew, Leon's dilled, 92–93
New England hot pot, 98
squash and chickpea stew, Paula's autumn, 96–97
stew with root vegetables, Irish, 93–94
traditional Kentucky burgoo, 138–139
lamb shanks:
with rosemary, braised, 101

spiced, braised with tomatoes, 102–103
La Tertulia, 58
Lebewohl, Abe, 29
leek(s):
and lamb stew, Leon's dilled, 92–93
and lobster stew, Montauk, 230–231
parsnips and potatoes stewed in beer, 248–249
and veal ragout, sweet-and-sour, 114–115
lentil stew, Colorado curried, 266–267
Leon's dilled lamb and leek stew, 92–93
Lespinasse, 70
Lianides, Leon, 9, 92
lima beans:
beef and grits scramble, Alabama, 28
Kentucky stewed ham hocks and, 86–87
my chicken succotash, 128
Southern succotash, 246
turkey and corn mull, 145–146
linguiça sausages, 56
liver, beef, and raisin braise, 185
Liz Clark's Iowa coffee beef stew, 13–14
lobster:
Down East mixed shellfish stew, 215
and leek stew, Montauk, 230–231
stew, Jasper White's chunky, 228–229
storing of, 229
Louis' Basque Corner, 178
Louisiana:
Cajun crawfish étouffée, 225–226
Cajun ham, sausage, and shrimp jambalaya, 80–81
Cajun maque choux, 249–250
chicken gumbo ya ya, 132–133
Commander's seafood gumbo, 216–217
crawfish stew, 227

prunes:
  pork stew with apples and,
    55
  spicy stewed fruit compote,
    272
pumpkin:
  curmudgeon's pork and
    onion stew in, 59–61
  kidney bean and sausage
    pot, 260–261

Q

quail burgoo, Tennessee,
  183–184
quinces, Coach House beef
  stew with, 9–11

R

rabbit:
  smothered with onions, Low
    Country stewed,
    176–177
  stew, Carolina, 174–175
  Western jugged hare, 178–179
ragout:
  of chicken giblets and root
    vegetables, Craig's,
    140–141
  curried pork and yellow
    squash, 64–65
  Georgia venison, with root
    vegetables, 169–170
  Middlebury duck and
    rutabaga, 158–159
  Napoleon pork, vegetable,
    and olive, 65–66
  prairie oxtail, 36–37
  sweet-and-sour veal and
    leek, 114–115
raisin:
  and beef liver braise, 185
  -mustard sauce, braised beef
    tongue with, 192–193
  scones, 294
ranch ham hocks with
  sauerkraut, 85
Randolph, Mary, 256
red beans and rice, Delta,
  264–265
red cabbage and apples,
  stewed, 253

red plum and pork stew, spicy,
  63–64
red shrimp and scallop stew,
  Maine, 219–220
reindeer mulligan, Great
  Northern, 172–173
rice:
  in bogs, 223
  Delta red beans and, 264–265
  Ritz-Carlton pork goulash,
    67–68
root vegetables:
  Craig's ragout of chicken
    giblets and, 140–141
  Georgia venison ragout with,
    169–170
  Irish lamb stew with, 93–94
rosemary:
  bourbon beef, braised,
    25–26
  braised lamb shanks with,
    101
Roussel's, 80
rutabaga and duck ragout,
  Middlebury, 158–159
rye biscuits, New England,
  291

S

salmon solianka, Northwest,
  202–203
salt pork, Southern collard
  greens stewed with,
  255–256
San Antonio venison and corn
  chili, 171
Santa Fe posole, 58–59
Santorini's, 102
sauerkraut:
  and pork goulash,
    Charlevoix, 69
  ranch ham hocks with, 85
sausage:
  Arizona cocido, 30–31
  chicken and hominy gumbo,
    plantation, 134–135
  chicken gumbo ya ya,
    132–133
  and chickpea stew, Mrs.
    Zodas's glazed, 77–78
  goose and chestnut stew,
    East Hampton, 160–161

ham and shrimp jambalaya,
  Cajun, 80–81
pilau, Uncle Tom's, 79
pumpkin and kidney bean
  pot, 260–261
stew, Southwestern venison,
  167–168
and white bean pot, Garden
  State, 83
Savannah shrimp pilau,
  220–221
scallops:
  Down East mixed shellfish
    stew, 215
  Neal Myers's seafood stew,
    212–214
  and red shrimp stew, Maine,
    219–220
scones, raisin, 294
seafood:
  gumbo, Commander's,
    216–217
  stew, Neal Myers's, 212–214
Seattle oyster and spinach
  stew, 234–235
Second Avenue Delicatessen
  cholent, 29
Sheboygan cider pork and
  apple stew, 61–62
shellfish stew, Down East
  mixed, 215
short ribs of beef, Paw Paw's,
  39–40
shrimp:
  bog, Sullivan's Island,
    223–224
  broth, 223
  Carolina gumbo, 218–219
  cioppino, 210–211
  Commander's seafood
    gumbo, 216–217
  Creole, classic, 222–223
  Down East mixed shellfish
    stew, 215
  Neal Myers's seafood stew,
    212–214
  Old Stone fish stew,
    209–210
  pilau, Savannah, 220–221
  red, and scallop stew, Maine,
    219–220
  sausage and ham jambalaya,
    Cajun, 80–81

turkey wings, 118, 148
ham and pea bog, 146–147
Twentieth Century Limited
Hungarian goulash, 23–24
"21" Club, 240

U

Uncle Tom's sausage pilau, 79

V

veal:
and artichoke stew,
Castroville, 109–110
corn and mushroom burgoo,
111–112
and fennel stew, Barbara
Kafka's, 107–108
and leek ragout, sweet-and-
sour, 114–115
and pea stew, country,
112–113
stew with fiddleheads,
Aroostook, 103–104
zucchini and eggplant stew,
summer, 108–109
veal kidney braise, Kansas
City, 188–189
vegetable(s):
and chickpea chili,
California, 258–259
minted lamb fricassee with,
105–106
pork and olive ragout,
Napoleon, 65–66

vegetables, root:
Craig's ragout of chicken
giblets and, 140–141
Georgia venison ragout with,
169–170
Irish lamb stew with,
93–94
venison:
and Bing cherry stew, Ann
Arbor, 166–167
and corn chili, San Antonio,
171
ragout with root vegetables,
Georgia, 169–170
sausage stew, Southwestern,
167–168
verde, Colorado chile, 72–73
Vermont, Middlebury duck
and rutabaga ragout,
158–159
Virginia Country Captain,
original, 126–127

W

walnut, pheasant, and wild
mushroom stew, 181–182
Washington, Seattle oyster and
spinach stew, 234–235
Western cream biscuits,
283–284
Western jugged hare, 178–179
White, Jasper, 56, 228
white bean:
and oxtail braised in stout,
38–39

and sausage pot, Garden
State, 83–84
and tomatoes stewed,
262–263
white wine, Michigan cabbage
stewed in, 252
wild mushroom(s):
Jack Czarnecki's stewed,
257–258
pheasant and walnut stew,
181–182
Philip's chicken cacciatore
with black olives and,
129–130
wild rice, Minnesota
braised pheasant with,
179–180
Wisconsin:
Sheboygan cider pork and
apple stew, 61–62
stewed red cabbage and
apples, 253
Wolfert, Paula, 96

Y

yeast biscuits, crackling,
282–283
yellow squash and pork ragout,
curried, 64–65
Yturria, Mary, 254

Z

zucchini, veal, and eggplant
stew, summer, 108–109